DISCOVERING YOUR OPTIMUM
"HAPPINESS INDEX" (OHI)
PROJECT

Marjorie and I introduce "Discovering Your Optimum 'Happiness Index' (OHI) Project" as our way to engage people, communities, and nations in a global dialogue about the *inherent* benefits of happiness. It fills a "gap" in knowledge as an alternative to happiness as primarily a lifestyle. It introduces "Optimum Happiness" (OH), underpinned by "Joy" as a 'higher value proposition' than "happiness." The tools of the OHI Project are fourfold *(1)* "Discovering Your Optimum 'Happiness Index' (OHI)," *(2)* "Discovering Your Optimum 'Happiness Index' (OHI) Quotes Handbook," *(3)* eBooks, and *(4)* an OHI app for mobile devices. We envision the design of the app in the year 2017, to take advantage of digital connectivity and mobile lifestyles. The photo on the front cover personifies this next phase of "Discovering Your Optimum 'Happiness Index' (OHI) Project."

"I am still determined to be cheerful and happy, in whatever situation I may be; for I have also learned from experience that the greater part of our happiness or misery depends upon our dispositions, and not upon our circumstances."

— *Martha Washington (1731–1802)*

DISCOVERING
YOUR OPTIMUM
"HAPPINESS INDEX" (OHI)

"Time, as it grows old, teaches all things."
— Aeschylus (BCE 525–BCE 456), Prometheus Bound

"This book is a timely and relevant encapsulation of the multi-faceted dynamics encountered in one's 'search for happiness.' Not only have the authors opened up a panorama of ways to view happiness, but their self-directed guide also challenges the reader to examine their personal past, present, and possible future states of happiness. Their extensive body of work speaks to individuals from all lifestyles and professions."

— Karla A. Hutchinson-Skeete, MSEd (Educator)
(Current Doctoral Candidate)
Decatur, Georgia, USA

"As we go about our busy lives, time afforded for reflection is limited. The 'Happiness Index'(HI) with its well-researched and equally well-presented information, gives us pause. Marjorie and Errol Gibbs have focused on the question of our time with self-guided material to help us understand this age-old question, 'What is happiness?'"

— Honourable Dr. Jean Augustine PC CM CBE
Former Educator and former Canadian Parliamentarian
Toronto, ON, Canada

"Errol and Marjorie have given us a fascinating body of research that answers the age-old question, 'What is Happiness?' They offer a 'ground-breaking' and compelling analysis of the 'search for happiness.' This book will revolutionize the way we view happiness. It is destined to influence contemporary writers, researchers, visionaries, and great thinkers on the subject of happiness."

— Carina Maharaj, LLB (Hons)
Currently completing an L.L.M. and Legal Practice Certificate (LPC)
University of Westminster, London, United Kingdom

"Many would say, 'Only you can make yourself happy.' Gibbs and Gibbs dispel such a notion in their comprehensive analysis of 'What is Happiness?' They bring to the world a broad perspective on happiness, utilizing their 'Happiness Index' (HI) Process Methodology to inform our interdependent nature, our happiness, and our HI."

— Dr. Lincoln Gibbs, EdD, MPH, CHES
Associate Dean of the College of Health Professions
Ferris State University, Michigan, USA

"Gibbs and Gibbs' guide to your 'Happiness Index' (HI) is a profound work that begins with a cogent narrative on Discovering Your Optimum 'Happiness Index' (OHI). Their genius shines through in their unique 'Happiness Index' (HI) Process Methodology. You will never view happiness the same — again."

— *Roderic Southwell, BA, Psychology, Researcher*
Ajax, ON, Canada

"Gibbs and Gibbs have done a phenomenal job of exploring the happiness conundrum. All readers, whatever their beliefs on the subject, will find much to stimulate their thinking in this guide. Its breadth and scope, the variety of data explored, and the sheer nature of the discussion will evoke both thought and emotion. Discovering Your Optimum 'Happiness Index' (OHI) proves itself to be an excellent, practical, and very timely much-needed publication."

— *Natasha-Janine Gibbs-Watson, CYW, BSW*
Program Manager
Toronto, ON, Canada

"If you fail to read this book, you will miss out on some revolutionary thoughts. Marjorie and Errol Gibbs have put together a masterpiece of insightful research and foresight. Indeed, they have compiled a piece of work that genuinely shows their tremendous understanding of man and the happiness quest that eludes most."

— *Nigel H. Waterman, BA, MPA*
Senior Legal Adjudicator
Toronto, ON, Canada

"Marjorie and Errol introduce to the happiness marketplace 'new' and thoughtful insights that profoundly change the way in which people understand the complexity of the 'search for happiness.' Their 'Happiness Index' (HI) model will create a 'new' dialogue on happiness and start a global HI movement."

— *Dr. Hazel Ann Gibbs DePeza, Assistant Professor*
University of Trinidad and Tobago (UTT)
The Republic of Trinidad and Tobago

"This self-directed guide to discover our 'Happiness Index' successfully captures the complexity of pathways to happiness. It is hard to find a corresponding text on this philosophical issue that simultaneously inspires, empowers, and enlightens in such a profound yet understandable way."

— *Iris Hewitt-Bradshaw, PhD*
Senior Educator, Specialist in the field of Linguistics
University of Trinidad and Tobago (UTT)
The Republic of Trinidad and Tobago

"Discovering Your Optimum 'Happiness Index' (OHI) is what the world needs. This innovative and revolutionary book crosses all cultural boundaries. It presents insightful and thought-provoking answers to the age-old question, 'What is Happiness?'"

— Tabitha Herd, MEd (Educator)
Darwin, Australia

"This book is a 'must-read' for anyone in 'pursuit of happiness.' I am impressed with the depth and breadth of the research of this masterpiece. It is evident from the book that the writers are living their dream of Optimum Happiness."

— Cynthia Kwakyewah, BA
International Development Studies
Toronto, ON, Canada

"Errol and Marjorie have opened a discussion on a subject we all think about from time to time but resist serious contemplation. As society continues to repackage and sell a universal notion of happiness with success, we drift farther away from truths. The Happiness Index is a catalyst for pause as it brings us back to universal truths and forces us to think about the concrete elements around us that actually bring happiness. It is a pleasant, easy to read, intellectual work, with anecdotes, cadence and rhythm all combined to bring the reader joy."

— Caline Derota Carter, Author
Milton, ON, Canada

"It gratifies me to know that Errol and Marjorie have recognized both the 'spiritual' and 'physical' components of happiness in their masterpiece, 'Discovering Your Optimum "Happiness Index" (OHI).' These skillful writers reveal their foundational belief in 'joy' as the most permanent state of happiness with poise and self-assurance."

— Wendell J. Gibbs, MDiv
Toronto, ON, Canada

"This is what you have been waiting for, to answer many of your questions about genuine happiness. You will enjoy reading this amazing work. Errol and Marjorie combined their knowledge and unique ability for research and insightful observation, with sound biblical, doctrinal foundation, reliable historicity, and insightful global perspective to aid our 'search for happiness.'"

— Randolph Neptune
A fellow traveler

DISCOVERING
YOUR OPTIMUM
"HAPPINESS INDEX" (OHI)

Edited by: *Marcia S. Samsoodin-Gibbs*

DISCOVERING
YOUR OPTIMUM
"HAPPINESS INDEX" (OHI)

A Self-Directed Guide to Your "Happiness Index" (HI)
(Including Questionnaire and Self-Improvement [SI] Templates)
© 2016 Errol A. and Marjorie G. Gibbs.
Edited by: *Marcia S. Samsoodin-Gibbs*

ERROL A. GIBBS
MARJORIE G. GIBBS

EMG

authorHOUSE®

AuthorHouse™
1663 Liberty Drive
Bloomington, IN 47403
www.authorhouse.com
Phone: 1 (800) 839–8640

DISCOVERING
YOUR OPTIMUM
"HAPPINESS INDEX" (OHI)

A Self-Directed Guide to Your "Happiness Index" (HI)
(Including Questionnaire and "Self-Improvement" [SI] Templates)

Published by AuthorHouse 06/09/2017

ISBN: 978-1-5049-8319-8 (sc)
ISBN: 978-1-5049-8320-4 (e)

Library of Congress Control Number: 2016903552

Printed information available on the last page.

This book is printed on acid-free paper.

Genre: Personal & Practical Guide/Self-Help General/ Religion (Christianity)
/Inspiration/ Enlightenment/Empowerment/ Philosophy (General)

Email: Info@gibbshappinessindex.com
Website: www.gibbshappinessindex.com

DEDICATION

Marjorie and I dedicate this book in memory of our parents Adolphus (1917–1956) and Virginia Gibbs (1918–present), and Robert (1915–2000) and Jemima Lindo (1917–2005), for their dedication to the health, safety, and happiness of our lives. We also dedicate this book to our children, grandchildren, and great-grandchild; to our brothers and sisters; to people throughout the world who are in "search of happiness"; and to those whom happiness seems to elude despite the sufficiency of the resources on the Earth. The goal of this book is to help people live *healthier, happier,* and *wholesome* lives. Notwithstanding life's circumstances, the "indomitable human spirit" enables us to triumph over challenges. Our hope is that *"Discovering Your Optimum 'Happiness Index' (OHI)"* will shine a bright light on your path to "joy" and "happiness" as it brightened our path.

BOOK COVER DEDICATION

Marjorie and I dedicate the book cover perspective to women. The front cover photo is only a representation of the **"Mothers' of Civilization."** We congratulate the great women in history for their contribution to the growth of civilization. The male genius tends to lead from the "head" — hence significant advancements in science and technology, space exploration, and growth in industrial complexes that underpin human progress — from a material perspective. The greatest opportunity that people have to create a better world of peace and prosperity and to achieve "Optimum Happiness" (OH) must include both "heart" and "head" leadership.

Women lead, united by "heart" (soul) and "head" (intellect) with "empathy" and "authenticity," and with "athletic" (physical) and "academic" (educational) prowess. Women have the capacity to create other sustainable ecosystems (spiritual, moral, social, intellectual, and physical) that are essential in the quest for a happier world that underpins *all* dimensions of human progress. Women have the capacity to imbue happiness in the lives of their partners, their children, their communities, and the world. A true measure of human progress, though, is the status of women as *co-equals, co-partners,* and *co-owners,* working together with their male counterparts to create a happier and healthier world for the present and future generations. Women are the original **"Practitioners of Happiness."**

"No language can express the power, and beauty, and heroism, and majesty of a mother's love. It shrinks not where man cowers and grows stronger where man faints, and over wastes of worldly fortunes sends the radiance of its quenchless fidelity like a star."

— *Edwin Hubbell Chapin (1814–1880)*

"MOTHERS OF CIVILIZATION" AND HAPPINESS

"Since a time has come, Mademoiselle, when the severe laws of men no longer prevent women from applying themselves to the sciences and other disciplines, it seems to me that those of us who can, should use this long-craved freedom to study and to let men see how greatly they wronged us when depriving us of its honor and advantages."

— *Louise Labé (1524–1566)*

This brief treatise is our contribution to awakening the world to the great benefits to humankind when we acknowledge the noticeable and the inconspicuous attributes of women that hold their families, communities, and nations together. Some may attempt to distinguish "mothers" from the generic term "women," but years of empirical observation teach that biology is not essentially the main ingredient. The main ingredient that constitutes "womanhood" is the "heart" of the woman.

A woman can nurture children whether she is a mother or has never tasted motherhood. A woman is neither jealous nor envious of her counterpart with children. Instead, she embraces them with her "heart" and "arms" as though they are the "fruit of her womb." Women have a boundless capacity to imbue happiness in the lives of their partners, their children, their communities, and the world.

When future generations examine the "flight recorder" from the wreckage of human history, the most important piece of evidence they will find is a male-dominated leadership. Where are our nurturing and caring "mothers of civilization"? Where are our "keepers of compassion"? Where are our "prayer worriers"? Has our male-dominated leadership relegated (theoretically) *fifty* percent of the world's population to silence? Can civilization progress without the "heart" of our "mothers of civilization?"

The current state of our world demands that we begin to make new history that should include women at every level of leadership in every sphere of human development (spiritual, moral, social, intellectual, and physical). The six thousand years of historical records testify to great leadership on the one hand and great failure on the other hand. Have we denied the legacy of great women of the past, though, not without some controversy as well?

The legacies of the great women of yesteryear live on in a new generation of women in every profession, even those occupations that were once the domain of men. From science and engineering to medicine to law, women now dominate the campuses of many prominent universities. Women are finding their place in the media as reporters and news anchors, and war correspondents, and in every level of government and private corporations from the ground floor to board chairpersons, including directors and chief executive officers (CEOs). Empowering women empowers the whole of humanity.

The courage of many great people of every race, color, and creed have brought civilization out of the Dark Ages (500–1000) (www.Britannica.com/events/Dark-Ages) and into the Era of Enlightenment 17th–18th centuries (https://www.britannica.com/event/Enlightenment-European-history). People have also used their genius to engineer better living through artificial intelligence, from the microwave oven to jet engines. They have given to humanity great institutions of learning, governmental agencies, and peace organizations.

Pharmacologically, modern medicines have all but eradicated and brought under control such diseases as smallpox, the bubonic plague, yellow fever, and even the dreaded polio (poliomyelitis). Why has humanity not found a cure for the aberration of the mind that promotes war, genocide, apartheid, and avarice, as well as the hoarding of strategic resources? Women and children are the most affected by these aberrations of the human mind.

Despite our leaders' successes and failings, the twenty-first century has ushered in significant demands for "heart" and "head" leadership. Women have become more involved in the affairs of their nations. Historically, issues such as civil liberties and demands for higher living standards inspired civil rebellion. Today, women bring a wider range of issues with a deeper sense of purpose to the table. Women also bring a more sophisticated and informed dialogue that is demonstrably more morally and politically motivated.

Women have agitated for change in various movements, including (but not limited to) the suffrage movement of the early 1800s to the mid-1900s (www.britannica.com/topic/woman-suffrage), feminism, the women's rights movement, feminist rebellion, social feminism, and gender equality legislation. Over one hundred years ago, in 1909, the recognition of women's place in society began through National Women's Day. March 8, 2016, marked another historic day for women, International Women's Day (first celebrated in 1911). Notwithstanding, the corporate boardrooms of our great organizations and institutions where life-saving and life-threatening decisions are made do not reflect a balanced representation of women.

Women are the "lanterns" that shine through the darkness of the modern church and other religious institutions. In times of family turmoil, women stand between fathers and sons. In periods of international conflict, they heal the felled soldier in battle. When the child cries at midnight, the mother awakens to attend to him or her. Women cry not for themselves but for humanity. Women endure when their mate leaves for another. Without the love of "women" and "mothers" in the world, the entire world would plunge *catastrophically* into a sea of UNHAPPINESS. Conversely, the very presence of "women" and "mothers" in the world imbues HAPPINESS.

"A father may turn his back on his child, brothers and sisters may become inveterate enemies; husbands may desert their wives, wives their husbands. But a mother's love endures through all."

— *Washington Irving (1783–1859)*

CONTENTS

ILLUSTRATIONS

Scientific investigations teach, "All human beings belong to a single species and are descended from a common stock. They are born equal in dignity and rights and all form an integral part of humanity."[1]

[1] Declaration on Race and Racial Prejudice (adopted by the General Conference of UNESCO at its twentieth session, Paris, November 1978), Article 1, Copyright © UNESCO 1979 (United Nations Education, Scientific and Cultural Organization), p. 11.

AUTHORS' NOTE

The interest in happiness dates back to the time of Aristotle (384 BCE–322 BCE). The postmodern era (1940–2016) is unprecedented in the interest of happiness. Googling the word "happy" returns 2,940,000,000 results; "happiness" returns 394,000,000 results; "happier" returns 74,200,000 results; and books about "happiness" and related topics return 53,200,000 results (extracted date: August 10, 2016). The "Discovering Your Optimum 'Happiness Index' (OHI) Project" is our brainchild. Marjorie and I put forward that everyone has a "Happiness Index" (HI). Our HI has a direct correlation to our well-being (spiritual, moral, social, intellectual, financial, and physical).

In the year 2000, we began to explore the question, "what is happiness?" We focused our attention on events that alter human life from perspectives of *happiness* and *unhappiness*. Events such as engagement, marriage, graduation, or career contribute to social, economic, and material well-being and *happiness*. Likewise, events such as marriage breakdown, financial failure, unemployment, or a major illness can contribute to *unhappiness*.

Marjorie and I introduce the OHI Project to the world, as our way to engage people, communities, and nations in a global dialogue about the *inherent* benefits to happiness. It fills a "gap" in knowledge as an alternative to happiness as primarily a lifestyle. It introduces "Optimum Happiness" (OH), underpinned by "Joy," as a higher 'value proposition' than "happiness."

The tools of the OHI Project are fourfold *(1) "Discovering Your Optimum 'Happiness Index' (OHI)," (2) "Discovering Your Optimum 'Happiness Index' (OHI) Quotes Handbook,"* (3) eBooks, and *(4)* an OHI app for mobile devices contemplated for 2017 to take advantage of digital connectivity and mobile lifestyles.

Marjorie and I live OH and successful lives, but success does not imply that we have great wealth, live in a mansion, drive exotic automobiles, or socialize with prominent figures in society. Our perspective on happiness means a commitment to God, marriage, children, family, and friends; likewise, to *recognize, acknowledge,* and *embrace* the "oneness" of the human family.

Happiness means to discover one's genius, which is to determine one's highest capability and develop it to the "Optimum." Happiness means to understand that all people have a common desire for universal *love, fairness,* and *justice.* Happiness means honesty and integrity, competency in business, and generosity to others.

Happiness means to listen to and empathize with others who live in fear and suffer anxiety. Happiness means to strive daily to improve relationships. Regardless of race, culture, or religion, or being single or married, learned or unlearned, wealthy or poor, this guide will challenge your perception of happiness and the "search for happiness." You will discover that this Self-Directed Guide to Your "Happiness Index" (HI) presents innovative perspectives and engages you in thinking about happiness in "new" ways. Whether you are a lawyer, engineer, sociologist, politician, minister, teacher, student, athlete, academic, or layperson, it will enlighten your "search for happiness."

Irrespective of your upbringing and experiences, we hope that this book will become your constant companion as you strive for Continuous Self-Improvement (CSI) and growth in areas that rob you of happiness, which is your birthright (spiritual, inherent, and constitutional). Marjorie and I have concluded from our religious teachings that happiness was central to the creation mandate, hence our "social and emotional interdependence."

Women have a unique role to create the ecosystems (spiritual, moral, social, intellectual, and physical) that sustain "joy" and "happiness" in human lives. Women also have the capacity to empower the world through leadership in various fields of science and technology previously dominated by their male counterparts. Women lead unified by "heart" (soul) and "head" (intellect) with "empathy" and "authenticity," and with "athletic" (physical) and "academic" (educational) prowess.

We also bring to the attention of readers excerpts from the works of thought leaders, philosophers, researchers, and writers who inquire about the correlation among faith, health, healing, and happiness. Institutions such as Harvard University, Harvard School of Public Health, and Mayo Clinic lead in research into the relationship between health and happiness. Likewise, researchers and professionals such as Gretchen Rubin, author of *The Happiness Project*, provide their relevant findings and perspectives on happiness.

The Happiness Project has been a blockbuster bestseller. It spent more than two years on the *New York Times* bestseller list, including hitting #1; has sold more than 1.5 million copies; and has been published in more than thirty languages. The global market appeal for original works and projects on happiness has set in motion "new" ways to think of happiness in the postmodern era. We now join the global conversation with a unique perspective, our "Discovering Your Optimum 'Happiness Index' (OHI) Project."

ACKNOWLEDGEMENTS

SPECIAL ACKNOWLEDGEMENTS

Marjorie and I acknowledge and express eternal gratitude to those who have granted us permission to include copyrighted materials that we have quoted; likewise, the work of others whom we have mentioned to help validate our inquiries and to provide visibility of their scientific and insightful research. We are also thankful for the academics, philosophers, humanitarians, and prophets of yesteryear and the present for their contribution to our understanding of the complex human condition of *happiness* and *unhappiness*.

We have stood on their shoulders to get a better view of the twenty-first century and of the new millennium with hope and optimism for a happier world. We also thank family and friends who have accompanied us during various stages of this remarkable journey in our boundless "search for happiness."

This chronicle is an accumulation of our faith, belief, and practice, nurtured by our *transformation* and *progression* from the knowledge of yesteryear to today's new knowledge, wisdom, and understanding, which we put forward as we continue our journey together. We trust that this text will *engage, enlighten,* and *empower* you to further "search for happiness," not merely as a temporary material state but as a permanent state of "joy" as you travel life's path.

"In order to undertake any journey we need assets at hand. The more resources, friends, support, discipline, education, etc. that we can gather-together, identify and create, the better. The bigger the change, the more necessary it is to have a large supply of things to help us on the path."

— Kathy Gottberg (Kathy@smartliving365.com)
smartliving365.com

INTRODUCTION

Over many centuries, the world has experienced exponential growth in world religions, human knowledge, science, and technology, and considerable financial and material wealth. Humanity has made significant progress in academia, science and technology, space exploration, and medical research, and in the treatment and eradication of some common diseases such as smallpox, measles, yellow fever, and polio (poliomyelitis).

The thoughtful observer could conclude that our world should blossom into a "new era" of high civilization with peace and prosperity, and hope and happiness. Instead, humanity has been ushered into a "global village," observably unprepared to manage past challenges, present challenges, and looming challenges of the twenty-first century and the "new millennium."

Some of these challenges resonate in the lives of people throughout the world who experience feelings of "unhappiness" in daily life. The impetus behind the "Discovering Your Optimum 'Happiness Index' (OHI) Project" is our earnest desire to share some inquiries and insights into our "search for happiness" and the great benefits (spiritual and material) that Marjorie and I have experienced on our "happiness journey." We have discovered that although material things can bring happiness, it is temporary. A "materially driven life" boosts one's lifestyle, but it is not fundamentally *intrinsic* to happiness.

This guide is not a scientific treatise on happiness. We do not make any claim of training in psychology, sociology, or any of the social science disciplines. We present our discourse as an alternative approach based on experiential knowledge; intuitive, intellectual, and empirical observation; multigenerational family life experiences; nurturing children; and business experience.

Marjorie and I have had the privilege of combined global travel on four continents—Africa, Europe, North America, and Oceania—approximately twelve countries, twenty-four states, and about one hundred cities, towns, and villages over several decades. Global travel afforded us a "panoramic view" and put us on the "front lines" to observe how people in these parts of the world experience *happiness* and *unhappiness*. The observation is the same in every culture—the need for love, peace, hope, happiness, and "joy" resonated in people's lives.

The twenty-first century (in primarily the Western world) is a stark contrast between *happiness* and *unhappiness* despite financial and material wealth in an era of wellness and lifestyle coaches, therapists, and psychological and psychiatric counselors. Researchers in corporations, universities, and university hospitals have provided scientific data to demonstrate a correlation between happiness and productivity, and lifestyle and wellness of individuals. We have cited excerpts from a variety of perspectives from some of their research.

We have witnessed unhappiness among the haves and have-nots. The human compulsion for material wants over deeper spiritual and psychological needs has led some to behave (intuitively, subconsciously, or consciously) in a manner that is often counterproductive to the universal goals of happiness.

Behaviors such as dishonesty, unfairness, unkindness, and inequity gratify the *head* instead of the *heart*. These practices rob us of "joy" and cause unhappiness. Conversely, behaviors such as honesty, fairness, kindness, and empathy gratify the *heart*. Many in the field of research and many ordinary citizens are astutely aware that intangible human attributes such as love, care, and hope have a greater influence on people's health and happiness than tangible assets such as money and material possessions.

Some of the ideas in this guide might be new to you, but we hope that you consider them as "new" discoveries to add to your toolbox of knowledge in your "search for happiness." The guide takes you on a journey of discovery where you can find happiness in the midst of *plenty* (wealth); likewise in the midst of *scarcity* (poverty). It offers the reader a broad spectrum of inquiry into the influence of human attributes, achievements, and customs on one's health, well-being, and happiness.

We have taken the same pathways that we share with you in this discourse on happiness as we endeavor to give something back to our nation and humanity. In other words, we have *"walked the talk."* We have a great capacity to imbue happiness in the lives of others when we accept the notion of our interdependent human relationship as innate to happiness and survival as a viable species.

Over past decades up to the present, we have observed many events that are world changing *(www.futuretimeline.net)*. Many will agree that poignant events and circumstances in life (the past and current), and even contemplated future events have contributed to different levels of *happiness* and *unhappiness*. We trust that this guide will shine a bright light on your path to "Optimum Happiness" (*OH*).

CHAPTER
1

BEGINNING THOUGHTS

"The heart of a father is the masterpiece of nature."

— *Antoine-François, Abbé Prévost d'Exiles (1697–1763)*

I had three days to live at birth; so said the midwife. I survived — happily. When I was a boy of fourteen years of age, my father passed suddenly. Dad was experimenting with a liquid-gas-burning stove in the home annex. The gas was under pressure. A release valve failed, and a burst of gas sprayed all over his body. The pilot flame followed the mist of gas and engulfed him in an inferno in my presence. A terrified mom saw my dad in a fireball and shouted to him to roll on the ground, which he did intuitively.

Dad drove himself to the hospital with me in the passenger seat and my elder brother in the backseat. Dad seemed to have some inner force guiding him. I do not know what was on his mind because he never uttered a single word over the approximately one-mile journey that seemed to take forever. The silence was paralyzing and the air was thick with fear as Dad pulled in front of the hospital's main entrance and collapsed on the steering wheel.

The attendants rushed him to the emergency room. During that era, there were no burn centers for treatment and recovery of patients with severe burns. We did not have any idea of Dad's treatment modality. Mom was in transit to the hospital as I returned home to a scene of screaming siblings, not knowing what to expect.

The unexpected news came the following day. Dad had succumbed to third-degree burns and had left us without any last words. A stay-at-home mom and nine children survived Dad. Mom was eminently unprepared for such an untimely passing of her husband and our father, who left us within twenty-four hours of the fatal accident.

Marjorie and I share many experiences in common in life's journey. We were close to our fathers. We lost both of our fathers without having the opportunity to share last personal words or to receive their final blessings.

Marjorie was an adult when her father passed suddenly as well, but the impact was no less traumatic for her. It was the morning of July 26, 2000. We were living in Troy, Michigan, USA. Marjorie got an emergency call from a relative to leave immediately to be with her father, who was undergoing surgery.

While in transit from Detroit Metropolitan Airport, Detroit, Michigan, to Logan International Airport, Boston, Massachusetts, to Bangor International Airport, Maine, Marjorie's father (Robert) passed at eighty-five years of age. The untimely passing of any family member is a calamity and a challenge for close family members to endure, in particular the parent or one who is the sole provider, as was the case of my father. Future hopes and aspirations for the future turned to *uncertainty* and *anxiety* at Dad' passing.

Our relatively comfortable family life free from economic challenges became a daily struggle for our mother, my eight siblings, and me. In today's vernacular, we were a middle-class family because Dad owned a car, which was rare for families in those days. Dad socialized with the British elites who provided engineering expertise to the energy industry. Dad was highly regarded in those circles for his technical expertise, hence his passion for experimentation.

Our family began a journey through a dark tunnel with no visible light on the other end, guided by a mother who needed guidance herself for the journey that she had embarked on — involuntarily. Again I contend she was "eminently unprepared."

Our family managed to weather this great personal and financial misfortune because we did not have all of the material needs in the 1950s as we do in our postmodern era. "Spirituality" and "religion" were a natural part of the family; it was the beacon for guiding the affairs of families and community.

The loyalty of our multigenerational family structure and the village mothers who would pray and share with less fortunate neighbors was paramount to family survival. The yield of backyard gardens and livestock played a significant part in our survival, but the highest yield was cooperation among siblings, fueled by the enduring faith of our mother, which the experience tested.

We began to view life from a different set of lenses as our family joined the ranks of those who lived in the valley between the *haves* and *have-nots*. The first lesson that we learned was that the poor among us never seemed hopeless or unhappy. Likewise, when tragedy struck, rather than tear the family apart, it became the glue that held the family together.

I noted that for some families, every day was a challenge that would repeat the following day. I learned that being poor necessitated the need to be resourceful. The poorer you are, the more *knowledge, wisdom,* and *understanding* you must have to survive, and these attributes are "spiritual attributes" as opposed to "natural attributes."

Knowledge, wisdom, and understanding were the bedrock of earlier generations, but they have always meant the knowledge, wisdom, and understanding of God that inspire human action.

In the succeeding years, I would often contemplate the source of Mother's capacity to endure under the prevailing circumstances. Mom needed a "cast of characters" to survive that included aunts, uncles, distant relatives, friends, and neighbors. "It takes a village" was more than attribution as an "African" proverb for us. Village mothers were the giants in their families. They are still the giants in our postmodern age.

Marjorie's mom (Jemima) passed at eighty-seven years old. My mom (Virginia) is alive. She is ninety-eight years of age, a resident of a seniors' home in Toronto, Ontario, Canada. Physical incapacity confined both of our mothers to a wheelchair and to their beds in their declining years.

Visiting our parents gave us a sense of their *formidable* strength and human *vulnerability* as the material world vanished from their memories. Spirituality became the guardian of their souls, and "joy" became the sentinel as their happiness of yesteryear took flight. The presence of their children became the only happiness that they knew and desired. In retrospect, we were a "very happy" family, although we did not realize it at the time.

Happiness was a "natural birthright" that families did not discuss in the *premodern* (beginnings to 1650s) and *modern* eras (1650s–1950s) as we do in the *postmodern* era (1950s to current) *(http://www.postmodernpsychology.com/)*. Yesteryear, happiness and unhappiness were not human psychological conditions that clinicians researched and measured. Happiness was simply "the life we lived." Common words such as *anxiety*, *mental illness*, and *depression* were unheard of when we were teenagers, although we imagine that those conditions existed but to a lesser degree than today.

The postmodern family seems to be in a state of significant adjustment, which might have begun during the Industrial Revolution (1800s–1900s). The Industrial Revolution ushered in new ways of life and financial and material prosperity for the masses. It also ushered in the commuter age and great mobility of individuals, which resulted in the separation of parents from children. The financial fortunes gained from the new era afforded a range of options for family members seeking to move out of crowded, centralized homes to establish their independence.

Today, the postmodern family is more educated than their counterparts of yesteryear. They have graduate and postgraduate degrees, and higher earnings. They are more sophisticated in their understanding of the world, and they have fewer children to nurture. Notwithstanding, the postmodern family is in need of a supporting cast including psychiatrists, psychologists, sociologists, drug addiction and family counselors, and local community workers.

Some parents and their children fall through the "proverbial" cracks in society and end up living "fruitless lives." Moreover, some end up as wards of the "deficit-driven" global Prison Industrial Complex (PIC), arguably the greatest bastion of unhappiness that we have near forgotten or perhaps abandoned in the "happiness equation."

This Self-Directed Guide to Your "Happiness Index" (HI) will enable the individual, the family, and the supporting cast to understand better the "crisis of unhappiness" that confronts them in daily life. It presents "new" perspectives on happiness to inspire hope for the individual, family, corporation, and nation.

o   THE SUPPORTING CAST

Today, not only is the family in need of a "supporting cast" to enable it to survive the rapidly changing times but individuals as well. Individuals need more than parents, grandparents, aunts, uncles, neighbors, and even matchmakers to cope in the twenty-first century.

The world comes to the aid of the postmodern family in every continent, country, city, and village. Billions of dollars in charitable donations, social safety nets, food banks to enable the family to cope with a myriad of challenges such as unemployment, violence, depression, poverty, hunger, and homelessness.

Some individuals and their families experience fear, anxiety, uncertainty, and unhappiness because they are essentially alone in their "search for happiness." There is no shortage of academic research, philosophical quotes, and personal stories of happiness to inspire us, but for some, the reality is often quite different from reading quotes and believing that happiness is strictly personal.

All types of media bombard us with impulses to *achieve, receive,* and *win* in a competition. These external motivations influence our happiness from childhood to adulthood. National lotteries have mushroomed across the human landscape as a well-lit path that promises that "winning" will lead to a happier and more fulfilling lifestyle, but does winning bring happiness?

A child who receives a new toy or completes a coloring book beams with pride and happiness in his or her achievement. A young woman who receives an engagement ring as her partner proposes marriage, and she responds—happily with a resounding yes! A postgraduate degree (summa cum laude) imbues internalized happiness in a youth and his or her parents. A mother who watches her child take his or her first step beams with pride and "joy." Our multigenerational family experiences have also taught us many lessons on our "happiness journey" that we are happy to share with you.

○   THE YEARS 2000–2015

Marjorie's father passed in the year 2000, which brought great unhappiness to their multigenerational family and to us as a shared "unhappy experience." It brought back instant memories of Dad's (equally) untimely departure from this side of our three-dimensional journey from "pre-mortal," to "mortal," to "immortal," generally underscored by Christian theology.

The year 2000 was a pivotal year in the decision to embark on the "Discovering Your Optimum 'Happiness Index' (OHI) Project." However, it was largely our beginning thoughts as we witnessed the decline in global happiness. Theoretically, our "journey of discovery" began some thirty-five years ago when we began to travel and observe people's *happy* and *unhappy* lives.

The year 2000 was also a time for reflection. It began the process of gathering data and making every moment a study of the challenges that human beings face in a world of plenty where so many have so little, and where they have relegated to society the custodianship of their happiness, *consciously* or *subconsciously*.

We have been witness to circumstances that have made Marjorie and me both happy and unhappy, but strong and tenacious. In January 2015, unlike a New Year's resolution, a torrent of inspiration descended upon us like a "decree" from the celestial to join in the global happiness movement with *"Discovering Your Optimum 'Happiness Index' (OHI)."*

In the year 2015, we also began to reflect on life, *past* and *present,* and we peered into the *future* and became overwhelmed by the universal nature of unhappiness in the world. We were also taken aback by the fundamental unawareness of the myriad of simple solutions (*untapped*) that are available to imbue and sustain happiness in human lives.

We answered the directive to begin immediately to chronicle fifteen years of "talks and dialogues," experiential knowledge, global travel, empirical observation, and findings to share our perspective on happiness with a global audience. Thus began the "life-transforming" journey to present the world with a "new" "value proposition" to begin its "search for happiness." With bursts of enthusiasm, we shared our directive with family members, friends, and associates in our "inner circle." They began to read and share their inner thoughts as well. Randolph Neptune penned these inspirational words for potential readers of our work:

"This is what you have been waiting for, to answer many of your questions about genuine happiness. You will enjoy reading this amazing work. Errol and Marjorie combined their knowledge and unique ability for research and insightful observation, with sound biblical, doctrinal foundation, reliable historicity, and insightful global perspective to aid our 'search for happiness.'"

— *Randolph Neptune, A fellow traveler (AD 2016)*

Reflecting on our repository of data, we began to examine words and their classical definitions; the meanings they transcend and their daily application to human lives. We evaluated many words, and ten began to take on different and more profound meanings than the way we understood them in the past.

Interestingly, these ten words are familiar household words that we have used throughout our youth and adult lives in casual conversations, and we have discussed their meaning with others, not recognizing they are the keys to open the doors to infuse happiness into our lives. The potency of these ten words became evident as we embarked on a journey to find the path(s) that happiness travels when it takes flight, knowing that happiness may return on another path(s). What is happiness? Why is there so much unhappiness in the world?

We recognized that the following words, which we refer to as "TEN KEY HAPPINESS INDICATORS" (TKHI), weaved "strands of interconnection" with *all* human activities as they relate to well-being (happiness), underpinned by our achievements, attributes, and customs. They form a pattern, a "solution matrix," to the plight of humanity regarding our *happiness* and *unhappiness*:

o   TEN KEY HAPPINESS INDICATORS (TKHI)

1. Career [C100] (Achievement)
2. Character [C100] (Attribute)
3. Education [E100] (Achievement)
4. Forgiveness [F100] (Attribute)
5. Health [H100] (Achievement)
6. Humility [H100] (Attitude)
7. Personality [P100] (Attribute)
8. Religion [R100] (Custom)
9. Self-Esteem [S100] (Achievement)
10. Socialization [S100] (Custom)

The superscript [100] (with the prefix) denotes the maximum score that the "Aspirant," who is in search of "Optimum Happiness" (OH), can achieve when answering the questions associated with each Ten Key Happiness Indicators (TKHI).

We do not argue that these are the only keywords that embody our "search for happiness" or our unhappiness plight, but they underpin the "Happiness Index" Planning Process Methodology (HIPPM), which we present in extensive detail in Chapter 5 (pp. 149–239).

Human beings are destined to be happy, so why is it only a few can find lasting happiness, and why do so many miss opportunities to be happy, knowingly or unknowingly? Can human beings discover and sustain happiness? These poignant questions inspired our "quest for happiness." In our quest to find happiness, we have witnessed the potency of "joy," which we will also share with you as a higher pursuit and a state that transcends happiness and greater purpose. We share with you briefly the PURPOSE, the WITNESS, and the FINDINGS that directed our path.

THE PURPOSE, THE WITNESSES, THE FINDINGS

"The secret of happiness, you see, is not found in seeking more, but in developing the capacity to enjoy less."

— *Socrates (469 BCE–399 BCE)*

o   THE PURPOSE

We have dialogued with individuals from all "walks of life" and from a myriad of disciplines. We have challenged long-held concepts of happiness and have introduced many "new" concepts to test and validate our proposition against the "age-old" question, "What is happiness?" The higher purpose of the "Discovering Your Optimum 'Happiness Index' (OHI) Project" is fivefold.

First:

To bring "new" and valued perspectives on happiness to the world in "search of happiness." "What is happiness?" This age-old question began our inquiry in the year 2000. Subsequently, in 2015, our research gave birth to the broader-based enterprise OHI Project, as we observed the rise of unhappiness in the world.

To introduce "new" tools to aid in the "search for happiness" such as this text, "*Discovering Your Optimum 'Happiness Index' (OHI);*" a handbook, "*Discovering Your Optimum 'Happiness Index' (OHI) Quotes Handbook;*" and companion eBooks. Likewise, to design an OHI app to take advantage of digital connectivity and mobile lifestyles.

Second:

To present readers with an extensive narrative to validate the ten human achievements, attributes, and customs that underpin our "Happiness Index" Planning Process Methodology (HIPPM) (Reference: Chapter 5). The overall goal is to bring to the "Table of Civilization" another perspective to broaden the conversation about happiness. We present a "new" set of building blocks to increase national and global happiness with the individual in the nucleus.

Third:

To introduce a nonscientific assessment tool, "A Self-Directed Guide to Your 'Happiness Index' (HI)." The tool is a predicate of the "Ten Key Happiness Indicators" (TKHI), underpinned by achievements, attributes, and customs described in detail later in the book (Reference: Table 3). The output of the self-directed guide, though nonscientific, implies the Aspirant's HI, which further introduces a "Self-Improvement" (SI) tool that the "Aspirant" can utilize as a basis to optimize his or her HI.

Fourth:

To facilitate "Self-Improvement Planning" (SIP) to help the "Aspirant" improve his or her HI. Improvement in one's HI is analogous to the aggregate improvement of our overall health, happiness, and well-being. More significantly, the benefits of SI can extend beyond self to marriage, family, and community. Likewise, the benefits of SI can reach within corporations, institutions, nations, and throughout the world.

Fifth:

To establish a basis to pilot additional HI models to help a broad range of communities such as religious, academic, corporate, political, justice, and military groups, to better understand the complex and comprehensive nature of impediments to happiness; moreover as a "human value proposition."

Marjorie and I formulated our HI model without any differentiation in weight or value among the THIK. Regardless of the complex nature of any one of the ten indicators, it will be a challenge to any branch of inquiry (scientific or nonscientific) to attempt to weigh one entity against another, or to measure the influence of the *happiness* or *unhappiness* on different individuals.

Aristotle (384 BCE–322 BCE) alluded to this complexity thus:

The Pursuit of Happiness: Bringing the Science of Happiness to Life, Introduction: Aristotle's Definition of Happiness: "Aristotle was convinced that a genuinely happy life required the fulfillment of a broad range of conditions, including physical as well as mental well-being. In this way, he introduced the idea of a science of happiness in the classical sense, in terms of a new field of knowledge."[2]

Happiness is a composite of the "*Optimum*" of the best of human achievements, attributes, and customs. We have witnessed many people who have tried to differentiate what would make them happy: a new car, a new home, engagement, marriage, or winning the lottery. The desire to achieve and sustain happiness is not exclusive to the physical realm. Intangible human attributes such as mutual love, social relations, and loyalty to family and friends are primary factors in the "happiness equation."

o   THE WITNESSES

Our travels to different parts of the world over the past thirty-five years have enabled us to observe up front the "search for happiness" by individuals from parts of the underdeveloped, developing, and developed world. People everywhere seem desirous to be happy, yet few can define their "search for happiness." This vagueness in the ability to describe the "search for happiness" informed us of the "complexity" of the search.

Unhappiness is part of the legacy of the human family, but our Creator has given us "joy" as the "sentinel" to watch over our emotions when unhappiness visits upon us. We have presented our arguments to individuals of different races, religions, cultures, and social and economic backgrounds. We have *listened, learned,* and *witnessed* the "rolling wave" of happiness and unhappiness of many in their respective "search for happiness," with different levels of awareness of the broad perspective of the aggregate nature of happiness.

Some individuals perceive happiness as a series of events such as birth, birthday, baptism, graduation, engagement, marriage,

---

[2] Pursuit of Happiness, Inc., a 501(c)(3), EIN: 26–475641, Copyright © 2015, www.pursuit-of-happinessorg/history-of-happiness/asistotle. Extraction date: October 18, 2015.

exotic living, the purchase of a new home or automobile, or a new job. These events and materially driven perspectives became the impetus that led us to embark on a more comprehensive search, to strive to discover a more permanent state of happiness. This quest was not only about travel to faraway destinations but also to meet and experience how people cope with daily life within our multigenerational families, in corporate settings, and within the "spiritual family" of religious adherents. The *inquiry* and *pursuit* were a mirror of daily life all around us.

o   THE FINDINGS

We have reasoned that everyone has a "Happiness Index" (HI), whether or not he or she is astutely aware of it. Likewise, there is an index for every known entity, quantity, and the human condition such as height, weight, body mass, learning, intelligence, and the internationally known stock index.

Whether by scientific or unscientific inquiry, Marjorie and I contend that there is not a singular (universal) definition of happiness. However, we proffer that each one of us can recognize various states of *unhappiness* and *happiness* in self and each other that we refer to as their HI (Reference: Table 5). We discovered that the HI was a dynamic rather than static measure influenced by the human condition, though it is possible to achieve and maintain a consistent state of "*Optimum* Happiness" (*OH*).

An "*Optimum*" state of happiness can transform individuals, marriages, families, workplaces, governments, and nations. We discovered that happiness exists in the "spiritual" and "physical" realms of our lives. To achieve *OH*, we must embrace both perspectives because they are mutually inclusive.

We discovered that for some, happiness is a measure of their possessions and lifestyle, and the lifestyles of their friends and associates. We discerned that many whom we encountered on our journey envisioned a plan for their lives only to be awakened by the reality of the "Master's Plan" for our lives, speaking in a biblical context. The "search for happiness" ought to take into consideration the ancient Book of Ecclesiastes. The Counsel of Living with Vanity,

p. 655—757. King Solomon, the wise King of Israel (circa 970 BCE– 931 BCE).[3]

We began our "search for happiness" knowing that the "discovery of happiness" does not mean that "happiness," more importantly "Optimum Happiness" (OH), would shield us from disappointments and trials in life. "Joy" keeps the light of happiness burning even when the trials of life seem unbearable.

Many whom we encountered on their "search for happiness" seemed contented with the temporary feelings that infuse the soul, underpinned by events, achievements, acquisition of material things, winning in competition, physical exchange of gifts, and companionship.

We have discovered that happiness does not come naturally or that we can be happy by merely envisioning ourselves as happy. Happiness has a deeper meaning that demands action such as to love, to care, to give, and to receive. These activities create great memories and bring great happiness that permeates the souls of many, and though these conditions are impermanent as we advance in life, they create lasting memories.

We can discover the keys to unlock the "doors to happiness" both internal (spiritual) and external (physical) when we find purpose and meaning in life. More importantly, our interdependence, more than any other expression of human life, gives us purpose. Marjorie and I were not satisfied with the mere "search for happiness" or "pursuit of happiness," but rather OH as a "higher value" proposition. OH empowers individuals, families, and nations.

Our inquiry revealed a significant number of benefits to happiness that can improve human communications, transform relationships, elevate peaceful coexistence, better inspire human relationships, better inform our understanding of the oneness of humanity, and promote the overall well-being of nations.

Below, we have provided a summary of some of our findings (randomly ordered). As an aggregate, they underpin the "Happiness Index" Planning Process Methodology (HIPPM) (Reference: Chapter 5).

---

[3] Copyright © 1985, 1983 by Thomas Nelson, Inc. The Book of Ecclesiastes, p. 655—757. Chapters: 9:13, 11:6 − 7, 12:1 − 7.

SUMMARY OF TWENTY-FIVE
"OPTIMUM HAPPINESS" (OH) FINDINGS

In summary, we provide the following random sample of findings on our "search for happiness." • Everyone has a "Happiness Index" (HI). • Happiness is *personal, interpersonal, transactional*, and *transformational*. • With the right tools, people can improve their HI. • A happy world hinges on a happy marriage, happy children, and a happy family. • Happier people are more calm, creative, and productive. • There are specific keys to a happier life. • Happier people have a happier personality and vice versa.

   • Material *success* is not the same as a *successful life*. • Rich or poor, neither group is happier than the other group. • People who travel are happier and better informed about the world and our interdependence. • The "pursuit of pleasure" is not the same as "pursuit of happiness." • Happy leaders are better managers of people. • Unhappiness does not have to be permanent. • Much of human behavior is counterproductive to happiness. • Happy people are charitable. • A happy nation constitutes happy people.

   • Happy employees are more dependable, more productive, more loyal, and more creative. • Good character traits imbue happiness. • The soil of our "interdependent human nature" nurtures the "roots of happiness." • Happier children and people are less destructive and foster relations more easily. • Happiness can help to mitigate much of the violence in the world. • Happy people get restful sleep. • "Joy" is a higher imperative of happiness. • Happiness exists in the "spiritual" and the "physical" realms of our lives. • "Optimum Happiness" (OH) is *achievable* and *sustainable*.

Notable Toronto, Ontario, Canadian theologian Wendell J. Gibbs has this to say:

> "It gratifies me to know that Errol and Marjorie have recognized both the 'spiritual' and 'physical' components of happiness in their masterpiece, 'Discovering Your *Optimum* "Happiness Index" (OHI).' These skillful writers reveal their foundational belief in 'joy,' a permanent state of happiness, with poise and self-assurance."

— *Wendell J. Gibbs, MDiv*
Toronto, ON, Canada

Global travel, informal surveys, and engaging philosophical discussions have also led us to conclude that there is also a need to develop a compendium of specific guides to help elevate the "Happiness Index" (HI) of some of the critical leadership faculties in society. Our "talks and dialogues" with many in society gave expression to the stressful nature of a myriad of disciplines that can benefit from our search and discoveries.

Some of these disciplines include (but are not limited to) religious leaders, professors, school principals, schoolteachers, lawyers, police officers, prison officers, doctors, nurses, firefighters, air traffic controllers, and truck drivers (in random order). Likewise, society expends vast sums of money to facilitate solutions to fundamental human problems caused by war, fear and anxiety, emotional stress, and the general conflict between people and nations.

Marjorie and I proffer that the vast majority of human problems have organic solutions. There is no doubt that leadership in the twenty-first century demands the great exercise of "heart" and "head" leadership. History teaches what we were like in the past and could be in the future. Leaders understand that they are leading for the present and future generations.

Women lead, unified by "heart" (soul) and "head" (intellect) with "empathy" and "authenticity," and with "athletic" (physical) and "academic" (educational) prowess. Women have the capacity to create sustainable ecosystems that are essential in the quest for a happier world that underpins all dimensions of human progress. Human development includes scientific and intellectual, in addition to spiritual, moral, social, economic, and physical.

Women have the capacity to imbue happiness into the lives of their partners, their children, their communities, and the world. A true measure of human progress is the status of women as *co-equals*, *co-partners*, and *co-owners*, working together to create a happier and healthier world for the present and future generations.

We can also help to change the world utilizing the three greatest powers on Earth that humankind can assemble: the *"power of love,"* the *"power of dialogue,"* and the *"power of the pen."* The following fifteen pledges can profoundly influence our lives and help to set our hearts right and make a pledge to each other, to spouse, family, friends, associates, community, and nation.

FIFTEEN PLEDGES FOR A HEALTHIER
AND HAPPIER LIFE

1. I pledge to engender loyalty and happiness
in my life, in my marriage, in my family, and in my friends.
2. I pledge to be a more loving and caring mother, father, brother,
sister, uncle, aunt, and grandparent.
3. I pledge to listen more, to be more patient, to be more attentive,
and to give more of my gifts.
4. I pledge to engender happiness in my home, my school, my
workplace, my place of worship, and in my community.
5. I pledge to exercise more compassion, more empathy, and more
nurturing, and to be less judgmental about others.
6. I pledge to strive for a balance between work and life, to afford my
family and myself more time to rest, to relax, and to enjoy the
"fruits of our labor."
7. I pledge to seek the ideal in *all* situations and to speak positively
about fellow human beings.
8. I pledge that when I am down, I will look to a higher "moral
power" to imbue "happiness" and "joy" in my life.
9. I pledge to stand with others when they are down, regardless of
their race, culture, color, or creed.
10. I pledge to seek the good in every situation and to not
dwell on the evil that is seen easily.
11. I pledge to care more for my spiritual, mental, and physical health.
12. I pledge to seek higher spiritual ground, to be a deep thinker,
and to entertain other schools of intellectual thought.
13. I pledge to be more resolute in the things that I pursue
and to be more determined to achieve my goals.
14. I pledge to strive for "Optimum Happiness" (OH) in my life and
share with others its "higher value" proposition
than "happiness."
15. I pledge to seek to understand better the "oneness of
humanity" and our mutual desire for love,
life, hope, liberty, and happiness.

— *Marjorie G. and Errol A. Gibbs*
Optimum "Happiness Index" (OHI) Mantra

CHAPTER
2

WHAT IS HAPPINESS?

"We tend to forget that happiness does not come as a result of getting something we don't have, but rather of recognizing and appreciating what we do have."

— *Friedrich Koenig (1774-1833)*

"What is happiness?" To define happiness and live happy lives, we also need to understand "what is unhappiness?" Throughout this guide, we will compare and contrast these two contradictory imperatives. We define *happiness* as a state of contentment with one's personal life, generally expressed as spiritual, moral, social, intellectual, and physical well-being. *"Happiness"* is a prescription for our postmodern era of *"unhappiness."*

Happiness is much more valuable to human existence than we might have contemplated thus far. It is not merely a temporary human condition underpinned by feelings and emotions, receipt of gifts, or life's events such as university graduation, birthdays, weddings, and anniversaries. When we are happy, every part of our being is in harmony.

Happiness is an outward expression of feelings and emotions that transpire from happy memories that imbue personal happiness. Happiness is *(1) Personal*, and as we interact with others, happiness becomes *(2) Interpersonal*, *(3) Transactional*, and *(4) Transformational*. These four perspectives of happiness provide "new" insights into what makes us happy and how we might help to influence our happiness and the happiness of others.

To clarify these four perspectives, we define "PERSONAL HAPPINESS" as the feelings and emotions that permeate our soul when we invoke memories of happy events in our lives such as our graduation or wedding day. Each one contributes in *conscious* or *subconscious* ways to our personal happiness, but we must take ownership of the mistakes we make that bring unhappiness, and we must strive daily not to repeat the same action, and moreover, to be mindful of every action and interaction with fellow beings.

We define "INTERPERSONAL HAPPINESS" as feelings and emotions derived from an interpersonal relationship with a husband or wife, with children, with good friends, and with associates, and their devotion to the happiness of others and ourselves.

We define "TRANSACTIONAL HAPPINESS" as feelings and emotions derived from external stimuli such as the exchange of gifts, receipt of an award, and sale or purchase of a new automobile or home. These transactions ought to bring happiness to each person involved in the transaction.

We define "TRANSFORMATIONAL HAPPINESS" as feelings and emotions derived from being at an opera, or being witness to a daughter or son taking their marriage vows, or watching a father or mother take his or her first steps after recovery from a debilitating illness.

Happiness is to *recognize, acknowledge,* and *celebrate* our shared human heritage (the oneness of humanity). Any divergence from this fundamental premise can lead to unhappiness, evidenced by the political, religious, racial, color, and cultural divides between people and nations. Genuine happiness is to find *contentment*, avoid *resentment*, and foster love for fellow human beings. Happiness is to rise beyond life's existence as a daily routine to a life of purpose, to building a legacy of hope and happiness for the future.

Although one cannot theoretically store the happiness of one day and then recover it another day when we are in a state of gloom, happiness means that *today* is more hopeful than *yesterday*, and *tomorrow* is more hopeful than *today*. Nevertheless, happy experiences are stored in the labyrinth of our mind, no different from the memory of a great poem we read as a child or a song or scenery that comes to mind vividly.

For instance, in June 2014, Marjorie attended a wedding on the beautiful Fiji Island of Viti Levu. A beautiful sunset lit up the magnificent landscape. The scenic view left her with a lasting memory of the happy event and happy feelings.

Marjorie and I will never forget the experience we had visiting the Spanish Steps (*Scalina Spagna*), built in (1723–1725), Rome, Italy, Roman Baroque Style, a gathering place consisting of 138 steps placed in a mix of curves, straight flights, vistas, and terraces, a great place to just sit down and enjoy the atmosphere, the magnificent mixture of people from diverse countries and backgrounds and cultures, overshadowed by [beautiful] views of the Eternal City (http://romeonsegway.com/7-facts-about-the-spanish-steps/).

Likewise, some experiences infuse unhappiness throughout some of our lives, such as being at the scene of the fatal accident of my father and the untimely passing of Marjorie's dad, creating a lasting memory of the incident and unhappy feelings. These experiences etched in our minds evoke happy and unhappy feelings.

It is a cliché, though, to say, "No one can make us happy," or "We alone can make ourselves happy." Happiness is not merely about the personal desire to be happy but also about how we contribute to the *happy* or *unhappy* state of others, and how they contribute to our *happy* or *unhappy* state as well.

A son or daughter who brings home an excellent school report brings happiness, but a suspension report for truancy brings unhappiness, not just for himself or herself, but also for his or her parents, siblings, family members, and friends of the family. Each person faces a unique set of circumstances in his or her life that contribute to his or her happiness or unhappiness. Happiness is not "generic emotion." What makes one person happy may not inspire happiness in another.

A fatal automobile accident may cause unhappiness for all who witnessed the particular tragedy. The loss of investment, employment, or material possessions may cause a person to be unhappy, though the unhappiness might be temporary. Some may have the financial means to overcome these circumstances. Others may seek solace from God (a divine being) for their loss and the resultant suffering, and thus maintain a tranquil state.

Tranquility and happiness are co-equals because tranquility can lead to happiness, and happiness can result in tranquility. Tranquility also leads to contemplation on another age-old question, "What makes us happy?"

Whether we are mindful of the fact or not, we depend on each other for our source of "happiness nurturing." When we *love*, *care*, and *share* with each other, it makes us happy. Our Creator made us fellow beings; hence we thrive on human interactions, which is the lifeline for a "happy existence.

The words of Mary Baker Eddy put happiness in its broadest perspective:

"Happiness is spiritual, born of truth and love. It is unselfish; therefore, it cannot exist alone, but requires all [humanity] to share it."

— *Mary Baker Eddy (1821–1910)*

WHAT MAKES MARJORIE AND ME HAPPY?

What makes Marjorie and me happy? The answer is fundamental to our survival because happiness is a "mutual" "human survival proposition." Happiness brings *contentment*, but unhappiness brings *discontentment*. Most, if not *all*, of humanity desire to be happy, but not all people are aware that a change in their circumstances informs their "pursuit of happiness." Following are the twenty attributes, behaviors, and activities that make us happy, engender contentment, and help to elevate our "Happiness Index" (HI) level.

o   TWENTY ATTRIBUTES, BEHAVIORS, AND ACTIVITIES
    THAT MAKE MARJORIE AND ME HAPPY:

1. Taking responsibility for each other's happiness.
2. Knowing and trusting God's guidance.
3. Nurturing a friendly marriage.
4. Reading books together.
5. Loyalty in marriage.
6. Sharing dreams.
7. Reliable friends.
8. Co-partners.
9. Co-equals.
10. Co-owners.
11. Peaceful home.
12. Peaceful living.
13. Common vision.
14. Sharing research.
15. Cooking together.
16. Optimistic future.
17. Intelligent conversation.
18. Practicing healthy eating.
19. Laughing out loud (LOL) regularly.
20. Traveling companion (>1,000,000 KM).

It does not matter how strong and independent we are; we need spiritual, social, emotional, intellectual, and physical connections to make us happy, not merely for ourselves but for others as well. Happiness in the world hinges on human relationships, but where do we begin the process of transformation into a world of happiness?

We can strive daily to uphold the bond of marriage, to maintain family and community relations, to be loyal to employers and employees, and to be patriotic to our nation, compelled by a mutual need to be happy.

We can start immediately with our attitudes, such as the attitude of forgiveness toward family members, friends, and associates. We can begin with our attitude toward our employer and our employees, work, and community. We can start by caring for those who are less fortunate than we are, as well as our attitude toward other races, cultures, colors, and creeds. Furthermore, we need to be aware of our attitude toward self and accept those things that we cannot change. It is worth introducing the "Serenity Prayer" as a daily watchword. American theologian Karl Paul Reinhold Niebuhr (1892–1971), author, provides the best-known form:

"God, give us grace to accept with serenity the things that cannot be changed, courage to change the things which should be changed, and the wisdom to distinguish the one from the other." Justin Kaplan, ed., *Bartlett's Familiar Quotations* 735 (17th ed., 2002) (attributing the prayer to Niebuhr in 1943).[4]

The greatest benefit of happiness is that it is not strictly a material imperative, but it is first a "spiritual imperative" of the highest order, manifested as "joy." Marjorie and I espouse "joy" as the essential form of happiness, but it begins with a "new" understanding. Bolstered by understanding, love is the most powerful human resource that can transform human lives from *(1) Very Unhappy, (2) to Unhappy, (3) to Happy, (4) to Very Happy,* and *(5) to "Optimum Happiness" (OH)* (Reference: Table 5). Happiness is a global necessity that can improve the state of humankind and help to improve the lives of millions.

Today, in our affluent middle class or lower-income families, some members are in need of an escape from domestic violence, abuse, loneliness, impoverishment, overcrowding, or despair. Depression in children and adults is indicative of internal and external stressors on the family, which cause unhappiness, but small actions can change the "unhappiness dynamics."

---

[4] You will find many references online to some not being sure who really wrote the above prayer, some claiming that Reinhold Niebuhr was not actually the author. Many have researched it including trying to find out if it even goes back to 500 AD. Despite all the research, though, it still goes back to Niebuhr being the author (http://skdesigns.com/).

When I was a boy, I would walk for about a half mile along the railroad tracks to my uncle's home on Saturday mornings as a routine, to ask for a few dimes and nickels for the Saturday 12:30 p.m. matinee, mostly Western movies. The larger-than-life images of Western cowgirls, cowboys, and Indian chiefs "lighted the life" of this teenage boy and his pals.

Who knows what a young fatherless boy would have experienced without the "money," the "movies," and the "memories"? My uncle never failed to locate a few dimes somewhere on his dresser to make good my Saturday morning visits. He is Dr. Sylvan Saunders. In June 2005, at seventy-three years of age, he received a Doctor of Theology degree from a Christian university in the United States.

Many in the academic community research, study, and write in the field of human behavior. The focus is on groups and individuals, but it is important to understand that the benefits of being a happy person come from the four perspectives delineated earlier as *(1) Personal, (2) Interpersonal, (3) Transactional,* and *(4) Transformational.* Happiness is not "mutually exclusive" or just personal. It is the most positive of *all* human interpersonal experiences.

Youths in multigenerational families who have graduated with postgraduate and graduate degrees bring their parents, family members, and friends a wealth of happiness that one can discern in each of the four perspectives of happiness delineated above.

Childhood experiences, material status, social standing, family conflicts, internal prejudices, and even financial and material standing can affect one's happiness. Experiential observation reveals the pervasive effects of both *happiness* and *unhappiness* as they affect individuals of all races, cultures, religions, and socioeconomic classes.

Many of us are aware of what makes us happy, but there is a need for a deeper emphasis on the myriad of relationships that can elevate our happiness and "Happiness Index" (HI). We can be happy as an imperative of national happiness when we accept human needs for material resources, food, and shelter; education and healthcare; and international peace and security. Following are fifteen essential practices, achievements, attributes, behaviors, and customs that can make us happy in spite of human relationships.

o   FIFTEEN ESSENTIAL PRACTICES, ACHIEVEMENTS, ATTRIBUTES, BEHAVIORS, AND CUSTOMS THAT CAN MAKE US HAPPY:

1. *Spirituality* as a first imperative of human survival.
2. *Love* as the highest imperative of human survival.
3. *Education* as a relationship and happiness enabler.
4. *Respect* for authority as a primary responsibility.
5. *Character* as the first imperative in relationships.
6. *Personality* as a communication enabler.
7. *Honor* and *loyalty* in all relationships.
8. *Career* as an economic essential.
9. *Health* as a survival necessity.
10. *Mutual* respect for all humanity.
11. *Forgiveness* as a moral imperative.
12. *Justice* with fairness and transparency.
13. *Humility* as a cornerstone of leadership.
14. *Socialization* as an interdependent reality.
15. *Integrity* as the first imperative of business.

Notwithstanding the transformational power that is inherent in the above fifteen essential practices, achievements, attributes, and customs, nothing exceeds the "power of love" to transform human relationships.

LOVE AND HAPPINESS

"Love many things, for therein lies the true strength, and whosoever loves much performs much, and can accomplish much, and what is done in love is done well."

— *Vincent Willem van Gogh (1853–1890)*

It is possible for nations to co-exist happily when people and nations view civilization through the prism of higher human virtues such as loving, caring, and sharing, underpinned by "love," and not merely through social, political, and economic prisms. Principles of love for humanity underpin the philosophies of the great world religions and add force to the exercise of love. "Love must be sincere. Hate what is evil; cling to what is good. Be devoted to one another in brotherly love. 'Love one another as I have loved you'" (John 15:12, NKJV). "Honor one another above yourselves. Never be lacking in zeal, but keep your spiritual fervor, serving the Lord. Be Joyful in hope, patient in affliction, faithful in prayer" (Romans 12:9–13, NIV).

Love underpins all of the happiness that we seek. Love is the most powerful force in the universe. God's selfless love, *agápē*, taken from Greek writers, provides the spiritual bond that holds humanity together.

God's love (*agápē*) inspires us to include more of others. It heightens our capacity for empathy and brings us closer to the spiritual purpose of our existence.

The ultimate transforming form of this love is expressed when we allow God's love (*agápē*) to flow through us and from within us, as it penetrates into every sphere of human existence and removes any inclination toward fear, hate, and aggression.

This love (*agápē*) can uproot all forms of conflict between spouses, siblings, relatives, neighbors, employees, communities, and nations. Love is vital to the survival of humanity. Love is not merely an emotion. Love transcends all other human attributes.

This preeminent human characteristic inspires hope and happiness in people. Ancient Greek writers made a distinction between various forms of love, such as *philia*, which refers to a special relationship between husbands and wives or between close associates.

The characteristics of these relationships are the focus of the intimate bond between two individuals who share their lives and experiences. They refer to *storge* as a form of love or deep relationship between family members, such as the bond between parents and children and brothers and sisters.

Abbreviated below, Roman Krznaric, Australian cultural thinker, shares a broad insight into his book *The Ancient Greeks 6 Words for Love (And Why Knowing Them Can Change Your Life)*, in *Yes!* Magazine. Roman says:

"The ancient Greeks were just as sophisticated in the way they talked about love, recognizing six different varieties. They would have been shocked by our crudeness in using a single word both to whisper "I love you" over a candlelit meal and to casually sign an email "lots of love."

So what were the six loves known to the Greeks? And how can they inspire us to move beyond our current addiction to romantic love, which has 94 percent of young people hoping—but often failing—to find a unique soul mate who can satisfy all their emotional needs?"

Eros:

"The first kind of love was *eros,* named after the Greek god of fertility, and it represented the idea of sexual passion and desire. But the Greeks didn't always think of it as something positive, as we tend to do today...."

Philia:

"The second variety of love was *philia* or friendship, which the Greeks valued far more than the base sexuality of *eros. Philia* concerned the deep comradely friendship that developed between brothers in arms who had fought side by side on the battlefield...."

Ludus:

"[The third variety of love was *ludus].* This was the Greeks' idea of playful love, which referred to the affection between children or young lovers. We've all had a taste of it in the flirting and teasing in the early stages of a relationship...."

Agapé:

"The fourth love, and perhaps the most radical, was *agapé* or selfless love. This was a love that you extended to all people, whether family members or distant strangers. *Agapé* was later translated into Latin as *caritas,* which is the origin of our word "charity...."

Pragma:

"Another [fifth variety of] Greek love was the mature love known as *pragma*. This was the deep understanding that developed between long-married couples. *Pragma* was about making compromises to help the relationship work over time, and showing patience and tolerance...."

Philautia:

"The Greek's sixth variety of love was *philautia* or self-love. And the clever Greeks realized there were two types. One was an unhealthy variety associated with narcissism, where you became self-obsessed and focused on personal fame and fortune. A healthier version enhanced your wider capacity to love...." "It's time we introduced the six varieties of Greek love into our everyday way of speaking and thinking."[5]

A materially driven lifestyle seems to reduce our expressions of love for humanity to love for objects. The love that we exhibit for objects can lead to many forms of aggression and violence when the object of our veneration is threatened or taken away. Some individuals, perhaps unintentionally, seem to view material possessions as more valued than human health, life, safety, and goodwill toward others. An unintentional automobile accident can quickly escalate into "road rage" and create a lethal situation that spells unhappiness for all those who are affected by the situation.

Our material lives cause us to associate the meaning of love with a particular object, person, or idea. On occasion, we give expensive gifts to others as an expression of our love, though the "happiness effect" may be short lived.

---

[5] Reproduced by permission of Roman Krznaric, c/o The Hanbury Agency Ltd, 53 Lambeth Walk, London SE11 6DX. Copyright ©2013. Roman Krznaric is an Australian cultural thinker and cofounder of the School of Life in London. This article is based on his new book, *How Should We Live? Great Ideas from the Past for Everyday Life* (BlueBridge, Copyright ©2011 Roman Krznaric). Website: www.romankrznaric.com.   Tweets   at   @romankrznaric. http://www.yesmagazine.org/happiness/the-ancient-greeks-6-words-for-love-and-why-knowing-them-can-change-your-life.

This parallel relationship between material gifts and expressions of love begins at birth with gifts for the newborn, and it extends through old age with gifts for the bereaved. Likewise, our birthplace, our race, our language, our culture, our religion, and our family members and friends have an influence on to whom we extend our love and courtesy. Notwithstanding, the human family strives for unity despite being shuttled into the "global village" unprepared.

We joyfully extend our love to those with whom we are familiar, often with the expectation or assurance of their love in return. In contrast, the Synoptic Gospel writer Luke tells us that we should love our enemies and our neighbor as ourselves, without preconditions (Luke 10: 29–37).

Who is our neighbor? The word *neighbor* has deep significance for the unity of the human family, for which geographic limitations no longer exist. Without such an understanding, we can only love in the natural, human sense of the word. What is love, and why is it such a potent and unifying force in our world?

Love for humanity informs the teachings of the main world religions, yet the practice of universal love for humankind still seems to be a great challenge in our postmodern world. The Apostle Paul, writing in the book of Corinthians (AD 56), speaks of love thus:

"Love is patient, love is kind. Love does not envy, is not boastful, is not conceited, does not act improperly, is not selfish, is not provoked, and does not keep a record of wrongs. Love finds no joy in unrighteousness but rejoices in the truth. It bears all things, believes all things, hopes all things, and endures all things. Love never ends. But as for prophecies, they will come to an end; as for languages, they will cease."

— *1 Corinthians 13:4–8 (HCSB)*

The lack of love (agápē) for our neighbor can translate into unrestrained violence among rival street gangs. We have become accustomed to seeing others suffer the consequences of human conflict, and our response has been the same over the centuries, up to the present.

We mobilize significant humanitarian efforts in our quest to relieve human suffering throughout the world, only to repeat the same acts or to be spectators to the same acts on another stage with a greater cost to human suffering and unhappiness.

The prevailing divorce rates seem to challenge the concept of marriage and family as the ideal first society in which to practice "altruistic love" and the happiness that love transcends. Despite challenges, marriage will prevail as the most important foundation upon which to build stable families and nations.

MARRIAGE AND HAPPINESS

"A man leaves his father and mother to get married, and he becomes like one person with his wife."

— *Ephesians 5:31 (CEV)*

Marriage includes a "conscious" and "subconscious" search for *love*, *happiness,* and *longevity*. It is implicit in the bond of marriage as the loving couple recites the marriage vows, solemnized by one who represents the spiritual or civil aspect of the wedding, and generally witnessed by a throng of family members, friends, and well-wishers.

"What counts in making a happy marriage is not so much how compatible you are, but how you deal with incompatibility."

— *Leo Tolstoy (1828–1910)*

The traditions, counseling, the marriage "vow," and the life of marriage come from "love," the love (*agápē*) of God. The husband and wife are co-equals, though some roles and responsibilities in marriage are *shared, unique,* and *dissimilar,* founded upon universal principles of love, care, and longevity of the marriage. The love of God and not natural love is the "bond" that holds the marriage together. Without love, which is a "reciprocal affection," no relationship can flourish.

It is only by mirroring God's love for humanity that marriage partners can attain the ultimate state of fulfillment in marriage: "till death do us part." What a fascinating foundation upon which to build a marriage. The website *By the Knot* provides a compilation of thoughts on various marriage "oaths":

> *By the Knot*: "Each religious faith has wedding traditions and practices—including standard wedding vows—that have been passed down through generations. Exact phrases vary slightly from place to place and among the different clergy, so ask your officiant to tell you what he or she prefers."
>
> The basic Protestant vows: "…from this day forward, for better, for worse, for richer, for poorer, in sickness and in health, to love and to cherish, till death do us part…"
>
> Traditional Hindu wedding ceremonies have many elements and rituals. Technically, there are no "vows" in the Western sense, but the Seven Steps, or Saptha Padhi, around a flame (honoring the fire god, Agni) spell out the promises the couple makes to each other: "…Let us take the fourth step to acquire knowledge, happiness, and harmony by mutual love and trust…" "Let us take the sixth step for self-restraint and longevity…" "Finally, let us take the seventh step and be true companions and remain lifelong partners by this wedlock."[6]

People marry for love, companionship, and family. Most, if not all, marriages begin with the notion that it is a lifelong commitment by the couple. However, based on available statistical data, the trend seems to indicate that many marriages fail to deliver longevity and happiness, which are implicit in the wedding vows. The probability of a successful marriage increases when the couple seeks professional marriage counseling before they get married.

Marriage is a "Happiness Contract" that is underwritten by our birthright to be happy. Failure to uphold the agreement can spell trouble for the marriage partners. Marriage is more than two people

---

[6] https://www.theknot.com/content/traditional-wedding-vows-from-various-religions.

living in harmony. It is the *first* institution of "altruistic" love. Unfortunately, many marriages end in separation and divorce, often resulting in unhappiness for the spouses and their offspring. Nevertheless, many divorced couples often move on and live happy lives, even with children in blended families.

> "When there is love in a marriage, there is harmony in the home; when there is harmony in the home, there is contentment in the community; when there is contentment in the community, there is prosperity in the nation; when there is prosperity in the nation, there is peace in the world."
>
> — *Chinese Proverb*

Happiness can blossom when the spouses strive to maintain the "vows" of marriage and reject the notion of "irreconcilable differences." We have a choice to take "ownership" of our marriage and "strive" to "reconcile differences."

Separation and divorce trends will continue in light of the ever-increasing stresses of daily living, predominantly the demands of work, career aspirations, and raising children. These challenges often impede the capacity of many couples who would wish to spend quality time with their families to build relations necessary for family stability. Marriage relationships today are under great stress due to the demands of commuting, work, and family commitments.

Statistical observation indicates that married couples who live longer, healthier, and happier lives have a compassionate nature; they mutually espouse shared values and responsibilities, have a keen sense of loyalty, and a healthy work–life balance.

The economics of survival relegate both husband and wife to the workplace, which sometimes creates a shift in roles and responsibilities, bringing stress into the relationship. Various forms of blended families will emerge in the future, but the family will survive. The natural desire for human companionship will prevail in spite of the domestic violence, "irreconcilable differences," and broken marriages.

God is the "Author" and co-partner in the marriage relationship (Reference: Figure 1). For better or for worse, many of us get married; hence, the critical need to strengthen the institution. The biblical (religious) view of marriage affirms the presence of a divine element in marriages. The couple must differentiate the wedding sacrament from the wedding.

GRAPHICAL DEPICTION OF
HUSBAND AND WIFE AS CO-EQUALS AND CO-PARTNERS
WITH GOD, AND WITNESSES TO THE MARRIAGE VOWS

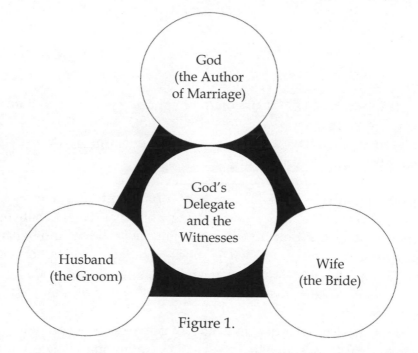

Figure 1.

His representative officiates in the capacity of "spiritual" and "civic" authority to perform the sacrament in the presence of witnesses. The witnesses become a testimony to the wedding "vows" that the married couple exchange as a public declaration.

The wedding sacrament solemnizes and symbolizes a couple's commitment. Marriage represents a unity of *mind, soul*, and *body*; it likewise involves an understanding of God's purpose for the spousal union. Husbands and wives are no longer two but one flesh (Matthew 19:5).

This biblical metaphor may be difficult to comprehend, but the reality is for the *unity, stability,* and *longevity* of the union. This deeper meaning of marriage is the "permanent foundation" upon which marriage rests. It is the most significant source of happiness in the lives of the couple, and it spills over into the family, neighborhood, community, and nation.

Marriage also rests on five foundational principles — *(1) Companionship, (2) Completeness, (3) Enjoyment, (4) Procreation,* and *(5) Protection* — to ensure security, longevity, and happiness in marriage and family life, and the stability of nations. These five biblical principles for *unity, stability,* and *longevity* in marriage are *intrinsic* to the reality of the bonds of marriage. These are the first canon of marriage, as the spiritual bonds upon which to build a foundation and to establish happy families.

Other systems of belief, religions, and cultures subscribe to other perspectives to keep and maintain their bond of marriage, but the desire is the same for most, if not all, married couples. Some follow the strictures of their particular faith while others may not follow any religious stricture at all. The five biblical principles may be "new" to some, but they have the capacity to foster unity, stability, longevity, and happiness, described briefly as follows:

o FIVE BIBLICAL PRINCIPLES FOR UNITY, STABILITY, LONGEVITY, AND HAPPINESS IN MARRIAGE:

Principle 1: Companionship *(Mark 10:8)*
Principle 2: Completeness *(Genesis 2:23–24)*
Principle 3: Enjoyment *(1 Corinthians 7:5)*
Principle 4: Procreation *(Psalm 127:3)*
Principle 5: Protection *(Ephesians 5:25–28)*

o PRINCIPLE 1: COMPANIONSHIP

The principle of COMPANIONSHIP affirms, "I am alone without you." I am unable to achieve my fullest potential in life without you. With you in my life, I can experience the oneness of "heart" and "head" working together to achieve "our" fullest potential, which is best, expressed by the words *us* and *ours,* no longer *me, my,* or *mine.* Companionship does not merely imply being in one's presence. It begins with an understanding of the needs of each other. It means a spiritual, emotional, and physical connection to each other.

Companionship means setting aside quality time to share conversations and listen to each other's needs, hopes, dreams, and aspirations. It means sharing some common indoor and outdoor interests. Most of all, it means nurturing an unbroken bond of friendship, which says, "I will never abandon you for another."

o   PRINCIPLE 2: COMPLETENESS

The principle of COMPLETENESS affirms that each married couple is saying, "I have checked and examined my life carefully and concluded that you are the best person to meet and fulfill my needs. Since my needs are not temporal but permanent, I, therefore, need you in my life permanently. My life is incomplete without you. I will live a life of trustworthiness, loyalty, and fidelity, and will forsake all others until death do us part."

The marriage vow is the most important proclamation of "global happiness." No other statement when put into action can bring more happiness to marriage, family, and the world than the marriage vow, *powerful, profound,* and *far-reaching* in its capacity for completeness.

o   PRINCIPLE 3: ENJOYMENT

The principle of ENJOYMENT affirms that the sexual act is not only for the consummation of marriage, but it also strengthens love in marriage. This physical expression within marriage is not merely a privilege and pleasure but also a lifelong responsibility.

The married couple affirms, "I enjoy the physical expression of marital sex with you, and I am responsible for the child or children that result from the sexual act." The mutual enjoyment of sex in marriage helps the married couple to develop self-control and to maintain *trustworthiness, loyalty,* and *fidelity* within the marriage to the exclusion of all "others."

o   PRINCIPLE 4: PROCREATION

The principle of PROCREATION affirms that children are a gift from God to parents (Genesis 1:28). Children are the fruit of the womb as His reward (Psalm 127:3). Children replenish the earth (Genesis 1:28). Children in the lives of parents ought to make a family happy.

Do parents with children live happier lives? Children make a man happy (Psalm 127:5). Parents with children enjoy the "fruit of their marriage" and the nurturing they provide that is an extension of themselves and the magnificent experience of marriage life. This experience becomes a family legacy when parents become grandparents and great-grandparents.

o   PRINCIPLE 5: PROTECTION

The principle of PROTECTION affirms the need for the nurturing and protection of children who will ultimately influence the direction of the world, "for better or for worse," as parents and future leaders.

The life of the wife also falls under the protection of her husband and vice versa as co-equals, as the *heart* and *head* of the married relationship. When a husband extends love for his wife, she becomes more beautiful in every aspect of her being, and her love becomes reciprocal.

The couple, therefore, must always remind each other of the sacredness of their union since it represents a vital union that is eternal in value, weight, and rewards. When married couples practice mutual protection of *heart* and *head*, it helps to increase longevity in marriage.

SUMMARY OF THE FIVE BIBLICAL PRINCIPLES FOR UNITY, STABILITY, LONGEVITY, AND HAPPINESS IN MARRIAGE

These five fundamental principles help the married couple to build bonds of friendship and a strong relationship based on mutual needs, hopes, dreams, and aspirations. These five relationship bonds underpin the mutual expectations of the married couple. When married couples maintain constant awareness of the five principles of marriage, and when they engage in the consistent daily practice of the bonds of the wedding, it helps to create stability in the family for not only the couple, but also for stable societies, a connection that is not always apparent.

In marriage, as in *all* relationships, the "power of dialogue" creates opportunities to build mutual trust and friendship. Following are twenty key points for dialogue to help build unbreakable bonds for a healthy and happy marriage relationship and the family foundation.

o   TWENTY KEY POINTS FOR DIALOGUE TO BUILD
    UNBREAKABLE BONDS FOR A HAPPY MARRIAGE:

1. *Understand* God's plan for the marriage.
2. *Foster* loyalty and fidelity in marriage.
3. *Engage* in long-term family planning.
4. *Keep* communication channels open.
5. *Establish* community activity goals.
6. *Support* each other's career goals.
7. *Honor* the marriage vows.
8. *Agree* on work–life balance.
9. *Build* each other up spiritually.
10. *Develop* mutual religious goals.
11. *Develop* mutual interests.
12. *Establish* realistic expectations.
13. *Share* responsibilities in the home.
14. *Mutually* agree on work–life issues.
15. *Develop* mutual (intellectual) objectives.
16. *Accept* responsibilities within the family.
17. *Practice* financial management and budgeting.
18. *Plan* for the future care and welfare of children.
19. *Create* plans for family vacations (rest and relaxation).
20. *Discuss* issues openly and with empathy for each other.

Ideally, the right starting point for couples contemplating marriage is as follows: "Increase the *dialogue*, increase the happiness." "Increase the *loyalty*, increase the happiness." "Increase the *friendship,* increase the happiness." "Increase the *love,* increase the happiness."

Some married couples take for granted that merely maintaining the marriage relationship equates to a successful marriage. The ability to understand and manage these twenty key points for dialogue in marriage will increase the probability of fidelity, longevity, marriage success, peace, and happiness. Marjorie and I have discovered that one of the most important human attributes that helps to sustain all human relationships is LOYALTY.

LOYALTY AND HAPPINESS

"Loyalty to the family must be merged into loyalty to the community, loyalty to the community into loyalty to the nation, and loyalty to the nation into loyalty to [humankind]. The citizen of the future must be a citizen of the world."

— *Thomas Cochrane (1775–1860)*

Loyalty and happiness go "hand in hand." *Love* and *loyalty* are two of the cardinal virtues that hold a marriage, family, friendship, corporation, and institution together. Love is universal. Loyalty brings out the best in human relationships in marriage, family, corporate, and national and international relationships. Loyalty is a great stabilizer of human relationships. Loyalty contributes to improving the "Happiness Index" (HI) of the marriage partners.

Love informs loyalty. Without love (*agápē*) in a relationship, loyalty cannot flourish. Likewise, loyalty in marriage, care for family, and integrity in business can surpass all other human attributes except love (*agápē*). The mere fact that a person knows that the other is loyal infuses feelings of peace, safety, security, and happiness, and it strengthens the relationship.

> "To maintain a joyful family requires much from both the parents and the children. Each member of the family has to become, in a special way, the servant of the others."
>
> —*Pope John Paul II (1920–2005)*

Although loyalty is critical to all relationships, it can flourish only in a nurturing and caring environment. Allegiance, constancy, consistency, dependability, devotion, faithfulness, fidelity, openness, reliability, steadfastness, and trustworthiness also underpin loyalty. Loyalty transcends feelings of happiness, contentment, and security. Loyalty also extends into the lives of children and all those who are a part of the family, group, corporation, institution, or organization that exemplifies loyalty. This human attribute transcends all barriers.

Loyalty is the bedrock of longevity in any relationship, good or bad. From street gangs to close-knit traditional families, loyalty is the glue that holds the relationship together. Loyalty can also be a double-edged sword; for instance, many leaders of past centuries held ideological views, and those loyal to them carried out their command, causing great carnage and unhappiness in the world.

Conversely, *disloyalty* is a destructive force that can instantaneously destroy relationships, along with everything that was built up over many years. Many factors in life underpin disloyalty; the most critical is "self-interest." In marriage, some may have selfish motives that satisfy their personal goals rather than mutual goals of the relationship.

Disloyalty can impair long-standing relationships, sometimes with a single act of betrayal. Divorced parents may move on to happier life experiences, but the statisticians tell us that the rising number of broken homes, fatherless children, and single-parent homes do not present a happy picture for children of the twenty-first century and the new millennium.

Statisticians also tell us that many juveniles who have an encounter with the justice system come from dysfunctional and fatherless homes; often these are unhappy homes. Wealthy homes with two parents can be similarly unhappy homes; often, some use material wealth as a substitute for human companionship that is lacking.

Lack of loyalty in the corporate arena often displays a similar dynamic in which some employees feel betrayed by corporations that do not demonstrate the corporate loyalty of the past when the human worker was essential to the industrial processes facilitated by machines; machines served people.

The rising cost of employee benefits—in particular, healthcare and pension benefits—may influence corporate loyalty or even the capacity to retain employees. Likewise, the employee may display disloyalty due to a workplace that may be unfulfilling. These situations lead to an "unhappy" workplace.

Rapid technological changes have an adverse impact on the culture of corporations and the relationship between employer and employee. The words *employer* and *employee* loyalty have all but disappeared from the lexicon of workplace vocabulary in the postmodern era.

This "new" challenge to the postmodern workplace can lead to an unhappy work environment. More importantly, neither employer nor employee expects or contemplates loyalty as salient to the relationship. An unhappy workplace does not bode well for the future of a happy work environment, but many innovative organizations are coming to the rescue. One such organization is Zappos, led by CEO Tony Hsieh, with creative work such as "Delivering Happiness."

Delivering Happiness is Zappos CEO Tony Hsieh's first book, which launched in 2010 and has since sold over 600,000 copies worldwide, hit #1 on bestsellers lists like the New York Times and USA Today, and been voted one of the best business books by NPR, Inc. Magazine and the Wall Street Journal....Tony shows how a very different kind of corporate culture is a powerful model for achieving success — and how by concentrating on the happiness of those around you, you can dramatically increase your own."[7]

Nations can measure the cost of happiness empirically in our twenty-first century, in which corporate loyalty is on the downturn with the same detrimental impact as the downturn of the economy. The effects of many of these changes, in which corporations refer to employees as "surplus," also invade the home as family stress while uncertainty rises and suffocates the happiness of individuals, families, and entire communities as well.

Corporate loyalty sustained and brought corporations through the Industrial Revolution (1800s–1900s) and up to the twenty-first century. Likewise, loyalty had once been the bedrock of marriage relationships. Today, marriage partners seek divorce citing "irreconcilable differences," which might be symptoms of chronic unhappiness with each other or a particular situation, behavior, or attitude.

The viability of great societies hinges on the integrity of the great pillars of marriage, family, productivity, and community, fortified by stable governments when nations contemplate the *potency* of loyalty at all levels of interaction. Following are five key attributes that transcend behaviors and that can enhance loyalty within marriages, families, and within businesses.

o   FIVE KEY ATTRIBUTES TO INSPIRE LOYALTY WITHIN
     MARRIAGES, FAMILIES, AND WITHIN BUSINESSES:

1. *Love* (friendship)
2. *Fidelity* (loyalty)
3. *Integrity* (honesty)
4. *Empathy* (understanding)
5. *Equality* (impartiality)

Daily practice of these five key attributes can have a profound influence on the happiness of all of the institutions and organizations that are essential to *worth*, *growth*, and *productivity*.

---

[7] http://deliveringhappiness.com/book/.

Some challenges will arise in the form of cyclic economic collapse, social unrest, rejection of religion, political apathy, early youth independence, infidelity, disloyalty, and a general state of unhappiness.

Differences in marriage are not "always" irreconcilable. The family should strive to remain loyal, and renew a "new" spirit of cooperation for the survival of families, corporations, and nations. Loyalty enables all human relationships with mutual benefits. It is an *indispensable* ally in our quest for happiness. What can postmodern societies do to foster a greater sense of loyalty?

Some individuals pursue their careers, money, wealth, and power to the detriment of a happy marriage and the well-being of children. The resultant marriage breakdown can lead to financial hopelessness. Children can become desperate and succumb to street life as an escape from the home, creating a "new" category of homeless individuals.

We must endeavor to maintain the "trajectory of loyalty" and pass on this salient human attribute to the next generation. We must maintain a conscious awareness of our relationships within marriage, family, community, corporation, and nation. To do otherwise is to flirt with a higher cost of survival, to make available less money to build needed "happiness infrastructure," and to lower the threshold of unhappiness for many. Money, when managed effectively, can be a source of *happiness* on the one hand and a source of *unhappiness* on the contrary when people mismanage money.

MONEY AND HAPPINESS

"Simple, genuine goodness is the best capital to found the business of this life upon."

— *Louisa May Alcott (1832-1888)*

Is money synonymous with happiness? Can money buy happiness? Money may not buy happiness, but it is a crucial factor in the happiness equation. Unlike agrarian societies, money is the principal exchange in postmodern capitalist societies. Many individuals would say that they are happy when they have sufficient money to satisfy their immediate needs and the needs of their children. For some others, wants supersede needs to fulfill a more comfortable life, and then there are those for whom only a lavish lifestyle will suffice.

Lack of money may present a major challenge to some marriages and the postmodern family. Having an adequate source of money is essential to our survival to purchase goods and services, though money is a "double-edged sword."

An anonymous writer puts money in an interesting context thus:

"Money will buy a bed but not sleep; books but not brains; food but not appetite; finery but not beauty; a house but not a home; medicine but not health; luxuries but not culture; amusements but not happiness; religion but not salvation."

—Author Unknown

There is a broad range of perspectives regarding money. For instance, Andrew Blackman, the *Wall Street Journal*, November 10, 2014, provides an answer to the age-old question. Blackman says:

"Can money buy happiness? Over the past few years, new research has given us a much deeper understanding of the relationship between what we earn and how we feel. Economists have been scrutinizing the links between income and happiness across nations, and psychologists have probed individuals to find out what really makes us tick when it comes to cash. The results, at first glance, may seem a bit obvious: Yes, people with higher incomes are, broadly speaking, happier than those who struggle to get by. But dig a little deeper into the findings, and they get a lot more surprising—and a lot more useful."[8]

---

[8] http://www.wsj.com/articles/can-money-buy-happiness-heres-what-science-has-to-say-1415569538.

Marjorie and I have nurtured five children, not including nieces and nephews. We understand that "it takes a village to raise a child" (African proverb), but in addition to the "village," it takes financial capital to raise children in a "capitalist" society. According to MoneySense.ca, "The average cost of raising a child to age 18 is a whopping $243,660." The more gifted children are, the more it costs to raise them in an environment in which postsecondary education is vital to their future careers. Furthermore, children with disabilities can also pose a financial challenge for their parents.

Money may not buy happiness in the permanent sense, but it can help to sustain happiness. Conversely, lack of money relegates the poor and disadvantaged to a life of less than "Optimum" nutrition, health, housing, transportation, education, and employment. Lack of money denies much of the world's population from participation in extraordinary acts of kindness. This inability to give also deprives people of the inner happiness and "joy" that come with sharing with others as a mutual reward.

Marjorie and I have aggregate travel on four continents to *underdeveloped*, *developing*, and *developed* countries. We have witnessed how the lack of money frustrates and challenges some families and the "financial complacency" of some with abundant of money. We have seen how their happiness takes flight due to poor nutrition, deficient diet, failing health, and inadequate housing and education, underpinned by the lack of money.

The level of frustration varies among peoples and nations. The more affluent societies also appear to have higher levels of frustration and unhappiness due to higher material wants and expectations, but the poor have a harder existence.

> "The poor are shunned even by their neighbors, but the rich have many friends....He who has mercy on the poor, happy *is* he."
>
> — *Proverbs 14:20 (NIV)*

The materially abundant lives of many living in affluent Western societies associate financial wealth and material possessions with happiness. The most admired people in our world are those with abundant material possessions.

Although happiness derived from such admiration is real, the challenge to sustain a viable material status can often result in behaviors that bring unhappiness. For instance, investment risks, gambling, stressful commutes, long working hours, and absentee parenting can contribute to challenges to sustain material success. More importantly, health, well-being, and family stability could be at risk.

One might postulate that material possessions contribute to happiness for the wealthy, but consider the gift of a four-million-dollar diamond ring to a blushing Hollywood bride and the gift of a five-dollar box of crayons to a dispossessed child in an underdeveloped country.

Can any scientific inquiry or observation determine that the Hollywood bride derives greater happiness from the diamond ring on her finger than the dispossessed child with the box of crayons in his or her hands? Moreover, can any scientific research or observation demonstrate that the disproportionate material value of the gifts can translate to disproportionate happiness of one over the other?

This parallel relationship between material gifts and expressions of happiness begins at birth with gifts for the newborn. This essential element of the human "happiness equation" is to give and receive, but by extension, to give more than one asks is not merely natural, but a divine command (Luke 12:48).

This national and international preoccupation to give and receive gifts at birth, birthdays, marriage, Valentine's Day, and Christmas Day, and though highly commercialized, contributes to happiness in the world, though temporary.

Religious individuals ascribe the love of God (*agápē*) as a gift to humanity, which is *eternal*, *absolute*, and *unconditional*, and the value of which is incalculable. When this love (*agápē*) radiates in our hearts, the universality of humanity becomes a reality, and we begin to experience the same happiness for others that we feel for ourselves.

Many individuals give money because they are wealthy or generous, thankfully, but giving (not strictly money) is a "spiritual" command that is the foundation of the great religions. Generosity is in the human DNA (deoxyribonucleic acid). We have witnessed generosity by poor individuals who give to others less fortunate than themselves sacrificially.

> "From a Christian perspective, the Bible is a vast repository of knowledge to foster a balanced view of money. Jamieson-Fausset-Brown Bible Commentary alerts that "the love of money—not the money itself, but the love of it—the wishing to be rich (1Timothy 6:9)—"is a root (Ellicott and Middleton: not as English Version, 'the root') of all evils." (So the Greek plural).
>
> The wealthiest may be rich not in a bad sense; the poorest may covet to be so (Psalm 62:10). Love of money is not the sole root of evils, but it is a leading "root of bitterness" (Hebrews 12:15), for "it destroys faith, the root of all that is good." "Keep your lives free from the love of money..." (Hebrews 13:5). "In everything I did, I showed you that by this kind of hard work we must help the weak, remembering the words the Lord Jesus himself said: 'It is more blessed to give than to receive.'" (Acts 20:35, NIV).

Our conscience compels us to give, but observably, the general spiritual, mental, social, and physical health, and stability and happiness of disadvantaged people in the world, are under greater threat than for the general population.

Paradoxically, being a wealthy person is not a guarantee of spiritual, mental, social, or physical health, or happiness any more than being poor is a guarantee of unhappiness. A debilitating illness can plunge a family into poverty or even bankruptcy, likewise a loss of employment or failure of a family business.

Ruth Alexander, BBC News, June 198, 2013, Magazine-22935692, points us briefly to some of the enormous challenges that the poor face in daily life. Ruth states:

> "Every 15 seconds a child dies of hunger [mainly in the underdeveloped countries], says a campaign by charities urging G8 leaders to pledge more aid for the world's poorest families—or every 10 seconds, according to the latest version of the slogan. But does this paint an accurate

picture? There is enough food for everyone, but not everyone has enough food, says the Enough Food for Everyone If campaign."[9]

"*Happy Money* offers a tour of research on the science of spending, explaining how you can get more happiness for your money. Authors Elizabeth Dunn and Michael Norton have outlined five principles—from choosing experiences over stuff to spending money on others—to guide not only individuals looking for financial security, but also companies seeking to create happier employees and provide 'happier products' to their customers. Dunn and Norton show how companies from Google to Pepsi to Charmin have put these ideas into action."[10]

We often think of money in the abstract, but where does the money come from that we need to satisfy needs and bring a temporary state of happiness? We immediately think of education as a primary source for the general population. Education (higher education) can be expensive and may pose a challenge for some career options as the age of robots, cobots (collaborative robots), and supercomputers invade some job markets.

The paradox of this advancing need for new technologies to evolve the information age is the overshadowing of the critical need for "humanity" and "spirituality" in the "age of anxiety." "In 2012, about 3 million service robots for personal and domestic use were sold, 20% more than in 2011. The value of sales increased to US$1.2 billion" (World Robotics 2013 Service Robots, (http://www.worldrobotics.org/).

Notwithstanding, you can help to increase your "Happiness Index" (HI) by increasing your education, which is the gateway to better career choices, better employment prospects, and higher financial compensation. Other sources of money include creativity, innovation, invention, real estate investment, and inheritances. Unfortunately, there are those who live by "chance" with expectations of lottery winnings.

---

[9] http://www.bbc.com/news/magazine-22935692.

[10] http://www.amazon.ca/Happy-Money-Science-Happier-Spending/dp/1451665075.

King Solomon, the wise King of Israel (circa 970–931 BCE), writes:

"Wealth *gained by* dishonesty will be diminished, but he who gathers by labor will increase."

—*Proverbs 13:11 (NKJV)*

The twenty-first century has ushered in economic uncertainty for many households, both wealthy and poor. Businesses small and large face financial challenges as well. Some businesses reduce production and downsize their corporations to manage the uncertainty. Some families (wealthy and poor) are better able to overcome some of the situations that unhappiness can cause. Others rely on their religious beliefs and their inner "spiritual circle" to enable them to cope in times of economic challenges.

We provide the following ten *nonreligious* and *religious* principles that have guided our decision-making in times of economic challenges and as a regular practice.

o   TEN NONRELIGIOUS PRINCIPLES TO CONSIDER IN GOOD
     AND BAD ECONOMIC TIMES:

1. Stay focused.
2. Learn new skills.
3. Consolidate debt.
4. Plan driving trips.
5. Expand your circle.
6. Prepare a meal plan.
7. Create a monthly budget.
8. Repair rather than replace.
9. Postpone expensive vacations.
10. Reduce discretionary expenses.

Likewise, below we provide the following ten *religious* principles that have guided our decision-making in good and bad economic times and as a regular practice. These twenty principles are merely a starting point to avoid financial breakdown.

o   TEN RELIGIOUS PRINCIPLES TO CONSIDER IN GOOD AND
    BAD ECONOMIC TIMES:

1. Guard against the impulse to be unfair.
2. Choose prudence over extravagance.
3. Guard against the impulse of greed.
4. Be faithful to those who serve you.
5. Be cognizant of those less fortunate.
6. Be generous with excess wealth.
7. Seek wisdom ahead of wealth.
8. Exercise justice and mercy.
9. Develop a good reputation.
10. Be thankful for all things.

Although there are many ways of coping with economic challenges, from *nonreligious* and *religious* perspectives, many families, including ours, have experienced sporadic economic challenges. We have embraced both aspects because together they are more *potent* than embracing one or the other. One might surmise that they comprise both *intellectual* and *moral* perspectives.

The reality that faces rich and poor is that neither one is any more capable of buying good health when confronted with a catastrophic illness. Widely informed individuals are aware that a mentally and physically rested healthy body is synonymous with a clear mind and a happier predisposition. Other nonmonetary attributes are equally empowering such as *attitude* and *gratitude* for life.

ATTITUDE, GRATITUDE, AND HAPPINESS

"Gratitude bestows reverence, allowing us to encounter everyday epiphanies, those transcendent moments of awe that change forever how we experience life and the world."

—*John Milton (1608–1674)*

Happiness lives between the twin towers of *attitude* and *gratitude*. These twin towers of attitude and gratitude are powerful beacons of light that shine a path to *patience* and *humility*, which undergird the twin towers.

Attitude manifests thoughts and actions that are both positive and negative. A positive attitude demonstrates *hope, trust,* and *happiness*, and a negative attitude displays *despair, mistrust,* and *unhappiness.* Attitude and gratitude are not mere human attributes; they transform lives.

Patience and humility underpin attitude and gratitude. When things go wrong, the situation is "what it is." We should strive to remain calm and reasoned. A *negative* attitude will always have adverse outcomes, but a *positive* attitude can positively change the dynamics that underpin the situation.

You may have to postpone an important trip because of the weather but gain an opportunity to catch up on some household projects. When we accept a situation for "what it is," it creates *internal* harmony with self and *external* harmony with others.

The choice is ours to use the tools that are available to us—spiritual, moral, social, intellectual, and physical (the embodiment of happiness)—to nurture and sustain happiness. We can conjure up the "power of small gestures." We can begin with open minds and positive thoughts for the day. Every morning we rise, we can choose how we want our day to transpire.

We can enter the workplace with a readiness to respond to our work associates with unkind words and be the benefactor of an unhappy work environment, or we can decide to let kind words and high ideals guide our thoughts. Often, the universe blesses us with all the things that can make us happy. We may be in good health and have a successful career, a husband or wife, and healthy children yet feel unhappy.

One may be a corporate executive, earn a seven-figure income, be in the top tenth percentile of affluent people in the world, and live in a suburban neighborhood with one or two children yet experience chronic unhappiness or depression.

What can bolster happiness in our lives is an attitude of gratitude even for the things in life that we take for granted such as a beautiful sunshine, living in a peaceful neighborhood, or a loyal spouse and family members.

GRATITUDE has reciprocal benefits. When we exercise gratitude, the lives it influences radiate with happiness. The converse, INGRATITUDE, radiates unhappiness. Consider a business partner who benefitted from the success of the enterprise but walks away when the economy takes a downturn, leaving his or her business partner to cope with the financial dilemma.

Consider a husband or wife who rises to an executive management position in a corporation and then abandons the spouse because of a perception that the spouse does not fit his or her "new" image. This "unhappiness reality" confronts us in the postmodern age in which the aura of a person's image can dominate the social landscape and change perceptions in the public and private world.

Following are fifteen essential keys to unlocking the doors of *attitude* and *gratitude* that can lead to a happy and healthier life of fulfillment.

o   FIFTEEN ESSENTIAL KEYS TO UNLOCKING THE DOORS OF ATTITUDE AND GRATITUDE THAT CAN LEAD TO HAPPINESS:

1. Demonstrate love and care for others.
2. Be grateful for your work associates.
3. Genuinely compliment others.
4. Volunteer with a local group.
5. Be a good listener to others.
6. Be thankful for your health.
7. Be thankful for small things.
8. Greet others in a friendly manner.
9. Be thankful for spouse and children.
10. Let someone in a hurry go before you.
11. Donate regularly to a charity of choice.
12. Be grateful for every morning you rise.
13. Surprise a friend with a greeting card.
14. Maintain loyalty to friends and family.
15. Purchase some good reads for friends.

We can make a conscious effort to practice acts of gratitude daily. When we demonstrate visible acts of gratitude, they spill over into the lives of children and adults. Children then begin to display their acts of gratitude early in their lives as a positive influence on their upbringing. You may have to rearrange some parts of your life to engender a spirit of *attitude* and *gratitude*.

Even the small stuff can make us unhappy. For instance, a visit to the office of one of the many surgeons who care for my health can often include an extended waiting period. I would often become impatient. During one of those visits, I decided to change my attitude to gratitude. I began to internalize the fact that when the surgeon walks into the room, his radiant personality transforms the room.

I remind myself often that the surgeon is the embodiment of positive nurturing. He imparts a sense of youthfulness and rejuvenation through his conversations. I decided to take a journal, magazine, or laptop to the waiting room to change the experience. Now a visit to my surgeon is an experience that I wholeheartedly welcome, notwithstanding.

Gratitude is a term that encompasses a greater range of actions than we might contemplate, such as *appreciation*, *thankfulness*, and *gratefulness*. These attributes of gratitude inspire us to perform acts that we might otherwise consider simple acts of kindness and courtesy, but they have far-reaching positive consequences for the betterment of human relations.

Change may call for a commitment to rise above the "fear of failure." Fear can be as minor as a second or third attempt to obtain a driver's license or the challenge to overcome academic failure, or as major as fear of losing one's employment, fear of getting old, or fear of a catastrophic illness diagnosis.

Change may involve positive radical action and a willingness to do things that you have not done before, or it may require you to make sacrifices that you might not have contemplated. Some may say that they are too old to change or that their religion and culture may inhibit them from adjusting to a "new" way of life in a different country.

As a parent or guardian, you may have to adjust your schedule to spend more time with your children. You may have to adopt a new attitude, attend a baseball game, meet with teachers, or walk to the neighborhood church, synagogue, temple, or mosque with your children.

Change may mean to rise above pride and express remorse for a wrong, extend *forgiveness*, seek *repentance*, and provide *restitution*.

In the end, happiness will reign supreme. This magnitude of change will instill an attitude of hope and happiness in anyone touched by the "new" you, which will become evident by your "new" attitude.

ATTITUDE, HOPE, AND HAPPINESS

> "If a man insisted on always being serious, and never allowed himself a bit of fun and relaxation, he would go mad or become unstable without knowing it."
>
> — *Herodotus (circa 484 BCE–425 BCE)*

Attitude, hope, and happiness are principal factors that can bring about the greatest positive change in personal lives and the world. Our thoughts are fertile ground for a positive or negative attitude to flourish. The mass media environment has a significant influence on the way we think of the world, often contradictory to our beliefs.

Thoughts of hopefulness produce an attitude of hope. Thoughts of fearfulness create an attitude of fear. Thoughts of resentfulness produce an attitude of resentment, and thoughts of forgiveness produce an attitude that forgives.

The labyrinth of the mind is a storehouse of positive and negative thoughts. We were born with an infinite capacity to store our thoughts. Negative thoughts imbue the mind with unhappiness. Conversely, positive thoughts permeate the mind with happiness. Choose positive thoughts for a happy mind that is full of peacefulness and a healthy mental and hopeful attitude. Charles Rozell "Chuck" Swindoll, evangelical Christian pastor, author, educator, and preacher, profoundly states:

> "I believe the single most significant decision I can make on a day-to-day basis is my choice of attitude. It is more important than my past, my education, my bankroll, my successes or failures, fame or pain, what other people think of me or say about my circumstances, my position, or me. Attitude keeps me going or cripples my progress. It alone fuels my fire or assaults my hope. When my attitudes are

right, there is no barrier too high, no valley too deep, no dream too extreme, and no challenge too great for me."[11]

These positive attributes will engender a higher "Happiness Index" (HI). Let us examine the word *happiness* for a moment. Can there be *happiness* without *hope*, or *hope* without *happiness?* Most, if not all, human beings are in "search of happiness," but some may experience only fleeting moments of happiness even though they may search for the elusive state all of their lives.

The recurring state of unhappiness, underpinned by hopelessness around the world, makes evident the need for higher levels of intervention, not only as leadership, political, social, and economic imperatives but also as a *religious* and *spiritual* imperative as well.

For many, hope lies in the abundance of material things they have and the potential for acquiring more things that will supposedly bring greater hope and happiness.

Any notion of hope that relies exclusively on material things and upon the human intellect as its experienced guide exists within a narrow sphere of our material and our temporary existence. Material things are essential to satisfy human comforts, but whenever the human element takes second place to the accumulation of material wealth, it diminishes hope for the better world that we desire. Our search then becomes counterproductive to our desire and our "search for happiness."

Millions of individuals in underdeveloped nations rely on other people, their governments, NGOs, and the international community to provide occasional rays of hope. This hope provides the only architecture available for "rays of happiness" to shine forth in their lives.

CNN (Cable News Network, 2015) reports on heroes who help awaken our consciousness to the tremendous needs of people in the United States of America and throughout some parts of the world. More significantly, it helps us to realize the impact of individual initiatives, self-sacrifice, and enduring commitment to a better world for all humanity.

---

[11] "Charles R. Swindoll Quotes," *Quotes.net*, STANDS4 LLC, Dec. 8, 2015, http://www.quotes.net/authors/Charles R. Swindoll.

Many of these individuals have elevated their call to action as some have established permanent organizations to further their cause and to engage governments and other world bodies in their efforts. The CNN programs that recognize local heroes have positive benefits for the hero, who would otherwise not have the capacity to expand his or her "hope initiative;" likewise, they magnify the hopefulness for those whom they serve.

Human survival is the eternal "search for happiness" through hopefulness, but hope must encompass the desire for human survival not merely as a physical compulsion. The hope of humanity must take on universal dimensions. We must not relegate hope only to those with the social, economic, and technological means to engender hope, but hope must extend throughout the "global village," affirmed in the poignant statement below:

"I believe America has a unique ability, and a special calling, to fight this disease. We are blessed with great scientific knowledge. We're a generous country that has always reached out to feed the hungry, and rescue captives and care for the sick. We are guided by the conviction of our founding—that the Author of Life has endowed every life with matchless value."

— George W. Bush, Remarks on World AIDS Day,
Online by Gerhard Peters and John T. Woolley,
The American Presidency Project,
December 1, 2005
http://www.presidency.ucsb/edu/ws/?pid=65254.

What are we hoping for, and how can we attain it? Is the search rooted in one's single-mindedness, one's inclinations, one's maturity, and one's material and physical needs? Is the hope for happiness? We must answer these important questions for hope to become a meaningful and purposeful search.

Society should participate by doing *all* that it is capable of to engender hope for the less fortunate, but how does a hopeless person esteem himself or herself through the looking glass of his or her perceived hopelessness? Hope bolsters pride, the form of pride that *empowers, engenders,* and *enlightens* the mind. The core premise of the text is that there is hope for a better world, but this hope calls for a "new" understanding of the dichotomy between our "spiritual" and "physical" existence on Earth.

PRIDE, HUMILITY, AND HAPPINESS

"It is better to lose your pride with someone you love rather than to lose that someone you love with your useless pride."

— *John Ruskin (1819–1900)*

Every youth should experience great moments of pride as a positive motivator, especially when he or she is in the nurturing presence of his or her parents or nurturing adult, yet pride is a double-edged sword.

On the one hand, we nurture a new baby with pride. Parents are overwhelmed with a sense of pride on graduation day when their child graduates from college or university. A man beams with pride after restoring a vintage automobile. This form of pride brings about feelings of happiness in self and others.

On the other hand, when a person makes a statement that is unjustified or inflammatory about another, and he or she refuses to apologize, it is because of stubbornness and pride. This form of pride causes resentment, tension, unfriendliness, and unhappiness in self and others.

Pride has its roots in our weak human nature. When we give in to the mastering nature of pride, it leads down the path of hopeless struggles that eventually overtake and overwhelm people and nations. Human pride can influence the decisions we make daily, for "better or for worse."

Pride undergirds all selfishness, all human suffering, all egotistic behavior among families and friends, and all broken marriages. Pride is the "cause" of the violence that occurs on the streets. Pride can also be the catalyst for national and international conflicts. Pride has been responsible for the downfall of many so-called great empires. In our postmodern era, leaders of nations have chosen the destructive nature of *pride* over *prudence*.

Pride is an outward emotion in response to an inward feeling that one highly regards himself or herself above others. The proud person creates a barrier between himself and others, and it impedes spiritual, moral, social, and intellectual growth; mental health; and happiness.

These conditions often cause some to view others who are not as sophisticated and prominent as undeserving of our love, respect, and attention. They give rise to pride, which suffocates our humility. Pride also erodes our humanity and may misguide us and cause us to regard humility as a weakness and an undesirable quality. Rather than the relentless pursuit of service to other human beings, self-elevation leads us on a path of inhumanity and lack of humility and pride.

King Solomon, the wise King of Israel (circa 970–931 BCE), has this to say about pride:

"Pride goes before destruction and a haughty spirit before a fall. It is better to be of a lowly spirit with the poor than to divide the spoil with the proud."

— *Proverbs 16:18–19*

Pride is a spirit that we can conquer only in the spiritual realm. When we overcome pride, we unlock the "power of humility," which promotes peace and harmony in our lives, families, communities, nations, and the world. Pride suffocates happiness; therefore, we should avoid the paralyzing nature of pride so that our lives transcend selfless relations, humility, and servanthood.

We must be on guard that our ego does not create a barrier between others and us. The "spirit of pride" is a human condition that we should avoid in our "search for happiness."

Insightful observation leads us to understand that lack of humility toward each other is typical of the human condition, such as our social and economic class status, color, race, gender, and culture.

Pride can be a positive or negative motivating factor. Therefore, we should avoid the negative aspects of pride that damage relationships. It is easy for us to display personal and national pride in our material accomplishments, but these are small achievements in comparison to the significant benefits of *humility* and *servanthood.*

These two great pillars bring out the best in human relations and happy outcomes. Humility transcends happiness. Insightful observation leads us to understand that lack of humility toward each other is typical of the human condition, often underpinned by pride in our social and economic class status, our race, and our culture.

Humility does not demand that we humiliate ourselves or eliminate character or personal integrity, but rather that we give preference and honor to others. It does not mean weakness; neither does it mean that one has to relinquish personal ambition to adopt a humble disposition.

When we recognize the importance of humility as a prerequisite for breaking down barriers, we advertently lift our understanding to greater heights of humility, humanity, and happiness. No group in society should assume a monopoly on happiness, whether by their words or by their actions.

It would be audacious for any "school of thought" (religious, moral, social, intellectual, scientific, or physical) to attempt to demonstrate any variance from the fundamental premise that *all* human beings are born equal in human rights and privilege.

Six thousand years of record of the "wreckage of human history" is a testimony to the egregious nature of the assumptions of "equal" and "unequal" human beings. These assumptions, *conscious or subconscious*, underpin much of the unhappiness in the world.

Scientific investigations teach:

"All human beings belong to a single species and are descended from a common stock. They are born equal in dignity and rights and all form an integral part of humanity."[12]

---

[12] Declaration on Race and Racial Prejudice (adopted by the General Conference of UNESCO at its twentieth session, Paris, November 1978), Article 1, Copyright © UNESCO 1979 (United Nations Education, Scientific and Cultural Organization), p. 11.

The search for answers has led us to the distinct conclusion that, from the perspectives of *religion, science*, and *observation*, we are not different from each other. Are we different? Marjorie and I proffer that there are "intrinsic linkages" among all humanity. Regardless of our station in life, *all* human needs, priorities, emergencies, rights, and privileges are the same.

World travel, experiential knowledge, and intellectual and empirical observation teach that there are more similarities in human beings and their behavior than there are differences.

Most, if not all, people have a similar desire to be happy, but when we observe the manner in which we behave toward each other, one could conclude that we are born *equal, unequal, equally unequal, unequally equal*, or, paradoxically, *unequally unequal*.

In every continent where we have traveled — every country, every city, every village — and in every history book, we have encountered visible and written evidence of a common human heritage. As a species, we subconsciously and sometimes consciously set up barriers to human relationships that create unhappiness for millions throughout the world.

The "Discovering Your Optimum 'Happiness Index' (OHI) Project" awakened Marjorie and me to an important question that humanity should contemplate: "Why is it, despite exponential growth in world religions, science and technology, human knowledge, and great financial and material wealth, that people lack the capacity to build and sustain great civilizations?" What is it in human nature that acts as an *impenetrable* barrier to the "lessons of history"?

The ultimate test of our humility confronts us in the twenty-first century. Nations of the world are meeting at the crossroads of the civilization that has become a "global village." Circumstances beyond any nation's control have shuttled humankind *into* the "global village" with unresolved past challenges, present challenges, and emerging future challenges.

Marjorie and I put forward that as humankind systematically removes or eliminates inequity and unfairness regarding the following twenty relationship barriers, *humility* and *humanity* will give rise to wellsprings of hope and happiness.

o TWENTY RELATIONSHIP BARRIERS THAT WHEN LIFTED
   WILL CAUSE NATIONS TO RISE TO WELLSPRINGS OF
   HOPE, HUMANITY, HUMILITY, AND HAPPINESS:

1. *Race, Color, and Language* Barriers
2. *World Economic and Trade* Barriers
3. *Social and Economic Class* Barriers
4. *Religious Communication* Barriers
5. *Religious Denominational* Barriers
6. *Educational Achievement* Barriers
7. *Marriage Relationship* Barriers
8. *Employment Equity* Barriers
9. *Age and Disability* Barriers
10. *Height and Weight* Barriers
11. *Technological* Barriers
12. *Generational* Barriers
13. *Immigration* Barriers
14. *Nationalism* Barriers
15. *Patriotism* Barriers
16. *Healthcare* Barriers
17. *Interstate* Barriers
18. *Cultural* Barriers
19. *Voting* Barriers
20. *Gender* Barriers

These twenty relationship barriers have a definite influence on the way we relate to each other. They are complex, and if they are unmanaged, they can form an impenetrable barrier that suffocates human progress as the obstacles get more complicated for the ordinary person to navigate. When nations remove these barriers, they will rise to great heights of humanity, imbued with the capacity to *navigate* and *mitigate* many unresolved past challenges, present challenges, and emerging future challenges.

As an aggregate, these barriers (intentional or unintentional) create much of the human suffering and unhappiness people experience in daily life. They underpin the way we view the world ("worldview") through various lenses such as religion, race, color, culture, economics, academia, politics, gender, and transgender.

We must be mindful that our partialities foster our educational, political, social, and economic biases; as a result, many individuals and nations may never fully partake of the enormous benefits that humanity brings to the "Table of Civilization" (TOC). Empathy enables them to cope in a world where many experience denial of love, compassion, mercy, fairness and justice, equitable opportunities for employment, and fair compensation, which are the causes of great unhappiness for many.

Patience is one of the most indispensable requirements of peace and stability in our emerging global village. Without the exercise of patience, the racial, cultural, religious, social, and economic crossroads of our current civilization will lead to future genocide and wars between nations.

Perceptive observation and the clear records of six thousand years of history should make us acutely aware that patience, kindness, goodness, faithfulness, gentleness, and self-control are necessary for meeting such challenges in the future.

These challenges that face nations in the global village in the postmodern era are no different from internal problems encountered by individual countries with a high level of cultural diversity. The difference in the issues facing the "global village" lies with conflicting interests such as monetary policies, trade imbalance, political ideology, and *race, religion*, and *color*.

We often forget that we are the world composite of all of our needs, thoughts, feelings, hopes, and aspirations, and of our violent nature as well. Can a nation secure peace or its national interest apart from the international concern for humanity? The answer to this essential question must precede our "search for happiness."

We are nationalistic (even so, nationalism can be both positive and negative). We are African, American, Australian, British, Canadian, Chinese, French, German, Indian, Jamaican, and Russian, just to name a few nationalities. We are White, Black, and Brown. We are adherents of Christianity, Hinduism, Jainism, Sikhism, Buddhism, Judaism, and Islam, just to name a few religions.

Three of the major world religions speak to us in unambiguous language regarding our love for our neighbor, which brings peace. Christianity, in Matthew 5:43–45 NKJV; Judaism, in Leviticus 19:17, 18, Ta; and Islam in She Who is Tested Al-Mumtahanah 60:5–9. We are religious, but do our religions matter if they divide us and set us apart because of our superficial differences? Can our religions lead the way to peaceful coexistence and unite us as a human family?

YOU CAN FIND PEACE AND HAPPINESS

"Now and then it is good to pause in our pursuit of happiness and just be happy."

— *Guillaume Apollinaire (1880–1918)*

The "search for happiness" is not new. You can find peace and happiness. This guide will take you on a journey toward self-discovery. Neither doubt nor reservation must accompany you on this journey, but an open, objective, and peaceful mind. A peaceful mind is a happy mind, but how peaceful is the mind of the citizens of nations when *fear* is becoming a national preoccupation? Can we find peace or happiness by merely traveling to exotic lands?

The undeniable fact is that human beings cannot give nor bring about peace because peace is a "spiritual attribute" (John 14:27) as opposed to a "natural attribute." The world thinks of *peace* as the opposite of *war*, but the indisputable fact is that love, not peace, is the opposite of war. If we can find peace, we will find happiness. Therefore, to eliminate war from the human landscape, we must seek love; then "joy" and peace shall come.

Ancient and contemporary writers and researchers have penned great works that teach profound lessons, which help to elevate our understandings, thoughts, words, and deeds, and aid in our relationships. They advise us how to live and be happy. Likewise, there are psychologists, sociologists, psychiatrists, and counselors who teach how to enhance relationships and live fruitful lives.

The great experience that we share is the lesson of empathy for those whom some might deem inferior. It imbues them with feelings of inclusiveness and happiness. We urge all to search for happiness in their lives, despite the circumstances under which we live, because individual happiness aggregates to *(1) family, (2) corporate, (3) community, (4) national,* and *(5) universal happiness.*

Over the centuries, great classical Greek philosophers such as Aristotle, and writers such as Tolstoy and Proust have shared their thoughts thus:

"Happiness is the meaning and the purpose of life, the whole aim, and end of human existence."

— *Aristotle (384 BCE–322 BCE)*

"A quiet secluded life in the country, with the possibility of being useful to people to whom it is easy to do good, and who are not accustomed to have it done to them; then work which one hopes may be of some use; then rest, nature, books, music, love for one's neighbor — such is my idea of happiness."

— *Leo Tolstoy (1828–1910)*

"Let us be grateful to the people who make us happy; they are the charming gardeners who make our souls blossom."

—*Marcel Proust (1871–1922)*

Happiness will break forth like a magnificent sunset on an overcast day when all embrace happiness as a national agenda and a national preoccupation rather than as strictly a personal pursuit.

The search for happiness will take you along paths that you might not have traveled, although these paths may hold the secret to your happiness. Some paths that you have traveled or that you are currently traveling may be the path(s) that have suffocated your happiness and have robbed you of your "joy."

We have traveled the many paths herein that we share with you. This guide may signify the beginning of a "new" expedition along new paths of happiness and successful living for you.

Some disappointments may appear to impede your path to happiness, but embrace the disappointments, for there might be significant and potential benefits and meanings that demand an alert mind to the workings of the incomprehensible universe.

Marjorie was on standby to board a flight after she missed an earlier connecting flight in Miami. She was in transit to the Island of Jamaica, West Indies, for the 2009 Christmas holidays. The congestion of travelers spoke to her subconscious mind. An inner voice urged her to wait for a later flight as other delayed passengers seemed more anxious to get on the flight to the Caribbean island. Later that night, the news reported, "American Airline Jet Overruns Runway at Jamaica Airport after Landing: American Airlines flight AA 331 on December 22, [2009] originating out of Washington's Ronald Reagan International Airport, stopping in Miami and then heading to Kingston, Jamaica." The flight that Marjorie missed overran the runway at Norman Manley International Airport and broke apart after landing in a heavy rainstorm.

In 1995, I worked for a United States company based in Ontario, Canada, that decided to repatriate part of its operations back to the United States. The announcement gave rise to uncertainty for employment security with the company. Rather than becoming anxious and fearful, I committed my thoughts to a better opportunity and a peaceful mind despite the tenuous situation.

While I was negotiating a possible transfer to the United States, I received an invitation to interview with a different corporation in the United States. I accepted the latter position because of the growth opportunity and their corporate head office location that was close to a border crossing between the United States and Ontario, Canada.

An initial tenure of twelve months became a corporate journey of sixty months, a journey that was unsurpassed in its experience and the hospitality of the nation of the United States of America under the North American Free Trade Agreement (NAFTA). It is fascinating to share that the universe inexplicably resonates with our thoughts, hopes, dreams, and aspirations. Always think positive and wholesome thoughts about *self, people*, and *situations*, because thoughts lead similar to a pace car in the Indianapolis 500 (Indy 500) auto race.

In the summer of 1986, Marjorie and I shared thoughts about our dream home. It would be on a premium corner lot with features we imagined. One evening, a cousin said, "Let us drive out to a subdivision in Mississauga, Ontario, Canada, and look at new home sales." When we arrived at the subdivision showroom, there among the framed photos of available homes was our dream home. Amazingly, the framed photo of the home on the wall matched exactly what we imagined and discussed. More astonishing was the fact that it was the last available property in the particular model home of our interest.

We make no claim that the apex of happiness is strictly a by-product of one's imagination or that happiness is strictly a material compulsion. We merely share how thoughts that live deep in the labyrinth of our mind can manifest in the ethos.

The universe is a repository of collective thoughts. We must be mindful that as fish are immersed in the ocean and the body of air encapsulates the Earth, a universal spiritual cord intrinsically links all humanity. The happiness of the wealthy twenty percent of the world's nations ought to be concerned about the unhappiness of the eighty percent as a mutual survival responsibility.[13]

The whole of humanity benefits when we embrace every opportunity to elevate others according to God's divine plan for our existence. Conversely, we could choose to cultivate the growing international instability and unhappiness in the world.

Thoughts manifest in actions over which we do not have ultimate control, but *faith, belief,* and *hope* are our capable guides. The crucial "human survival mechanism" resides in positive thinking and positive actions that imbue the mind. The benefits of our crucial search for happiness are enormous when we consider that we are members of the human family, with a common heritage

---

[13] http://betterexplained.com/articles/understanding-the-pareto-principle-the-8020-rule/.

and *inseparable* by a common desire for peace, safety, health, hope, and happiness. The collective desire for a "wholesome" and happy life unifies the human family.

> "To enjoy good health, to bring true happiness to one's family, to bring peace to all, one must first discipline and control one's own mind. If a man can control his mind he can find the way to enlightenment, and all wisdom and virtue will naturally come to him."

— *Siddhartha Gautama Buddha (circa 563 BCE-483 BCE)*

We have delineated a list of twenty-eight multifaceted benefits of happiness among four essential happiness perspectives: *(1) marriage and family, (2) corporate, (3) community and nation*, and *(4) international community*. You can find happiness when you allow these twenty-eight multifaceted benefits to inform your search.

o SEVEN KEY HAPPINESS BENEFITS FROM A MARRIAGE AND FAMILY PERSPECTIVE:

1. *Happiness* in marriage
2. *Longevity* in marriage
3. *Greater* family loyalty
4. *Happier* life and home
5. *Fewer* unstable relationships
6. *Happier* and more creative children
7. *Higher* Personal "Happiness Index" (PHI)

o SEVEN KEY HAPPINESS BENEFITS FROM A CORPORATE PERSPECTIVE:

1. *Greater* employer loyalty
2. *Greater* employee loyalty
3. *Fewer* absentee employees
4. *Fewer* corporate challenges
5. *Greater* productivity at meetings
6. *Higher* efficiency and productivity
7. *Higher* Corporate "Happiness Index" (CHI)

o   SEVEN KEY HAPPINESS BENEFITS FROM A
    COMMUNITY AND NATIONAL PERSPECTIVE:

1. *Greater* volunteerism
2. *Lower* incarceration rates
3. *Fewer* neighborhood incidents
4. *Better* relations with law enforcement
5. *Higher* political and voting participation
6. *Happier* neighborhoods and communities
7. *Higher* National "Happiness Index" (NHI)

o   SEVEN KEY HAPPINESS BENEFITS FROM AN
    INTERNATIONAL PERSPECTIVE:

1. *Better* global governance
2. *More* peaceful negotiations
3. *Fewer* international conflicts
4. *Improved* international relations
5. *Better* management of the environment
6. *Fewer* infringements on national sovereignty
7. *Higher* International "Happiness Index" (IHI)

The preceding twenty-eight multifaceted benefits, delineated as marriage and family, corporate, community and national, and international, rest on the foundation that people and nations can aspire to a higher "Happiness Index" (HI). We trust that they will inspire your "search for happiness" motivated by a desire to achieve some of the benefits listed above.

How can the international community of nations find peace? Is peace a *military* imperative as opposed to a *spiritual* imperative? If we miss this most important distinction, our desire for peace becomes a vain pursuit, marked by futility and frustration, and a recurrent drain on valuable human and financial resources, while human suffering unhappily continues unabated as peace remains a grand illusion that we pursue. Where can we find the path to peace and happiness? Is there a defined path for humanity to follow? Marjorie and I have discovered five pathways that undergird all aspects of human lives. They lead to self-actualization, and they help to sustain "happiness" and "joy."

CHAPTER
3

FIVE CRITICAL PATHWAYS TO "OPTIMUM HAPPINESS" (OH)

"I have but one lamp by which my feet are guided, and that is the lamp of experience. I know no way of judging of the future but by the past."

— *Edward Gibbon (1785–1881)*

This chapter is about five critical pathways to "Optimum Happiness" (OH) that Marjorie and I have discovered and traveled. These five paths encapsulate our "search for happiness." We often think of life as a path or a journey, and largely it is, but in a broader sense, we travel along multiple paths to multiple destinations in the material world. We have discovered that at some point along life's journey, the ultimate path and destination become real, and everything else becomes an illusion.

The challenge is to recognize the path that leads to the greatest fulfillment of life and happiness. After traveling separately and together for several decades (metaphorically speaking) along multiple paths, we have discovered five illuminating pathways that we share with you. We delineate these five key pathways as *(1) Spiritual Happiness, (2) Moral Happiness, (3) Social Happiness, (4) Intellectual Happiness,* and *(5) Physical Happiness.*

Each of the five pathways underpins the human journey. They confer on us all of the spiritual and material gifts that we desire to experience a life of fulfillment. The benefits become real when we subscribe to a belief in the existence of a higher "Spiritual Intelligence" (SQ). Voltaire, writer and historian, makes an unequivocal claim in his words to us in the twenty-first century:

> "If God did not exist, He would have to be invented. But all nature cries aloud that he does exist: that there is a supreme intelligence, an immense power, an admirable order, and everything teaches us our own dependence on it."

> — *Voltaire (1694 –1778)*

PREPARATION FOR THE JOURNEY

It is possible to live a happy life despite the challenges we face daily and despite the things that we want for ourselves that elude us. The lives of some people resonate with unhappiness. More importantly, they may not know the ideal path to happiness.

Marjorie and I started our "happiness journey" self-assured that *all* humanity deserves to be happy and with a "new" understanding that *all* humankind can find the path to "happiness" and "joy."

We cannot wait for everything in our lives to be as we wish it were before claiming our happiness. There are very few moments when we feel that everything is going well. Realistically, most people do not have all that they hope for in life. That is life. If we had it all, what would our purpose be? From whence cometh our inspiration? What would we plan and strive to achieve? Who would we be grateful to for our achievements or thank for helping us to overcome challenges? Would we even entertain a belief in a higher moral authority or seek divine intervention? We may deceptively assume ourselves divine.

Nothing outside of our being will give us anything more than fleeting moments of peace, security, and happiness. Life may not always be easy, but it is a blessing. We are God's beloved children, and His favor is with us. "For I will look on you favorably and make you fruitful, multiply you and confirm My covenant with you" (Leviticus 26:9). The preponderance of evidence tells us that it is from these truths that positive outcomes originate and humanity realizes peace, safety, security, and happiness.

Whether we are rich or poor or whether we have all that we desire does not guarantee us a life free of adversity. We worry about the diminishing value of our worldly possessions because there is something in the ethereal that speaks to the "insufficiency" of our materially driven lives.

The endowment of "free will" provides humankind with the freedom to think, reason, and make choices, but these gifts can be either *creative* or *destructive*. They can bring happiness or unhappiness to the human family.

When the unimaginable happens, we become frustrated and even enter the realm of despair, but no matter how unfair life seems, there is a greater meaning to life beyond our earthly imagination.

No matter what happens, we must strive to stay centered by maintaining a calm awareness of our divine appointment. If we stay healthy in our spirit, we will always be capable of finding our way.

Obstacles may impede your path, but they are not necessarily to stop us; they are challenges to overcome. Life is a continuous experience. Many of us have challenges in our lives, but we have overcome them by *faith, belief,* and the *fervent* prayers of many family members and friends, and our positive attitude and *indomitable* spirit.

When we turn the pages of the "book of life," there will always be more positives than negatives. Our family and friends contribute to the positive side of the ledger. Life will continue to present challenges, but knowing that we are never alone significantly improves our capacity to cope with personal challenges. The most precious gift that we can present is the "Five Pathways to Happiness" that Marjorie and I have followed in our journey.

Humankind has taken many paths to bring itself out of many dark situations, from catastrophic wars, and natural, "humanly inspired," and "humanly caused" disasters, plagues, slavery, famine, world hunger, and economic collapse over the centuries.

Marjorie and I put forward that these five foundational pathways (aspects) can help to liberate the postmodern world from a growing state of unhappiness. Whether we are aware of the fact or not, every aspect of our lives and every action encompasses the five foundational perspectives, briefly discussed below:

THE FIVE CRITICAL PATHWAYS TO "*OPTIMUM HAPPINESS*" (*OH*)

o   PATHWAY ONE
SPIRITUAL HAPPINESS

SPIRITUAL HAPPINESS ("joy") transcends all other forms of happiness. This path is a noble way that brings both happiness and "joy" to others and ourselves because it is the realization of the whole purpose of human existence.

The spiritual pathway speaks to the foundation of God's love (*agápē*) for His creation, which is absolute and unconditional. His love, manifested within us, breaks down barriers of intolerance between human beings regardless of color, race, class, culture, nationality or religion.

Spirituality sustains us when everything else fails. "Spiritual Happiness" is the "*Optimum*" state of happiness. It rises above all other imperatives of happiness. It is the exception because it manifests both happiness and "joy," which is internal to the human spirit and is lasting; it is living a life of higher virtues.

Spirituality is not an abstract notion. A belief in God characterizes spirituality, but more than a conviction, one who is spiritual demonstrates the "fruit of the Spirit" in daily life toward others. The "fruit of the Spirit" is expressed in Christian writing as love, "joy," peace, long-suffering, kindness, goodness, faithfulness, gentleness, and self-control (Galatians 5:22).

Spirituality compels us to choose *light* instead of *darkness*, *love* instead of *hate*, *tolerance* instead of *intolerance*, *faith* instead of *fear*, *hope* instead of *despair, peace* instead of *war,* and *happiness* instead of *unhappiness.* On the other hand, material compulsion fosters the need for material things to satisfy temporary human material and physical needs and wants. Essentially, the human desire to *seek, acquire,* and *maintain* material possessions can satisfy only the outer person.

Nevertheless, we can maintain both spiritual and material happiness when we *consciously* and *consistently* seek to purify ourselves of the tendencies to act on selfish impulses. We must guard against inaction that can amount to shirking responsibility to bring happiness to the lives of others.

o   PATHWAY TWO
MORAL HAPPINESS

MORAL HAPPINESS is the pathway taken to *understand, embrace,* and *practice* moral laws. The principal foci of the moral foundation are the *transcendental* and *transformational* benefits to "moral leadership" in the world. Moral happiness promotes voluntary control of superfluous wealth and power, and helps individuals, families, and nations to grow and prosper equitably as a unified human family.

Moral happiness comes from knowing that our behavior and character are in conformity to higher moral authority, recognized universally as God's Word. It informs our understanding of our spiritual and natural relationships with God and neighbor. These two mutually inclusive relationships help us to maintain a perfect *spiritual* and natural *balance* between "moral" and "civic" duty, which often conflict in the corporate world.

Furthermore, God's transcendent power must be active in every facet of human endeavor to realize just societies and nations, and to exercise moral judgment (ethics, fairness, honesty, and integrity). A common spiritual purpose on Earth intrinsically links all humanity regardless of color, race, culture, language, nationality, or religion.

The moral foundation demonstrates moral discipline, moral courage, moral appeal, and moral persuasion. It helps individuals, families, and nations to prosper in health, happiness, and a virtuous life.

Moral authority is an indispensable attribute of leadership and power in the world. Violation of moral laws brings unhappiness, while attention to and the application of the universal moral code of behavior resonates peace and happiness among people. The Golden Rule or ethic of reciprocity is a maxim, ethical code, and morality. It essentially states, "Do to others as you would have them do to you" (Luke 6:31).

o   PATHWAY THREE
SOCIAL HAPPINESS

SOCIAL HAPPINESS is the pathway taken to build close social relationships with fellow beings, depicted in the following fifteen relationship types:

o   FIFTEEN RELATIONSHIP TYPES THAT ARE DISTINCTLY DIFFERENTIATED:

1. *Spiritual relationships* (between God and man)
2. *Marital relationships* (between husbands and wives)
3. *Parental relationships* (between parents and children)
4. *Sibling relationships* (between brothers and sisters)
5. *Romantic relationship* (between lovers)
6. *Platonic relationships* (between friends)
7. *Business relationships* (between business associates)
8. *Associate relationships* (between co-workers)
9. *Casual relationships* (between strangers)
10. *Subordinate relationships* (between employers and employees)
11. *Territorial relationships* (between neighboring countries)
12. *Sovereign relationships* (between nations)
13. *International relationships* (between nations)
14. *Constitutional relationships* (between government and people)
15. *Judicial relationships* (between state and judiciary)

Relationship bonds define all human interactions in a myriad of ways. Social Happiness is not merely with family and friends, or with our immediate neighbors, but with those in the diverse international community, religiously, morally, socially, culturally, scientifically, and environmentally.

Intellectually and intuitively, we understand that there are many distinct types of relationships, each with a unique bond and directive. The fifteen distinct relationships and the associated bonds provide a broad spectrum for understanding the uniqueness of each relationship and its particular bond. Without such an understanding, individuals may respond intuitively to each relationship and bond in a similar manner. Such a response is probably responsible for much of the breakdown of communications and unhappiness in the world.

The nature of these interdependent relationships makes us *happy* or *unhappy*. Strong relationship bonds enable us to build and weather the challenges that we may face in the myriad of relationships that we experience daily. The above fifteen relationships, unlike the impersonal world of social media and digital connectivity, put us in direct contact with others. The quality of these social connections is a function of our social well-being and happiness, and how we strive to mitigate and manage each situation relative to each bond.

o   PATHWAY FOUR
INTELLECTUAL HAPPINESS

INTELLECTUAL HAPPINESS is the pathway that informs the human intellect. It is being in an environment that stimulates and inspires people to reach greater heights, much beyond our rational reasoning. Many may view happiness generically, but intellectual happiness comes from the "intelligence capacity" to make critical life-saving and life-enhancing decisions.

We can all benefit from the outcomes of such decisions to maintain a well-informed diet and exercise regimen; likewise the decision to purchase "critical illness" insurance that can avert financial hardship that may result from a critical illness. On the grand scale, preservation of the environment benefits the whole of humanity, yet it is difficult to reach a mutually "intelligent agreement" on how to preserve the environment.

Where does intelligence come from, and why is intelligence essential for us to live happy and prosperous lives? Is intelligence the same as education, knowledge, wisdom, or understanding? Is "Human Intelligence" (HQ) the same as "Spiritual Intelligence" (SQ)?

Everyone has an "Intelligence Quotient" (IQ). Likewise, the appropriate environment offers intellectual stimulation to him or her. For instance, a group of engineers working on a major scientific endeavor and surrounded by his or her peers stimulate each other to states of "Intellectual Happiness" (IH) that inspire their imagination and creativity.

HQ guides our decision-making concerning the nature and purpose of every human action and endeavor, especially happiness. Our connection to God's source of SQ is the greatest source of happiness through acts motivated by HQ. SQ transcends and empowers *all* other forms of intelligence, such moral, social, scientific, and leadership intelligence. It enables us to understand things beyond our natural comprehension.

When we analyze the "flight recorder" of the wreckage of human history and current world conditions, the analysis will reveal a world littered with fallen empires and casualties of wars, deficit-financed in trillions of dollars, in the pursuit of peace. We are not yet aware that when history repeats itself, the price grows exponentially. SQ is a prerequisite for global leadership; only SQ can help humanity to change its destructive path and rein in the peace and happiness that we seek.

o PATHWAY FIVE
PHYSICAL HAPPINESS

PHYSICAL HAPPINESS is the pathway that exists in the physical realm, which comes from a sense of physical well-being, but understanding all of the complexities of our physical well-being is critical to living healthy and happy lives. For instance, we cannot experience physical health and happiness to the exclusion of spiritual and mental health and a clean environment.

From the medical scientist to the layperson, all will agree that the human body is complex but marvelously made (Psalm 139:14–16). We are also, as living beings, an integral biological component of the living and breathing universe. Even the living trees exchange matter with people. The trees cleanse the environment of toxins for our health, survival, and happiness.

Medical practitioners tell us that we are predisposed to inherit diseases from parents. They also say that an unhealthy environment has adverse effects on human health; likewise that diseases that afflict current generations genetically link us to our foreparents and future generations as well.

Physical happiness is achievable when we have good physical health, which is a function of diet and nutrition, sleep, exercise, and general wholesome (stress-free) living. Medical researchers advise of the significant value of certain herbs, grains, fruits, and vegetables in our dietary regimen. What do clinicians think?

> William R. Miller (ed.), Washington, DC, United States, "American Psychological Association, in his book titled: Integrating Spirituality into Treatment provides clinicians with practical advice on clients' spiritual perspectives in the therapeutic relationship. The book offers a history of the often tense relationship between spirituality and psychology and addresses broad, transtheoretical aspects of spirituality, including acceptance, forgiveness, hope, prayer, and meditation."[14]

The capacity to maintain the *purity* of the atmosphere that encapsulates the Earth is a monumental task. Mass manufacturing, which began with the Industrial Revolution of the 1800s–1900s, was inadvertently also the beginning of its effects on the integrity of the environment and human health. The effects have now become life-threatening to humans as the Earth's ecosystem falls out of balance.

The co-relation between the environment and human health and happiness is debated and documented in scientific literature, and it is a major concern to governments around the globe, with global warming taking center stage as the clarion call of scientists as the greatest potential threat to human survival as a viable species.

One can postulate that there is a direct correlation between the "abundant life" of nations and the physical well-being and

---

[14] PsycINFO Database Record (c) 2012 APA, all rights reserved.

happiness of nations. We have provided for your benefit the following ten healthcare criteria to help sustain a healthy and happy body. They are not the only criteria, but they have been helpful in sustaining us on our path to physical happiness.

o TEN HEALTHCARE CRITERIA TO SUSTAIN A HEALTHY AND HAPPY BODY:

1. *Get* a yearly physical.
2. *Avoid* stressful situations.
3. *Strive* for work–life balance.
4. *Manage* stressful situations.
5. *Seek* spiritual and mental nurturing.
6. *Exercise* frequently (daily if practicable).
7. *Maintain* a healthy diet rich in natural foods.
8. *Research* the family predisposition to illnesses.
9. *Strive* for adequate *exercise*, *rest*, and *relaxation*.
10. *Eat* foods from the *ground*, the *sea*, and the *tree*.

These ten healthcare criteria for a healthy and happy body enable us to counteract the challenges that postmodern lifestyles inflict on our bodies and make us unhappy physically.

From an environmental perspective, is there any wonder why the forest is green? Perhaps God is sending humans a message. Today, emerging scientific research is discovering the calming effects of a green environment on people. We have finally understood it with our "Green Revolution."

We could have known the concept that "green is good" thousands of years ago. The 1992 United Nations Conference on Environment and Development (UNCED) defines deforestation as "land degradation in arid, semi-arid, and sub-humid areas resulting from various factors including climatic variations and human activities."

It is important to observe that as we deforest, we face significant challenges ranging from ecosystem imbalances and loss of animal species to land erosion, to climatic danger, and to food shortages that will ultimately foster global hunger and even wars for food.

Food shortages can lead to land grabs in underdeveloped and developing nations as wealthy nations' domestic food production continues to decline. This brief discourse on physical happiness should awaken us to the importance of the relationship between good *governance* of the planet and *health* and *happiness*.

"The secret of health for both mind and body is not to mourn for the past, not to worry about the future, or not to anticipate troubles, but to live the present moment wisely and earnestly."

— *Siddhartha Gautama Buddha (circa 563 BCE-483 BCE)*

Developed nations have some capacity to engineer their recovery from natural and manmade disasters, but underdeveloped and developing countries may never recover from natural disasters, the ravages of resource and economic exploitation, or armed conflicts with their neighbors.

The world has demonstrated its capacity to take a stand against great human catastrophes such as the ravages of wars, famines, genocide, and natural disasters. The human capacity to answer the call of human goodness prevails despite the repetition of history (premodern, modern, and postmodern).

The next frontier is the development of consistent national and international policies that can predict and prevent, when possible, "humanly caused" and "humanly inspired" catastrophes. Thus, intelligence becomes a catalyst that enables individuals and nations to rise above the lack of cooperation and to appeal to our higher "survival predispositions."

Undeniably, intelligence is our "moral guide," our "moral compass," and critical for our physical safety. Intelligence, therefore, is the greatest asset for human survival. Over the centuries, people have dominated and killed each other for no other reason than their religion, race, culture, color, creed, or possessions.

With high intelligence, it is possible to create a happier world for millions, even for billions on the Earth, when we choose to exercise hope. Hope inspires the "intelligent capacity" that helps humanity to envision rays of light that shine through otherwise darkened clouds of life for many.

This path of *darkness* and *unhappiness* rather than *light* and *happiness* seems to prevail in parts of our postmodern world despite postmodern "enlightenment." Upon closer examination, the five key pathways — (1) *Spiritual Happiness*, (2) *Moral Happiness*, (3) *Social Happiness*, (4) *Intellectual Happiness*, and (5) *Physical Happiness* — that we have delineated in the preceding discourse may hold the key to "joy" and "happiness."

The reality of our postmodern era is that we have come to a crossroads of undeniable financial and material progress on the one hand, and to a decline in spiritual, moral, social, intellectual, and physical growth on the other hand. With this "new" knowledge, there is "no excuse," no "moral alibi" for not embracing this "new" path.

This dividing line between *material* and *spiritual* progress punctuates our primary focus on scientific knowledge and scientific experimentation as the means by which to create a better world despite human challenges that point to the need for nonscientific approaches as well. Advances in science and technology are not the underlying cause of unhappiness in the world, but they also are not leading to permanent solutions to fundamental problems of human survival.

For instance, vast expenditures in medical research strive to determine the causes of new diseases and to control their incidence. Ironically, the impact of common diseases such as cancer, diabetes, and heart disease continues to afflict young and old alike despite medical research and burgeoning healthcare budgets. On the other side of the healthcare equation, some medical practitioners put forward that inadequate diet, a sedentary lifestyle, lack of adequate rest, and stressful living are working against the gains in healthcare research and advancement.

We applaud the scientific minds for their great efforts to help us to understand and manage health issues and to better comprehend the magnitude of catastrophic diseases that confront us. Unfortunately, some of the great efforts of medical science are negated by the incalculable harm that some of us cause to our bodies by not exercising regularly, by neglecting sleep and proper nutrition, or by working excessively, often pushing the limits of our mental and physical capabilities, ultimately impacting our health and happiness.

CHAPTER
4

COMPLEX DIMENSIONS OF HAPPINESS

"We frequently pass so near to happiness without seeing, without regarding it, or if we do see and regard it, yet without recognizing it."

— *Alexandre Dumas (1802–1870)*

Our "happiness journey" led Marjorie and me to conclude that there are complex dimensions of happiness, though we were born to live happy lives on the Earth. Every human deserves to be happy, but on the grand scale, millions, perhaps even billions, of people live unhappy lives. Unhappy lives demonstrate that we are not benefitting from the bountiful blessings bestowed upon us by our Creator, who gave to fellow beings of every race, color, and creed the keys to our mutual "happiness existence."

We have concluded from our journey that as a human family, many are not taking full advantage of the tools (spiritual, moral, social, intelligence, and physical) that are available to create a happier life and a happier world. Instead, we have stealthily focused on physical and material progress, primarily at the expense of equally important spiritual and moral growth that bolsters happiness.

The human genius engineered better living through "Artificial Intelligence" (AI) from the microwave oven to jet propulsion engines. The human genius has given to us great private and public institutions of learning, and significant governmental and nongovernmental peace organizations.

More importantly, the human genius has labored to find cures for human illnesses. Pharmacologically, medicines have all but eradicated and brought under control such diseases as smallpox, the bubonic plague, yellow fever, and even polio (poliomyelitis).

Despite these remarkable medical achievements, human beings have not found a cure for the aberration of the mind that promotes war, genocide, slavery, apartheid, avarice, and the hoarding of strategic resources that bring *unhappiness* to the human family.

Happiness eludes many in the West. Often, we give in to our state of unhappiness, not realizing that it may strengthen and prepare us for challenges that are more difficult or for an eminent breakthrough. Our progress in the physical mastery of our material world yields great comforts, great advances, and significant material benefits, but despite the material abundance of Western nations in the twenty-first century, happiness is merely a temporary state in the lives of many underpinned by a series of events.

For some teenagers, high-school graduation and prom night sit at the apex of happiness. For some youths, a new car or college or university graduation sits at the top of their happiness. For some young adults, it may be engagement or marriage, the birth of a baby, or the purchase of a new home.

For some middle-aged adults, happiness may be the acquisition of a retirement residence. Nevertheless, happiness is not essentially a material compulsion. Something innate within the human spirit cries out for something deeper, something more lasting, and something more profound than material things to bring us to a more sustained state of happiness.

Notwithstanding the genius of the human mind, it seems we are unhappy due to three converging states of mind: *(1) unresolved issues from the past, (2) present unmanaged circumstances, and (3) fears and anxieties for the future.*

We, voluntarily or involuntarily, yield to these three converging states of mind, and we often allow them to permeate our *conscious* and *subconscious* minds. In the process, we inhibit our creative energies, our relationships, our happiness, and our "joy." Where and how should the "search for happiness" begin? Should it start in the "spiritual" or the "natural" realm of our lives?

The search must first recognize the human family as one indivisible whole with a common need for universal love, hope, "joy," peace, patience, compassion, forgiveness, gentleness, kindness, and happiness. Without such an explicit recognition, the "search for happiness" can become futile.

We must begin with a positive mental attitude that bolsters happy thoughts to promote better relationships with others. Inner "joy" and outer happiness can then reign supreme in the life of self and of others.

There are political, religious, racial, cultural, and color components that underpin such factors as "country of birth" and "worldview" that permeate cultures. These *intrinsic* and *extrinsic* attributes have both a positive and negative influence on human relations despite our upbringing.

Travel around the world and you will experience religious and cultural behaviors as far apart as the East is from the West. For instance, a "pledged bride" (where parents decide for them) in some traditional Eastern cultures may not experience the same happiness as an "autonomous bride" (who decides for herself) in Western cultures or vice versa. Relaxnews provides some insights thus:

"In Western cultures, happiness is an essential goal of people's lives, and appearing unhappy is often cause for great concern. Yet in certain non-western cultures, happiness is not considered an important emotion. Ideas of harmony and conformity often clash with the 'pursuit' of happiness and personal goals. Studies have found East Asians are more likely than Westerners to view public expressions of happiness as 'inappropriate.' The Japanese, for example, are less likely to 'savor' positive emotions than Americans."[15]

The mass movement in the global village has brought people from all corners of the globe into various cultural communities on every continent voluntarily. On the other hand, the rise of refugees throughout the world involuntarily contributes to a "Happiness Gap" (HG) fueled by *differences* or *indifferences* to race, religion, culture, color, and other social and economic factors.

To bridge these "gaps," the global community could strive to achieve a deeper understanding of human needs, priorities, and emergencies at the primary cultural level. Conflict and unhappiness can take root when human needs at the primary level are unfulfilled with little hope for fulfillment.

Fundamentally, this perspective is essential for "mutual survival," for peaceful coexistence in harmony and happiness with others, as the mass movement of legal, illegal immigrants and refugees of war becomes a norm in disaster-prone and war-torn nations. Paradoxically, when the world powers intervene, they create even greater conflict and refugees of war.

Where can human beings find happiness when the homogeneous world no longer exists, and the postmodern world has become a focus of racial, cultural, political, religious, and ideological thinking that creates conflict?

GENEVA, June 18, 2015 (UNHCR) – "Wars, conflict and persecution have forced more people than at any other time since records began to flee their homes and seek refuge and safety elsewhere, according to a new report from the UN refugee agency. UNHCR's annual Global Trends Report: World at War, released on Thursday (June 18), said that worldwide displacement was at the highest level ever recorded. It said the number of people forcibly displaced at the end of 2014 had risen to a staggering 59.5 million

---

[15] Relaxnews, published Tuesday, March 18, 2014, 9:38 a.m. EDT, http://www.ctvnews.ca/health/happiness-not-valued-equally-across-cultures-review-finds-1.1734275.

compared to 51.2 million a year earlier and 37.5 million a decade ago. The increase represents the biggest leap ever seen in a single year. Moreover, the report said the situation was likely to worsen still further."[16]

THE SEARCH FOR HAPPINESS

"The happiness of your life depends upon the quality of your thoughts. When you arise in the morning think of what a privilege it is to be alive, to think, to enjoy, to love."

— *Marcus Aurelius (121 AD–180 AD)*

The search for happiness behooves us to consider three human conditions— *(1) Spiritual, (2) Mental,* and *(3) Physical* – that make us happy knowing that all three are essential to cultivating the search for and instilling happiness. When we think of happiness, we might think of a "generic" human condition, but this hard-to-define phenomenon permeates the three dimensions of human life.

The SPIRITUAL (divine) state of happiness requires a belief in a higher "Spiritual" power, not merely a belief but a transcendental belief. Most of humanity subscribes to a belief in the spiritual existence of God, gods, or a divine being because we did not create ourselves, and neither can we account for our existence as a natural phenomenon. The MENTAL (mind) state of happiness is very personal and speaks to our positive mental attitude, character, and personality, but we must nurture these attributes.

The PHYSICAL (material) state of happiness relates to our physical well-being and our material existence. To many individuals, the "search for happiness" is the quest for material success, which in our postmodern era is synonymous with financial and material wealth, and prominence in society. Evidently, the search for success and happiness must be a search for something that satisfies the higher purpose of our existence than mere material possessions.

---

[16] United Nations High Commissioner for Refugees | Haut Commissariat des Nations pour less réfugiés, ©UNHCR 2001–2015, http://www.unhcr.org/558193896.html.

What is success, and how do we measure success? Is success the same as a successful life? Consider the story of a wealthy businessperson (an abridged story) who lived a life filled with heartbreak, tragedy, and sorrow. Despite his financial and material wealth, he was unable to maintain stable relationships with his family. He experienced deep depression and failed marriages. He lost his money in an economic collapse.

Sitting in an upscale restaurant, he finished a "champagne breakfast" and then went and sat in his luxury automobile and ended his life. He left a parting note, but why did a successful, happy, and fulfilling life elude him, as it does so many, notwithstanding their affluence and the appearance of success?

Marjorie and I have researched similar stories throughout many countries. The account of this one person's tragic life is a mirror of so many wealthy individuals. We empathize with the surviving family members, with people throughout the world, and with those in our affluent Western hemisphere, many of whom, despite great wealth, struggle to find meaning and purpose in life and happiness.

Human life is often a parallel of the ancient texts; therefore, we began our "search for happiness" with a reading of the Book of Ecclesiastes, written by the great King Solomon of Israel, circa 935 BCE.

> "The key word of Ecclesiastes is *vanity*, the futile emptiness of trying to be happy apart from God. The wisest, richest, most influential king in Israel's history looks at life 'under the sun' (Ecclesiastes 1:9) and, from the human perspective, declares it all to be empty. Power, popularity, prestige, pleasure—nothing can fill the God-shaped void in man's life but God himself! But once seen from God's perspective, life takes on meaning and purpose....Skepticism and despair melts away when life is viewed as a gift from God....No amount of activities or possessions has satisfied the craving of his [man's] heart. Every earthly prescription for happiness has left the same bitter aftertaste."[17]

---

[17] The Book of Ecclesiastes, New King James Version, copyright © 1982 by Thomas Nelson, Inc., pp. 655–657.

Evidently, material prosperity cannot replace feelings of emptiness and lack of purpose experienced by affluent individuals and their families. Sadly, a loss of material wealth can often take the wealthy to the brink of hopelessness.

The great and wise King Solomon of Israel must have peered into the future of the postmodern world, seen the state of humanity, and decided to pen his most profound thoughts to enlighten humankind of the complexity of the "search for happiness." His words light a path like a beacon for humanity to follow in the twenty-first century and the new millennium (Ecclesiastes 1:1–2).

SUCCESS AND HAPPINESS

"Take up one idea. Make that one idea your life — think of it, dream of it, live on that idea. Let the brain, muscles, nerves, every part of your body, be full of that idea, and just leave every other idea alone. This is the way to success, that is way great spiritual giants are produced."

— *Swami Vivekananda (1863–1902)*

Success means different things to different people. For the majority of human beings, a moderate lifestyle might suffice. For some, success is having wealth, raising genius children, paying off a mortgage, or winning in the Olympics. The religious may claim success as God's love enabling his or her life in our temporary existence. The path that leads to success begins in earnest when we realize that our higher spiritual needs are at the apex of all other human needs.

The greatest success imperative is to understand that a common fate links people and nations, hence the need for a "spirit of cooperation" rather than self-interest and accumulation of superfluous wealth. Success is not a state of having or being but a state of doing and experiencing. A brain surgeon experiences success after performing major surgery as his or her patient experiences a full recovery. The humanitarian with little or no financial reward may consider his or her success as service to others.

Although happiness is not necessarily synonymous with material success, material *success* can engender temporary *happiness*. Likewise, *happiness* can produce *success*. There is a fundamental difference between *success* and a *successful* life. We share with our readers five key principles for success and a successful life that guided our lives (Reference: Figure 2).

FIVE KEY PRINCIPLES FOR SUCCESS AND A SUCCESSFUL LIFE

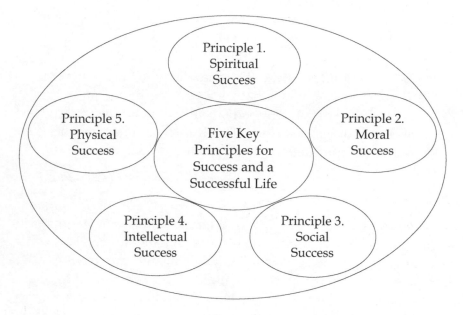

Figure 2.

The above five key principles for success and a successful life underpin both *material* and *nonmaterial* success. As a composite, they encompass an ideal formula for achieving a more permanent basis for a successful life.

No human companionship, no material possession, no money, and no power can fully satisfy the hunger of the human spirit for a successful life and happiness. Fulfillment can come only from a higher "search for spirituality," but there is no doubt that when we achieve material wealth, we engender a measure of worldly success that may bring us a measure of temporary happiness.

We often misappropriate the "pursuit of success," self-gratification, and material wealth for the "pursuit of happiness." The five principles briefly defined herein provide a "new" understanding of the "pursuit of success" that can bring lasting happiness. These five principles are mutually inclusive.

o PRINCIPLE 1

SPIRITUAL SUCCESS is the preeminent success criterion. It is to recognize and benefit from our higher "spiritual existence" as we give and receive the love of humanity. Spiritual success is the ultimate way to look at success through the prisms of love, peace, mercy, compassion, fairness, kindness, empathy, justice, generosity, and nonaggression against others. Spiritual success does not preclude entrepreneurship, creativity, or innovation; instead, it enables physical growth and progress in the physical world.

o PRINCIPLE 2

MORAL SUCCESS is to acknowledge the existence of a higher moral authority and to live with an awareness of our responsibility and accountability to fellow human beings. "Moral success" is to recognize that moral duty, moral courage, moral persuasion, and moral responsibility are at the front and center of leadership. Moral success demonstrates leadership capacity that *elevates, enlightens*, and *empowers* those who led and those who follow.

o PRINCIPLE 3

SOCIAL SUCCESS is to recognize our interdependent relationships with people and nations that lead to our higher social goals. "Social success" begins within the family, the first society. It is the testing ground for greater social responsibility in challenging environments in the public and private arenas. Social success manifests in the capacity to build and maintain social relationships with others who are not within our native social circle.

o PRINCIPLE 4

INTELLECTUAL SUCCESS is to recognize and to strive to achieve the highest levels of education and intellectual acumen of which each of us is capable. "Intellectual success" is critical for managing human affairs and the environment that supports our physical existence. Intellectual success gives the capacity to make life-saving and life-transforming decisions as leaders in family, public, and private life. Educational success is not substantially intellectual success, though there is a relationship between the two operatives.

o   PRINCIPLE 5

PHYSICAL SUCCESS is to recognize and practice healthy living that fosters a work–life balance to promote spiritual, mental, and physical well-being. "Physical success" is having the capacity to create and sustain a healthy environment for the preservation of a sustainable ecosystem. Without such a global perspective on physical success, the environment that we rely on for life to flourish on Earth will become a threat to the existence of *all* life.

In addition to these five key principles, when we put the following seven keywords into action, they further increase the potential for success and a successful life in every facet of life, including marriage, family, and business.

o   SEVEN KEYWORDS TO FACILITATE SUCCESS AND A SUCCESSFUL LIFE:

1. *Empathy* (understanding)
2. *Loyalty* (dependability)
3. *Integrity* (honesty)
4. *Knowledge* (understanding)
5. *Competence* (know-how)
6. *Transparency* (openness)
7. *Dependability* (reliability)

Material success does not always shield us from adverse effects of individual failures such as personal and business bankruptcy, separation, marriage failure, family breakdown, economic collapse, and corporate failure. Can human beings achieve a balance between material success and a successful life? One might consider winning a competition, the purchase of an exotic automobile and executive home, acquiring a doctoral degree, or becoming the

CEO of a Fortune 500 company as hallmarks of success, and they are the remarkable educational and material success we seek, but is there a finite limit to material success? What we may regard as success is not substantially a successful life.

The important question is how do we translate material success into successful living and imbue happiness in our lives and the lives of others? The "search for success" ought to underpin our desire to be on a continuum of happiness and not merely a search for financial and material wealth.

We rarely reflect on the critical need for *moral* and *ethical* leadership, good governance, and stewardship of the Earth and its diminishing resources as salient factors in the "happiness equation." Likewise, how often do we consider that our actions are instrumental in the unhappiness of others, in particular those close to us such as our spouses, family members, and friends?

An interesting observation in our journey is that people's desire for success seems to take on a very personal character, limitless and void of external influence. Although success requires entrepreneurial drive and determination, we must be cautious because the "pursuit of success" rarely comprehends the five principles discussed earlier at the foundation of our pursuit.

The essence of success is to be conscious of the needs of those whom we rely on as the ladders (metaphorically speaking) that we climb to reach the pinnacle of our success. More notably, we put forward that the beauty of success is also in the creation of ladders (metaphorically speaking) of opportunities for others to climb to the pinnacle of success for them as well.

Success from this perspective is wholesome. It helps to moderate the concentration of wealth in the hands of a few and among wealthy nations as the "wealth gap" (Reference: Figure 3) widens concurrent with the "unhappiness gap," which causes discord between the haves and have-nots throughout the world.

The dilemma that faces the human family is that we are always pushing the envelope of what we *know* and what we can do. Every day our knowledge of the world increases. We understand more and more the workings of our bodies, the delicate interactions that sustain our environment, and the majesty of creation. Despite our advances in the physical realm, we are not making similar progress in the spiritual realm.

We live in a closed system. Advances in healthcare, engineering, and space exploration do not change the fundamental truth of our existence, which is that there are finite resources available for the sustenance of *all* humanity. The luxury of life in the West is a stark contrast to the poverty, hunger, fear, despair, and unhappiness that persist in some of the underdeveloped and developing nations of the world. Race, religion, culture, and color are these dominant factors in the social, economic, and happiness infrastructure of the world.

RACE, RELIGION, CULTURE, COLOR, AND HAPPINESS

"We hold these truths to be self-evident: that all men are created equal; that they are endowed by their Creator with certain unalienable rights; that among these are life, liberty, and the pursuit of happiness."

—*Thomas Jefferson (1743–1826)*

There is breathtaking beauty in the diversity of the human family. Are any of these members of the human family less deserving of the "fruits of creation" such as mercy, compassion, technological empathy, and the opportunity to experience the "joy" of life, which are the inalienable rights of *all* of humanity? The accumulation of superfluous wealth and our reluctance to share knowledge and skills with those who desperately need them constitutes a formula for unhappiness in the world.

The great challenge that confronts the postmodern age is to invite *all* races, religions, cultures, and colors, and all social and economic classes to the "Table of Civilization" (TOC) in the "search for happiness." The universal desire of humankind is to strive to create a healthier and happier world and to elevate the "search for happiness" to a mutual happiness endeavor of *all* humanity.

Perpetual wars and strife among people and nations demonstrate that the goals of some members of the human family follow an alternate path fueled by indifference to the mutual happiness of humanity.

The "search for happiness" rarely considers race, religion, culture, and color as enabling or limiting factors. They often are both. Many of us can attest to some level of discomfort that we have experienced because of our race, religion, culture, color, or educational and economic status, and even our height, weight, and speech.

Biblical, *scientific*, and *observable* evidence points to the same origin and destination of all human beings. Some schools of thought remind us that we are mere travelers toward a common destination, with the same aspirations, pitfalls, challenges, rewards, and equal opportunities to be happy.

The daily news services are a litany of unhappy news. International terrorism, racial conflict, anti-Semitism, resource wars, religious fundamentalism, genocide, hunger, poverty, food shortages, political apathy, avarice, and corruption paint an unhappy picture, but there is nothing new under the sun.

The "search for happiness" is a problem for millions due to their race, religion, culture, color, and social and economic class differences. The legacy of the human family has left an indelible trail of unhappiness, underpinned by these *differences* and *indifferences*.

Despite the conditions that negatively affect the general state of our world, many, including ourselves, enjoy a life of "*Optimum Happiness*" (*OH*). The "Happiness Index" Planning Process Methodology (HIPPM) will help to establish a "new" basis upon which you too can enjoy a life of *OH*.

Although many would predicate their "worldview" on the premise that "all people are born equal" with fairness and justice for all, which is underwritten in the constitutions of Western nations, race, religion, culture, and color are the most identifiable characteristics of human beings. They influence every human action and interaction at some level.

Although many would say that *you* alone can make yourself happy, many external circumstances in everyone's life affect his or her *happiness* or *unhappiness.* Indisputably, characteristics such as a person's race, religion, culture, color, height, weight, and gender make some individuals unhappy with themselves. Moreover, these human characteristics can also foster "conflict of differences" by some members of society against others.

As human species, the anthropologists characterize us first by race as opposed to human beings created by God. Can the anthropological sciences better inform us of our *origin, purpose,* and *destiny*? The United Nations Education, Scientific and Cultural Organization (UNESCO) recognizes the degree to which this classification negatively influences human relations.

It declared:

"All human beings belong to a single species and are descended from a common stock. They are born equal in dignity and rights and all form an integral part of humanity."[18]

One might hypothesize (through observation) that variances in human behaviors are attributable to the conditions under which a person was born and raised such as their country of birth, cultural norms, religious upbringing and nurturing, and economic circumstances.

The unhappy person may internalize his or her feelings of helplessness, thus negatively influencing his or her self-esteem. The effects may lead to perpetual unhappiness by placing him or her at odds with peers, members of society, and even members from within the family unit.

---

[18] Declaration on Race and Racial Prejudice (adopted by the General Conference of UNESCO at its twentieth session, Paris, November 1978), Article 1, Copyright © UNESCO 1979 (United Nations Education, Scientific and Cultural Organization), p. 11.

Whether we view the human species from the perspective of *(1) religion*, *(2) science*, or *(3) observation*, it affirms the *intrinsic* linkages among all humanity and of the oneness of humankind, endowed by their Creator with the same inalienable rights and privileges to pursue a happy and wholesome life.

We are spiritual beings endeavoring to master human experiences. Out of the spiritual come love and fruitfulness. These general reflections have led to the conclusion that all races possess equal capabilities for great good and great evil. Moreover, we can observe from a historical perspective that every nation is at an "embryonic stage" in its evolution.

The awareness of this evolution should awaken humankind to the real issues that confront the underdeveloped, developing, and developed worlds. It should awaken the developed world to the need to lead and influence the underdeveloped and the developing world with spirit, presence, technological empathy, and authenticity to imbue some level of parallel growth and happiness.

How does the individual overcome unhappiness over which he or she may not have total control, such as living in an abusive situation or the inability to manage a delinquent child? We can begin with an understanding that every race and every culture reflects its fears, tears, suffering, joys, hopes, and happiness.

Happiness is a birthright (*Spiritual*, *Inherent*, and *Constitutional*). All human beings have a responsibility to make our greatest contribution to helping each other in our respective "search for happiness." To choose another path is to perpetuate a state of unhappiness that negatively influences humanity's hope for survival as a viable species.

One can further hypothesize that the main difference between any two human beings is in their responses to needs, wants, priorities, and emergencies. This understanding should help in the "search for happiness" as a "national happiness endeavor." We can accomplish such an endeavor when human beings awaken to the sacred trust of our interdependence.

Empirically observe the national dialogue on race, religion, culture, and color that speaks to the unity of the human family. Disunity has been the hallmark of human civilization, chronicled in six thousand years of the history of humankind. We hope that this awakening will *inform* better human relations and *transcend* happier relationships among races, religions, cultures, and colors that comprise the human family.

Some races, religions, and cultures exhibit behaviors that are different from others, and some of those behaviors may contradict societal norms. The mass media of the postmodern age can be the greatest agent to help modify *all* forms of human actions.

Marjorie and I have discovered that "communication breakdown" was the most significant predictor of unhappiness in human relations. We provide the following twenty attributes that should enlighten us about our commonality.

o   TWENTY ATTRIBUTES THAT SHOULD ENLIGHTEN US ABOUT OUR COMMONALITY:

1. *Understanding* as well as *misunderstanding*
2. *Hopefulness* as well as *hopelessness*
3. *Friendliness* as well as *unfriendliness*
4. *Lawfulness* as well as *unlawfulness*
5. *Happiness* as well as *unhappiness*
6. *Tolerance* as well as *intolerance*
7. *Intelligence* as well as *arrogance*
8. *Love* as well as *hate*
9. *Belief* as well as *unbelief*
10. *Kindness* as well as *unkindness*
11. *Admiration* as well as *contempt*
12. *Trust* as well as *mistrust*
13. *Humanity* as well as *inhumanity*
14. *Compassion* as well as *coldness*
15. *Generosity* as well as *avarice*
16. *Patience* as well as *impatience*
17. *Strength* as well as *weakness*
18. *Respect* as well as *disrespect*
19. *Caring* as well as *uncaring*
20. *Faith* as well as *fear*

As we observe the phenomenon of human life depicted in the twenty attributes listed above, we hope that it awakens you to a higher understanding of our commonness and informs our mutual "search for happiness." Cultural and racial forbearance can help to bridge "communication gaps" and inspire mutual hope and happiness.

The proliferation of radio, television, and Internet media communications can contribute to elevate the understanding of the need for interconnectivity of the "global village." Nations can promote cultural and racial forbearance, and the mass media can help bridge "communication gaps" to raise the national awareness of the need for mutual hope for survival.

The media could enlighten humanity to our commonality beyond our racial, cultural, religious, ethnic, and color differentiation and better inform international unity. Without great caution, our unhappiness with each other can rise to great heights of inhumanity and translate into catastrophic events in the world, such as *World War I (1914–1918)* and *World War II (1939–1945)*.

World War II was the single deadliest conflict the world has ever seen, causing tens of millions of deaths of both soldiers and civilians.

Paradoxically, nations of the world referred to *World War I* as the war to end all wars, yet the dawn of the twenty-first century has ushered in a series of violent upheavals throughout North Africa, the Middle East, and Europe, underpinned by fear of each other and fear of domestic and international terrorism. The following UNESCO articles, though dated, are relevant to shed light on this subject of race and culture.

©UNESCO (1979): "Neither in the field of heredity concerning the overall intelligence and the capacity for cultural development, nor in that of physical traits, is there any justification for the concept of 'inferior' and 'superior' races."[19]

"All peoples of the world possess equal faculties for attaining the highest level of intellectual, technical, economic, cultural and political development. The difference between the achievements of the different peoples is entirely attributable to geographical, historical,

---

[19] Declaration on Race and Racial Prejudice (adopted by the General Conference of UNESCO at its twentieth session, Paris, November 1978), III Proposal on the biological aspect of race, Moscow, August 1964, Article 13, Copyright © UNESCO 1979 (United Nations Education, Scientific and Cultural Organization), p. 39.

economic, social and cultural factors. Such differences can in no case serve as a pretext for any rank-ordered classification of nations or peoples."[20]

Fairness and justice must extend to *all* humanity without limits, in all of its universal dimensions, regardless of race, color, or creed. In a general sense, all humanity has a stake in the elevation of each other by helping to elevate each other's *self-image, self-worth,* and *self-esteem.*

SELF-IMAGE, SELF-WORTH, SELF-ESTEEM, AND HAPPINESS

"At bottom every man knows well enough that he is a unique being, only once on this earth; and by no extraordinary chance will such a marvellously picturesque piece of diversity in unity as he is, ever be put together a second time."

— *Friedrich Wilhelm Nietzsche (1844–1900)*

Some individuals consider self-image, self-worth, and self-esteem to be synonymous, but self-image and self-worth are predecessors of self-esteem. *Negative Self-Image + Negative Self-Worth = Negative Self-*

---

[20] Preamble, Article 1. 4, 5, Copyright © UNESCO 1979, p. 12.

Esteem. Conversely, *Positive Self-Image* + *Positive Self-Worth* = *Positive Self-Esteem*. We should all strive to achieve positive self-esteem, which puts us in a happy state.

Self-esteem is one of the most important attributes of human existence. Self-esteem is a subjective concept by which one identifies oneself. It underscores feelings of superiority or inferiority, a general result of comparing oneself with others who are better off or worse off than us. Regardless of how we esteem ourselves (high or low), the act of comparing ourselves with others can cause some level of unhappiness.

Mere observation teaches that an individual who displays high self-esteem is happy, outgoing, highly socialized, and self-confident in dealing with others and has a love for life. Likewise, individuals who display low self-esteem may exhibit a lack of confidence, general unhappiness, lack of an outgoing personality, and lack of general feelings of self-worth.

The images that we see in the mirror are often in contrast to the magazine and television images of movie stars and models. This phenomenon of looking at oneself through images of magazines or the media serves to perpetuate two different responses. First, individuals with high self-esteem use the images to boost their self-esteem and feelings of happiness with their image. Second, individuals with low self-esteem further provoke their feelings of unhappiness.

Children are born into homes with generally happy and loving parents regardless of the parents' social or economic circumstances or country of birth. Some children are born into families whose parents have the financial means to provide for their biological and material needs. Some children are born into homes where their parents' lack of financial resources may limit their capacity to meet their children's basic daily nutritional needs.

Children's self-esteem begins within the family. Children do not have a choice in the household of their birth or the environment in which they grow, happily or unhappily. Children may not be aware of these mitigating situations or of how their parents' circumstances may be shaping their lives and images of themselves. They may not be conscious of the positive or negative conditions under which they live or how these conditions may influence their behavior.

Some parents enroll their children in private school as opposed to public school. They enroll them in music classes and athletic programs to enhance learning and to develop talents. They purchase fashionable clothes and provide generous allowances even at an early stage in their children's lives to help motivate them and to build up their self-esteem.

We do not make this statement to suggest that money and material goods are the primary means to address problems of poor self-image and low self-worth in children, but we recognize money and material possession as "happiness enablers."

A peculiar phenomenon playing out on the twenty-first century stage is lingering "unhappy vestiges" of "Black" African slavery of the sixteenth to nineteenth centuries in the Colonies. These include slavery in Africa, the Caribbean, Central and South America, and the United States of America, and its aftermath still overshadows the happiness of many.

It was not until the early nineteenth century that "Black" people on the North American continent began to "mentally" resist the negative image of "Black" inferiority and to adopt a persona of being "Black" and proud as a *metaphor* for hope and self-esteem.

Over the centuries, American and Canadian Native Indian populations and other indigenous peoples of the world have faced a similar assault on their *self-image, self-worth,* and *self-esteem* as human beings. Moreover, for centuries, they were a people bowed under *low self-worth, low self-image,* and *low self-esteem* in the aftermath of their trials as well.

In the twenty-first century, in cultures that have entrenched racial bias, castes, and social and economic class structures, there are those who still struggle unhappily on a daily basis. However, over the centuries, Western nations have written and amended constitutions and Charters of Rights and Freedoms, enacted civil rights laws, and penned employment equity laws for the protection of citizens.

They have formed human rights commissions and other equity panels to combat racism and other forms of systemic discrimination in the workplace. Human leadership continues to evolve to more widely informed and democratic principles of leadership.

Organizations such as the UN (1946) created the United Nations Educational, Scientific and Cultural Organization (UNESCO) for the preservation of the rights of human beings throughout the world regardless of color, culture, language, creed, or race. The preceding discourse represents a change in attitude at the highest national and international levels of governance. Our hope is that these global initiatives will continue to inspire peace, hope, and happiness for a better world for future generations.

When Marjorie and I reflect on our lives, each of us can remember a period of our childhood and youth when we felt somewhat withdrawn and lacking in vitality. As we traveled on our journey through the tumultuous teenage years, we never envisaged that the challenge of self-image, self-worth, and self-esteem would so profoundly influence human lives.

We seek attention from our peers to boost our self-image as we struggle to navigate the unpredictable years of our youth. The rapid changes taking place in society and the rising tide of youth violence (against themselves and society) are indicative of low *self-image, self-worth*, and *self-esteem* as factors to consider.

Experientially, the lives of children of past generations and the lives of children and adults in the postmodern age are different. We have concluded from observation and experiential knowledge that the seven levels of infrastructure cited below could help to nurture, better, and bolster their self-esteem.

o   SEVEN LEVELS OF INFRASTRUCTURE TO NURTURE, EDUCATE, AND ADMINISTRATE THE LIVES OF CHILDREN AND ADULTS:

Governments (Level 7)
Business and industry (Level 6)
Neighborhood and community (Level 5)
Education institutions (Level 4)
Religious organizations (Level 3)
Parent(s) and family members (Level 2)
Individual (Level 1)

Every nation that is concerned about the *happiness* of its people and desires to increase their *self-image, self-worth*, and *self-esteem*, and ultimately their "Happiness Index" (HI), should involve all seven entities listed above in the development of children and adults as well. They are mutually inclusive for "*Optimum*" self-esteem, which underpins "*Optimum* Happiness" (*OH*).

Our society has a tendency to relegate the *challenge* of self-esteem primarily to the individual, oblivious to the fact that each life is "inexplicably linked" to *all* seven levels of entities above as they influence human growth and development. Each entity has an integral part to play in a *total* solution to *self-image, self-worth*, and *self-esteem* in children, youths, and adults. For instance, incarcerated adolescents and adults are probably the largest populations of individuals with challenges of *low self-worth*, *low self-image*, and *low self-esteem*.

Interestingly, their entanglement with the justice system may result from their attempts to elevate their image by engaging in *power-enhancing* behaviors that only cause unhappiness for themselves and their families. For this reason, it is essential to demonstrate *high self-esteem* within the family as a first indicator of the child's ability to cope happily in a postmodern world.

Although accountability for one's behavior is a significant factor in bringing about change, negative self-image, self-worth, and self–esteem may be the "root" cause of the myriad of problems of children, youths, and juveniles.

Despite the reasons for the delinquent's contact with the justice system, there are "windows of opportunities" for parents, businesses, religious institutions, industries, and governments to collaborate on solutions that could mitigate some of the challenges with children and youths.

Self-esteem, one might argue, is a very confusing facet of the human psyche because fundamentally, the person who we are exists on the inside. However, what seems to preoccupy people's mind is how others view them on the outside and thus allows one's color, race, culture, age, size, height, and looks to act against him or her and thus impair human relationships.

The demands and influences of postmodern societies can become an obsession, and some youths may succumb to wrongful behavior in a quest to satisfy their material wants. No amount of material possessions or financial and educational successes can make, engender, or indeed elevate self-esteem apart from the knowledge of our higher self-image.

Fortunately, the majority of individuals can cope with and manage feelings of lethargy and low self-esteem. The intuitive nature of parents often helps them to detect signs of low self-esteem in children. Family members and others such as teachers, ministers, and family physicians may also observe and respond to changes in children's behavior. We suggest the following twenty principles of childhood nurturing and development practices for parents and family members to consider for the growth of healthy, happy, and creative children.

o TWENTY PRINCIPLES TO TEACH CHILDREN FOR CHILDHOOD NURTURING AND DEVELOPMENT :

1. To believe in a higher moral authority and a higher purpose.
2. That religion, race, or color does not limit human capacity.
3. To have respect for their elders and authority figures.
4. To appreciate their image, worth, and self-esteem.
5. To perform daily acts of kindness and compassion.
6. To read extensively in a variety of diverse subjects.
7. To respect the cultural heritage of other children.
8. To strive to be truthful in all circumstances.
9. To value their higher "Spiritual" existence.
10. To be confident about their cultural heritage.
11. To appreciate the value of routine exercise.
12. To achieve their best in all undertakings.
13. That violence is not a solution to problems.
14. The importance of meeting goals and objectives.
15. That a healthy diet is essential to healthy growth.
16. To give care and respect to the property of others.
17. To practice recycling and care for the environment.
18. To appreciate and care for their siblings and friends.
19. To display care for children less fortunate than themselves.
20. To seek opportunities to volunteer under the care of parents.

The diligent daily practice of these twenty principles can overwhelm some parents in our fast-paced, materially driven society. These practices can begin a process to transform the lives of children and adults from *low self-esteem* to *high self-esteem*. Low self-esteem also has causal factors emphasized by the lack of education, lack of creative endeavors, endemic poverty, poor self-image and self-worth, and general feelings of powerlessness and an unhappy state of mind.

These principles do not preclude the need for psychologists, sociologists, psychiatrists, and counselors who teach how to enhance relationships and live fruitful lives. Often, it is only in retrospect that family members "cry out" that they knew that something seemed odd about the behavior of their child.

When children become adults, some of the challenges they faced as preteens and teens may surface in ways that challenge social scientists as they try to unravel the malady of the adult mind. Essentially, investments in the nurturing and training of children are a great benefit to the stability of the family and nation. One can surmise that a positive mental state of the people of a country contributes to the positive side of the economic ledger of nations.

LEADERSHIP AND HAPPINESS

"If your actions inspire others to dream more, learn more, do more and become more, you are a leader."

— John Quincy Adams (1767–1848)

Marjorie and I have observed that the happiness of many citizens is a symptom of the type of leadership of the respective country, evidenced by the general social and economic climate and standards of living. Citizens in democratic countries seem to enjoy a *healthier* and *happier* life than citizens of nations governed by nondemocratic systems of government.

Enlightened leadership is critical to the personal and aggregate happiness of those they lead. More importantly, the idea of "happiness" as a national leadership imperative, and as a line item on the agenda of global leaders is critical to "national happiness."

We encourage researchers in the field of "happiness" to use their scientific tools to understand better the correlation between "poor leadership" and "bad governance" and the unhappiness of individuals within nations.

The intelligent observer could conclude that the "enlightenment" of the twenty-first century should blossom into a "new" era of high civilization with social and economic equity, technological empathy, compassion for others, fairness and justice, health, and happiness.

Marjorie and I propose that spirituality ought to be a prerequisite for global leadership, whether we live in a *premodern*, *modern*, or *postmodern* age. Essentially, this new paragon of leadership should consign wars and "humanly caused" and "humanly inspired" suffering to history.

Current global trends should awaken us to the need for a *spiritual* and *intellectual* revolution in the way we look at our lives. The twenty-first century is a momentous period in human history. The new dynamics of the postmodern world demand new ways of looking at civilization, not just through political and economic prisms, but through religious, moral, social, and cultural lenses as well.

There is a need for a new revolutionary approach to leadership and "leadership intelligence," underpinned by "Spiritual Intelligence" (SQ) as a prerequisite for creating the better, safer, and happier world that we *all* envision. For instance, the millions of individuals whom society incarcerates (the "almost" forgotten) also deserve some measure of happiness.

A more enlightened "leadership worldview" could usher in a "new" era of peace, hope, and happiness for *all* humanity, including those who have walked a "crooked path" and whom society incarcerates. The hope is that nations will hold to the belief that rehabilitation is a practical reality for the majority of incarcerated individuals.

Recognizing that they are an impediment to the happiness of those who strive to walk a "straight path," it is still incumbent on enlightened leadership to facilitate their integration back into society "happy" rather than "unhappy." The benefits to countries can be enormous when *all* people are happy, but not merely "lifestyle happy."

The incarcerated should also be "happy" at the prospect of a better life and an opportunity for meaningful integration back into the community to make a viable contribution and restitution to the individual, nation, and community that they have violated, and to avoid the prospects of recidivism. Christopher Zoukis (February 10, 2014, *www.prisoneducation.com*) says, "Recidivism is a problem of the highest magnitude. Every year we, as a nation, spend over $60 billion on prison systems...money drained away from early education initiatives, state universities, and other essential social services."

> "National Statistics on Recidivism: Bureau of Justice Statistics studies have found high rates of recidivism among released prisoners. One study tracked 404,638 prisoners in 30 States after their release from prison in 2005."[21]

Enlightened leadership could require selected populations of incarcerated individuals to write a "life-changing" biography of five hundred to a thousand words about their journey from "birth to incarceration." Leaders of nations could deploy a uniquely crafted Incarceration Index Questionnaire Model (IIQM), similar to our "Happiness Index" Planning Process Methodology (HIPPM) (Reference: Chapter 5) to gather empirical data on their respective journeys.

Computer programmers can write algorithms to analyze the data that could yield critical criteria for social scientists to create policies to inform better the approximately $80 billion dollars in the yearly cost of incarceration across North America.[22]

"Rehabilitation happiness" as a criterion for releasing inmates back into the community may "come across" as revolutionary, but what is the alternative?

Marjorie and I proffer that "rehabilitation happiness" better informs the safety and security of a nation, and it can make a significant contribution to the positive side of the ledger in an age of mass incarceration at costs that are prohibitive, let alone the overall decline in the social and economic state of communities.

---

[21] Durose, Matthew R., Alexia D. Cooper, and Howard N. Snyder, *Recidivism of Prisoners Released in 30 States in 2005: Patterns from 2005 to 2010* (pdf, 31 pages), Bureau of Justice Statistics Special Report, April 2014, NCJ 244205, *date modified: June 17, 2014.*

[22] www.globalissues.org.

The expenditure demands of maintaining the global Prison Industrial Complex (PIC) threaten the economic viability of nations. A "new" leadership imperative is essential to face the emerging challenges of the twenty-first century. What makes a great leader?

Experiential knowledge also teaches that the following fifteen general leadership practices by leaders in both private and public practice can begin the process to promote and sustain a high national "Happiness Index" (HI) of nations.

o   FIFTEEN GENERAL LEADERSHIP PRACTICES THAT CAN PROMOTE THE "HAPPINESS INDEX" (HI) OF NATIONS:

1. *Create* a Minister (Ministry) of Happiness (MOH).
2. *Create* a National Happiness Awareness Program (NHAP).
3. *Establish* National Education Goals as happiness enablers.
4. *Create* a happy workplace — social, intellectual, and physical.
5. *Establish* national "Happiness Index" (HI) objectives.
6. *Conduct* yearly "Happiness Index" (HI) audits.
7. *Create* a Gross Social Progress (GSP) Index.
8. *Lead* with vision, mission, and objectivity.
9. *Lead* by example and with empathy.
10. *Lead* with commitment and stewardship.
11. *Set* high expectations for others to follow.
12. *Lead* with spirit, integrity, and authenticity.
13. *Understand* human capacity and limitations.
14. *Help* everyone to exceed his or her expectations.
15. *Be* ready to train and promote, and be slow to demote.

These fifteen general leadership practices can begin the process of transforming leadership from a passive role to active participants in the "happiness transformation" of their nation. Likewise, each leader can do something to make his or her country a happier place, beginning with a change from within each of us who lead and who follow as well.

HI of the individual is *central* to the aggregate HI of nations. The two are mutually inclusive. The government could create a "Minister (Ministry) of Happiness" (MOH) to foster the advancement of HI policy directives to manage social, cultural, and economic change at both the macro and micro levels. Other corporate institutions can do likewise.

The "Happiness Index" (HI) of nations will rise when leaders in the public and private sectors establish an HI criterion alongside quality, performance, and productivity standards. More significantly, they could conduct yearly a "Happiness Audit" (HA) concurrent with quality and performance audits. Marjorie and I also put forward that a positive HA better informs all other forms of audits, whether, safety, security, quality, economic, performance, or product.

Leaders of corporations are aware, intuitively and by practice, that happiness is synonymous with creativity and productivity, and a healthier working environment. Nations' leaders can modify the above fifteen general national leadership practices to accommodate the specific goals of their nation's initiative. As an aggregate, the fifteen leadership practices peened herein can help to elevate the HI of people and nations through national policymaking and the creation of leadership guides to underpin a National Happiness Awareness Program (NHAP).

For instance, the television series *Undercover Boss* exemplifies this level of involvement. Stephen Lambert, English television producer and executive who created the series, works in Britain and America. Stephen Lambert first introduced his program in the United Kingdom (UK).

> "In 2010, The Huffington Post selected Stephen as one of its Game Changers— '100 innovators, mavericks, visionaries, and leaders who are changing the way we look at the world.' In 2013, he received the C21/FRAPA Gold Medal and in 2014, he was inducted into Realscreen's Hall of Fame."[23]

Kathryn Goldman Schuyler writes:

> "Whatever people say, how they express it could be different....If you look at great leaders, how did they live their

---

[23] http://www.studiolambert.com/stephen-lambert.html.

lives? There are common threads: selfless love, endless passion, and uncompromising dedication to the truth."[24]

The benefits of a high quality of work–life to nations are innumerable, among other attributes considered by such organizations as the Organization for Economic Co-operation and Development (OECD).

"The Better Life Index *(www.oecdbetterlifeindex.org)*, released for the first time in May 2011, has been designed to involve people in the discussion on well-being and, through this process, to learn what matters the most to them. This interactive web-based tool enables citizens to compare well-being across countries by giving their own weight to each of the eleven dimensions explored in the OECD well-being framework....

"As of October 2013, the Better Life Index has attracted over 2.6 million visitors and over 6 million page views from 184 countries. Over 47,000 users have shared their indexes with the OECD, generating information on the importance that users attach to various life dimensions and on how these preferences differ across countries and the demographic characteristics of users. The feedback gathered from these users shows that, on average, life satisfaction, health status and education are the dimensions deemed as most important."[25]

Developing a healthy sense of nationalism can mutually inspire leadership of nations and citizens alike. Nationalism inspires the love for one's country that leads to a sense of duty toward fellow citizens, inclusive of national happiness. Each one of us can resolve to pray for our leaders, beginning with leaders in the family, in religion, in academia, in politics, in law, in the military, in medicine,

---

[24] Schuyler, Goldman Kathryn, *Leading with Spirit, Presence & Authenticity*, San Francisco, CA: Jossey–Bass, 2014, p. 16.

[25] http://www.oecd.org/std/Measuring%20Well-Being%20and%20Progress%20Brochure.pdf.

in sports, in media, and in entertainment, as well as leaders of the nation. Praying for leaders is not merely a "happiness imperative" but a "human survival imperative" that rests on an educated population, which equates to a more vibrant social and economic "ecology" to foster a happier nation.

Corporations could not function without a steady stream of advanced science and technology academics to engineer and develop mass production techniques. Thus, to satisfy the need for human genius, corporations recruit the best and brightest with advanced degrees in mathematics, science and technology, and advanced management disciplines. Corporate education should challenge both "Human Intelligence" (HQ) and the "Spiritual Intelligence" (SQ) as well.

The demand for advanced leadership training, popularized by the Master of Business Administration (MBA), mushroomed throughout universities and within private corporations over the past several decades as a core requirement for positions of corporate leadership.

A great vitality in global economies parallels the significant advancements in corporate leadership training. Nevertheless, the recurring economic collapse of the global economy poses an ongoing threat to the stability of nations.

A "crisis in global leadership" is evident by the complexity of political, social, and economic problems that modern thinkers refer to as "wicked problems." Wicked problems are more than complicated—they are complex, difficult to define, and changing.[26]

Wicked problems underpin great unhappiness in the world. The solutions to "wicked problems" demand an awakening to the need for higher "leadership intelligence" underpinned by SQ.

The critical need for higher "leadership intelligence" in our postmodern world to elevate the "Happiness Index" (HI) of peoples and nations inspired the listing of these reference books on leadership. There is a tendency to think of leadership primarily as political leadership. Notwithstanding, we provide herein a mere sampling of the innumerable books on leadership by writers with 'various perspectives' on leadership from each age—*premodern, modern,* and *postmodern.*

---

[26] Grint, 2010; Heifer, 1994; Ritter & Webber, 1973

REFERENCES

Barna, George. *Leaders on Leadership (Wisdom, Advice and Encouragement on the Art of Leading God's People)*. Ventura, California: Regal Books – A Division of Gospel Light, 1997.

Böckle, Franz. *Moral Theology – War Poverty Freedom (The Christian Response)*. New York, New York/Glen Rock, NJ: Paulist Press, 1966.

Covey, Stephen R. *The Seven Habits of Highly Effective People (Powerful Lessons in Personal Change)*. New York, New York: Simon & Schuster, 2013.

Fox, Emmet. *Find and Use Your Inner Power*. New York, New York: HarperSanFrancisco, 1937.

Friedman, George. *The Next 1000 Years*. A Forecast for the 21st Century. Melbourne, Victoria 3000, Australia: Black Inc., 2009.

Helms, Ludger. *Poor Leadership and Bad Governance: Reassessing President and Prime Ministers in North America, Europe and Japan*. Northampton, Massachusetts: Edward Elgar Publishing Limited, 2012.

Marturano, Antonio. *Leadership and the Humanities* (2014 Volume 2 Number 1), Abingdon, Oxfordshire, UK, 2014.

Maxwell, John C. *Developing the Leader Within You*. Nashville, Tennessee: Thomas Nelson, Inc., 1993.

Melina, Ruskai L., Burgress, Gloria J., & Falkman, Lena Lid. *The Embodiment of Leadership*. San Francisco, California: Jossey-Bass, 2013.

Nehil, Thomas E. *A Cultural Guide to the Global Village*. Midland, Michigan: Simon & Schuster Custom Publishing, 1997.

Rourke, John T. *Taking Sides (Clashing Views on Controversial Issues in World Politics* (Eighth Edition). Guilford, Connecticut: Duskin/McGraw-Hill A division of McGraw-Hill Companies, Inc., 1998.

Schuyler, Goldman Kathy. *Leading with Spirit, Presence & Authenticity*. San Francisco, CA: Jossey-Bass, 2014.

Schuyler, Goldman Kathy, Baugher, Eric John, & Jironet, Karin. *Creative Social Change (Leadership for a Healthy World)*. Wagon Lane, Bingley, UK: Emerald Group Publishing Limited, 2016.

Sowcik, Matthew, *LEADERSHIP 2050 (Critical Challenges, Key Contexts, and Emerging Trends)*. Wagon Lane, Bingley, UK: Emerald Group Publishing Limited, 2015.

Weaver, Grady Henry. *The Mainspring of Human Progress*. Irvington-on-Hudson, New York: The Foundation of Economic Education, Inc., 1997.

EDUCATION, INTELLIGENCE, AND HAPPINESS

"Educating the mind without educating the heart is no education at all."

— *Aristotle (384 BCE–322 BCE)*

An interesting observation is that people attribute the same meaning to the words *education* and *intelligence* in daily conversation. Is education the same as intelligence? A general assumption is that an individual with a high educational degree also possesses a high level of intelligence. Not essentially, because education and intelligence originate from two distinctly different sources. The first source, intelligence, begins with God.

Arguably, education comes from the "head," and intelligence comes from the "heart." God has granted us the highest of His creation, special blessings of intelligence, to enable us to grow as a human family with the mutual desire for health, prosperity, happiness, peace, and security for all humanity—"Not as the world gives" (John 14:27, ESV).

The father of adolescence, G. Stanley Hall, best known for his prodigious scholarship that shaped adolescent themes in psychology, education, and popular culture, made this prediction:

"The education of the twentieth century will develop the heart as well as the intellect."

— *G. Stanley Hall (1846–1924)*

Formal education is a human construct. In a general sense, boards of education (BOEs) decide for the masses in the cycle of education. BOEs have the responsibility to shape and develop moral character in the lives of their students. The shift to a new model of materially based education has fostered new scientific approaches to teaching and learning.

Education is responsible for the phenomenal growth of human knowledge. It is a base from which to build stable nations. Education must take us beyond the natural inclination to think of education as principally Academic Information Literacy (AIL). What can the forerunners of yesteryear teach the postmodern world about education and the challenges that humankind had to overcome, especially the education of women?

> "Since a time has come, Mademoiselle, when the severe laws of men no longer prevent women from applying themselves to the sciences and other disciplines, it seems to me that those of us who can, should use this long-craved freedom to study and to let men see how greatly they wronged us when depriving us of its honor and advantages."
>
> — *Louise Labé (1524-1566)*

These poignant statements of yesteryear resonate in our postmodern age. They call to mind the importance of the role of women in the affairs of the world. Historically, society relegated the role of caring and nurturing to women, the "heart" and soul of the family and the nation.

Conversely, men were the "hunters and gatherers," the "head" and protector of the family, with the instinct to hunt, conquer, gather, and kill. These survival instincts of yesteryear seem to underpin much of the competition, conflict, and unhappiness in our twenty-first century despite the transition to high-yield agricultural and industrial production of foods.

The growth of fatherless homes and child poverty around the world might have helped to inspire the education of women in certain parts of the world. Women in academia are responding to the call for a higher form of leadership fostered by "heart" and "head" to guide humanity along a better path to ensure our survival as a viable species. There is also an urgent need for women who are more capable of functioning as "head" and "heart" of business and industry as a life-altering necessity for humanity.

The vast number of women entering colleges and universities, and graduating at higher rates than men in a representative population is an answer to the higher call because women alone may have the capacity for "heart" and "head" management. A Pew Research Center analysis of US Census Bureau data shows that females outpace males in college enrollment, especially among Hispanics and Blacks.[27]

The great concern that Marjorie and I share in this brief discourse is that women preserve the potency of the "heart" as they gain knowledge and surpass their male counterparts as the "head." Education should inspire the practice of fairness, justice, reason, realism, integrity, and prudence.

Katharine Hansen (2001) writes, "Next to quality of life: Is there anyone who wouldn't like to live a longer, healthier [happier] life? Studies show that, compared to high-school graduates, college graduates have: [sic]

> longer life spans;
> better access to health care;
> better dietary and health practices;
> greater economic stability and security;
> more prestigious employment and greater job satisfaction;
> less dependency on government assistance;
> greater use of seat belts;
> more continuing education;
> greater Internet access;
> greater attendance at live performances;
> greater participation in leisure and artistic activities;
> more book purchases;
> higher voting rates;
> greater knowledge of government;
> greater community service and leadership;
> more volunteer work;
> more self-confidence; and
> less criminal activity and incarceration."[28]

The eighteen benefits of education articulated above present compelling arguments for education as a critical "happiness enabler." Education has a direct relationship to our happiness and

---

[27] http://www.pewresearch.org/fact-tank/2014/03/06/womens-college-enrollment-gains-leave-men-behind/.

[28] Hansen, Katherine, "What Good Is a College Education Anyway? Quintessential Careers," Nov. 5, 2001,
http://www.quintcareers.com/college_education_value.html.

"Happiness Index" (HI), but only a "Wholesome Education"[29] can achieve these objectives. A "Wholesome Education" is an approach to education that focuses on five essential foundations of a student's development—religious (spiritual), moral, social, intellectual, and physical. These five foundations must have measurable outcomes that are similar to Academic Information Literacy (AIL).

These new criteria of a "Wholesome Education" ought to provide the greatest social and economic benefit to individuals and nations while increasing the value and quality of life. Wellsprings of hope and happiness of people and nations would flow if education were free or partially free in *all* countries, and education were a critical line item in the budget of *all* nations.

The real potency of education is realized when education is underpinned by "Human Intelligence" (HQ), which is a life-saving gift from God; unlike animals that are limited to instinctive behavior, humans have the capacity to promote good or evil in the world through HQ.

Intellectual education is pertinent to aid students with the ability to develop their mental faculties to take on intellectual and academic pursuits. Intellectual education helps students to understand the different concepts of *intelligence* and *education*. It helps students to understand the role of intellectual leadership in the world, and it forms the basis for intelligent decision-making as they examine successful leadership styles as well as the failure of autocratic leadership styles.

Seldom would an individual think of intelligence as synonymous with happiness, yet HQ is a prime influence on the nature of human behavior and prudent decision-making. Likewise, behavior is a prime influence on happiness. These are the right lessons that enable success and a successful life.

HQ inspired by SQ guides decision-making concerning the nature and purpose of every human action and endeavor for the advancement and growth of humanity and the preservation of *life, liberty,* and *happiness.*

There are many "schools of intelligence" such as emotional intelligence, character intelligence, social intelligence, scientific

---

[29] Gibbs and Grey, *Five Foundations of Human Development (FFHD): What Is Education?* Indianapolis, Indiana: AuthorHouse, 2011, pp. 355–379.

intelligence, wisdom intelligence, and leadership intelligence. More importantly, "Spiritual Intelligence" (SQ) is the element that enables all other forms of intelligence. SQ helps to increase our understanding of human capacity and human limitations. SQ evokes the higher moral virtues such as character, integrity, fairness, empathy, loyalty, humility, servanthood, wisdom, knowledge, and understanding.

The aggregate of all forms of intelligence is essential to a life of fulfillment, but SQ is the primary focus of this discourse. Observe the rise of unhappiness in the world, buttressed by the use of legal and illegal drugs, anxiety, stress, depression, loneliness, and, worst of all, suicide and criminal behavior among children, juveniles, and adults.

SQ enables human beings to understand things that the natural mind cannot comprehend because only the spiritual mind can discern those things that are spiritual (1 Corinthians 2:10–14). Discernment enables the natural mind to understand how to manage human affairs and to release the higher virtues that embody the highest transcendental form of intelligence.

Leadership intelligence or lack thereof is responsible for much of the *happiness* or *unhappiness* of billions of individuals in families, corporations, and nations, and among the international community of nations.

Leadership intelligence demonstrates the capacity of the mind to comprehend complex problems and derive solutions based on knowledge, wisdom, understanding, character, sprit-mindedness, presence, genuineness, and mindfulness.

Great leadership is also three-dimensional. It demands a critical balance among *(1) education, (2) intelligence,* and *(3) experience,* sustained by moral imperatives such as *honesty, integrity,* and *authenticity,* empowerment of subordinates, and the sharing of the fruits of success. It is paramount that all three dimensions be in concord to achieve the highest imperatives of leadership, but none is a substitute for the other.

This "new" paradigm of leadership intelligence can bring forth dramatic changes in the lives of billions of people worldwide when leaders place the fifteen perspectives of human existence at the "front and center" of their leadership agendas. These leadership attributes are for *all*, and not limited to political leadership.

o   FIFTEEN PERSPECTIVES OF HUMAN EXISTENCE THAT
    SHOULD BE AT THE CENTER OF LEADERS' AGENDAS:

1. Servanthood leadership *versus* authoritative leadership
2. Gross Social Progress *versus* Gross National Progress
3. Humanly caused disasters *versus* naturally caused disasters
4. Preservation *versus* overconsumption
5. Moral restraints *versus* legal restraints
6. Rehabilitation *versus* recidivism
7. Cooperation *versus* obstruction
8. Spirituality *versus* materialism
9. Equity *versus* equality
10. Reparation *versus* charity
11. Forgiveness *versus* retaliation
12. Linear growth *versus* exponential growth
13. Botanical healthcare *versus* pharmacological healthcare
14. Faith and freedom *versus* fear and subjugation
15. Environmental preservation *versus* degradation

The above fifteen perspectives can empower leaders and result
in significant benefits that will resonate across every spectrum of
human leadership. Try to comprehend the wondrous world in
which we live or observe the vast and incomprehensible universe
that humanity cannot order, but the universe provides a viable
ecosystem to benefit the leader and follower alike.

"For since the creation of the world God's invisible
qualities—his eternal power and divine nature—have been
clearly seen, being understood from what has been made,
so that men are without excuse."

— *Romans 1:20 (NIV)*

The complexity of the world provides compelling evidence of
creation by a superior intelligence. Can any branch of inquiry deny
that human beings are the intelligent species on Earth, singled out
for a higher purpose, regardless of one's school of thought or
worldview (religious or scientific), or whether one is a defender of

"Creation" or "Evolution?" The words of Paul the Apostle share a biblical perspective with humanity thus:

> Gibbons (1776): "The great and incomprehensible secret of the universe eludes the inquiry of man."[30]

Humanity can accomplish higher visionary goals when *intelligence* underpins *education*, but there are preconditions. We must clear our minds of all unhealthy thoughts, all negativism, all preconceptions, all racism, all prejudice, all gender bias, all classism, all judgments and all fears. Fear of other cultures is a barrier to our ability to listen, learn, understand, and respond to all human needs, wants, priorities, and emergencies.

We must then fill our minds with wholesome and positive thoughts of "the great gift of intelligence," "the universality of humanity," "the sacredness of life," and "the higher purpose of human existence" — likewise the blessings of marriage, children, and family," and "our interdependent relationships" — to make us happy. God has given humanity the power of intelligence. It is in our "spiritual DNA" (the human mind) to enable us to comprehend our relationship with Him and to live healthy, happy, peaceful, and productive lives. Marjorie and I share with you the following five pillars upon which human survival rests as a viable species.

o FIVE PILLARS UPON WHICH HUMAN SURVIVAL RESTS
   AS A VIABLE SPECIES ON THE EARTH:

   1. *Worship* God.
   2. *Serve* Humanity.
   3. *Care* for Family.
   4. *Obey* Authority.
   5. *Manage* Creation (the Environment).

We have entrusted our lives and our *faith*, *belief*, and *practice* on these five pillars because they are the code to a "wholesome life" on

---

[30] Edward Gibbon (1737–1794), *The History of the Decline and Fall of the Roman Empire*, 1776, p. 50.

the Earth. We share them with everyone we encounter. You now have the privilege to be the recipient of our most poignant thoughts about how a universality of *peace*, *hope*, and *happiness* can reign supreme in *all* of our lives and throughout nations.

Humankind's responsiveness to these five pillars has the greatest capacity to transform the lives of billions as we use our resources intelligently and preserve the environment. The environment is the natural repository of air, water, fuel, food, land, and many of the cures for our physiological ailments. Human beings have control over this natural repository to sustain the needs of all humanity—physical health, longevity, and happiness.

Education is the base from which to build stable nations; hence education should rise above the principal pursuit of Academic Information Literacy (AIL) and help to shape the "worldview" of citizens and inspire a revolution of "new" thinking and happiness.

WORLDVIEW AND HAPPINESS

"Freethinkers are those who are willing to use their minds without prejudice and without fearing to understand things that clash with their own customs, privileges, or beliefs. This state of mind is not common, but it is essential for right thinking."

— *Leo Tolstoy (1828–1910)*

The "Discovering Your Optimum 'Happiness Index' (OHI) Project" recognizes that happiness is not merely about the individual but the human family, intrinsically linked as a "community of influence." The "worldview" of a person, community, or nation can have a profound influence on national and international relations. Even the "worldview" of religious people can be polarizing.

Our "worldview" can bring us in conformity (peace and happiness) with others—religions, races, and cultures—or in conflict with others. It begins in the family with the lessons that we learn as children in our homes and in other foremost institutions such as schools, colleges, universities, churches, temples, mosques, and synagogues.

Many private and public organizations and institutions conduct studies to obtain the "Happiness Index" (HI) of nations, which is a survey of comparative measures of happiness indicators among countries. Below are the highlights of one such UN study: *The Third World Happiness Report*, released by the UN's Sustainable Development Solutions Network, ranked 158 countries based on Gallup surveys from 2012–2015 and analyzed the key factors contributing to happiness levels.

"The *World Happiness Report* is a landmark survey of the state of global happiness. The first report was published in 2012, the second in 2013, and the third on April 23, 2015. Leading experts across fields—economics, psychology, survey analysis, national statistics, health, public policy and more—describe how measurements of well-being can be used effectively to assess the progress of nations. The reports review the state of happiness in the world today and show how the new science of happiness explains personal and national variations in happiness. They reflect a new worldwide demand for more attention to happiness as a criterion for government policy."

Chapter 2: *The Geography of Happiness*: "Average life evaluations, where 0 represents the worst possible life and 10 the best possible, range from an average above 7.5 at the top of the rankings to below 3 at the bottom. A difference of 4 points in average life evaluations separates the 10 happiest countries from the 10 least happy countries...."

"Comparing the country rankings in World Happiness Report 2015 with those in World Happiness Report 2013, there is a combination of consistency and change. Nine of the top 10 countries in 2015 were also in the top 10 of 2013. But the ranking has changed, with Switzerland now at the top, followed closely by Iceland, Denmark and Norway. All four countries have average scores between 7.5 and 7.6, and the differences between them are not statistically significant.

"The rest of the top 10 (in order) are Canada, Finland, Netherlands, Sweden, New Zealand and Australia, all with average scores above 7.28. There is more turnover, almost half, among the bottom 10 countries, all with average ladder scores below 3.7. Most are in sub-Saharan Africa, with the addition of Afghanistan and a further drop for Syria."[31]

The happiness of a nation is the "aggregate happiness" of its happy people, which are mutually inclusive. One might postulate that effective leadership, good governance, and hospitable ecological conditions of life are factors that contribute to a high national "Happiness Index" (HI). Conversely, poor leadership, bad governance, and inhospitable living conditions are factors that contribute to a low national HI in some nations.

The metrics used in these models provide policymakers with the basis upon which to address the human conditions to improve a nation's HI. Nations measure Gross National Product (GNP) and Gross Domestic Product (GDP)—economic growth and outlook monthly, quarterly, and yearly—as indicators of productivity and economic performance. GNP and GDP are not true barometers of a nation's overall health, living standards, quality of life, "Poverty Index" (PI), or happiness of its people.

It would be a noteworthy statistical asset to nations to develop a third statistical measure such as Gross Social Progress (GSP). This important measure is an essential barometer of a nation's social and economic health and a measure that would be consistent with the happiness of the people of the nation depicted in global studies in a nation's happiness indicator, such as the United Nations (UN) 2015 edition of *The World Happiness Report*.

Many other organizations that record world trends paint a bleak picture of the future of our world if global leaders continue to leave unchecked cataclysmic events such as global warming, global poverty, terrorism, and nuclear proliferation.

When researchers measure the HI of nations, they could highlight nondemocratic leadership and bad governance as a predominant factor in the "happiness equation." They should also

---

[31] *World Health Happy Report 2015*, edited by John F. Helliwell, Richard Layard, and Jeffrey Sachs, 2015, http://worldhappiness.report/.

highly recommend effective leadership and good governance as essential enablers to the happiness of their nations.

We can *all* influence the path to national and international unhappiness when each of us recognizes that we are responsible for the sum of human suffering, though we may not be directly involved. We are by our spiritual, moral, social, intellectual, and physical connection responsible for all of the genocide, the wars, the hunger, the brutality in the world, and all of the unhappiness.

Figure 3 depicts the widening social, cultural, racial, religious, economic, technological, and employment gaps among developed, developing, and underdeveloped nations (Line #6). Marjorie and I refer to these "gaps" as the "Horn of Discontent."

A HYPOTHETICAL STATUS OF THE WORLD DEPICTING THE "HORN OF DISCONTENT" (INCLUDING A BRIEF DESCRIPTION OF LINE NUMBERS 1–6)

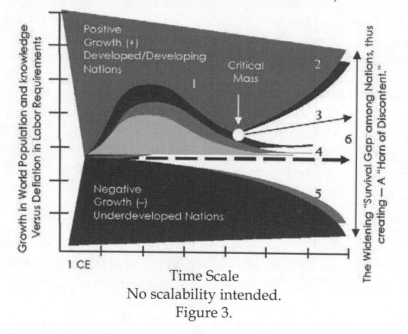

Time Scale
No scalability intended.
Figure 3.

Happiness will blossom when we reject any "moral alibi" for human suffering. We can do something to tap into the wellsprings of humanity that flow through a heart of love (*agápē*) for fellow human beings regardless of station in life. When we see the world through the eyes of our "neighbors," we can begin to understand their plight; we begin to communicate with them as a human family. It is only then that hope can exist for humanity, notwithstanding the unhappy "clash of cultures" playing out on the world stage within nations and between some nations in the international community.

BRIEF DEFINITION OF GRAPHIC LINES 1–6

1. Graphic Line 1: Shows a bell curve that depicts the rise and decline in labor requirements over the centuries. The decrease in labor requirements is concurrent with the massive shift away from labor-intensive economies to machine automation, and robots and cobots (collaborative robots).

2. Graphic Line 2: This line is indicative of the aggregate and exponential growth in science and technology and the world's population of 7,411,955,685 (March 29, 2016, 7:15 p.m.). Projected growth by 2050 is 9,725,147,944.[32]

3. Graphic Line 3: Depicts linear growth as opposed to exponential growth. Nations could benefit more from stable and linear progression in its growth infrastructure, represented in Gross National Product (GNP) and Gross Domestic Product (GDP). It would promote higher benefits in Gross Social Progress (GSP).

4. Graphic Line 4: Depicts flatline growth of nations, which may not be sustainable, relative to population growth and international competitiveness. This type of growth reflects a stagnant and flatline economy of some nations prone to a stalled economy.

5. Graphic Line 5: Depicts a negative growth in knowledge among underdeveloped nations. Underdeveloped nations cannot effectively benefit from globalization because of a lack of technical infrastructure. This includes countries in areas such as sub-Saharan Africa. Underdeveloped nations need technical support, beginning with the development of their nations' governance and education infrastructure.

---

[32] http://www.worldometers.info/world-population/.

6. Graphic Line 6: Depicts gaps in knowledge among underdeveloped, developing, and developed nations. Many of the great moral thinkers of our time would postulate that the present and emerging international unrest in the world is attributable to the ever-widening gap between rich and poor nations.

We cannot deny the reality of the circumstances that nurture unhappiness; neither should any of us assume that unhappiness is a pursuit by those with unhappy lives. Marjorie and I have conducted research, empirically observed human life, and engaged in discussions in our quest to discover a "worldview" that would help to bring humanity from the brink. A "worldview" that comprehends the *oneness* of the human family comes to the forefront as the most salient message to world leaders. We put forward that a change in "thinking" about humanity as *one* will begin to reverse our perilous path.

As we make progress in the physical sciences and as we create more luxuries for ourselves, we fall into the trap of self-reliance and fall victim to the illusion of self-sufficiency. Advances in healthcare, engineering, and space exploration do not change the fundamental truth of our existence, which is that there are finite resources available for the sustenance of *all* of humankind.

The luxury of life in the West is a stark contrast to the poverty, hunger, fear, and despair that persists in various parts of the underdeveloped and developing countries of the world. Despite advancements in military deterrent technology and the creation of national and international peace organizations, nations still face threats of terrorism, genocide, and war.

The increase in domestic and international instability provides compelling evidence of the need for a new paradigm in leadership education. We have listened to the honest and noble aspirations of and the promises of great leaders in religion, politics, academics and the military for a better society.

There is no doubt that most leaders want the best for their nations, but nations continue to *rise* and *fall* throughout history in undulating states of *hope* and *hopelessness,* and *happiness* and *unhappiness.* Why do human beings have to live on the brink of desperation? Is there a message that resonates for humanity that can radically change human destiny?

Our search for a "survival worldview" took us back to an earlier time in the history of humanity, when words spoken in the first century resonated up to the present twenty-first century. Marjorie and I present herein eight simple but profound biblical thoughts for your *contemplation*, not for your *conversion*. Speaking on a mountainside, these words resonated:

THE BEATITUDES *(Matthew 5:3–10 (NKJV))*

"³Blessed *are* the poor in spirit,
   For theirs is the kingdom of heaven.
⁴ Blessed *are* those who mourn,
   For they shall be comforted.
⁵ Blessed *are* the meek,
   For they shall inherit the earth.
⁶ Blessed *are* those who hunger
and thirst for righteousness,
   For they shall be filled.
⁷ Blessed *are* the merciful,
   For they shall obtain mercy.
⁸ Blessed *are* the pure in heart,
   For they shall see God.
⁹ Blessed *are* the peacemakers,
   For they shall be called sons of God.
¹⁰ Blessed *are* those who are persecuted
for righteousness' sake,
   For theirs is the kingdom of heaven.

Could this be the "view" that the world seeks that can bring humanity to a higher understanding of the purpose of human existence? Could this be the "view" that will culminate in our "search for happiness?" These eight simple but profound statements could provide confidence to the scholars and laypersons of this present age that there is a guaranteed path to peace and happiness.

On the path, you will find the answer to the most profound questions that one can contemplate. Paradoxically, one might question whether humanity could fully comprehend the magnanimous nature of these words or even live out their application in the postmodern era.

This path may not be easy to follow for some because it may call for a different form of spiritual awareness that might challenge one's "worldview." It may require us to broaden our belief system and "worldview," and even challenge our spirituality. It may bring one in conflict with his or her belief system, religion, race, or culture, but it will liberate us to a higher state of humanity, spirituality, and purposeful living.

SPIRITUALITY AND HAPPINESS

"This most beautiful system of the sun, planets and comets, could only proceed from the counsel and dominion of an intelligent and powerful Being."

— *Isaac Newton (1643–1727)*

The primary lesson that humanity can learn that will engender *happiness* and *"joy"* is the need for spirituality in our lives. The apparent decline in the display of international peace and harmony and the spread of violence worldwide among nations confirms a parallel decline in spirituality, worldwide as well.

There are fundamental relationships between "spirituality" and "happiness." Research demonstrates that persons who are spiritual and seek spiritual guidance exhibit a higher sense of purpose, well-being, and happiness than those who rely on other resources for happiness.

It is worth reiterating that most people subscribe to a belief in the spiritual existence of God, gods, or a divine being. Moreover, the visible presence of churches, chapels, cathedrals, monasteries, synagogues, temples, and mosques dispersed across nations is a testimony to a belief in a superior authority that extends from the premodern to the modern and up to the postmodern era.

The headline reads: "Religion is a sure route to true happiness. Catherine Sanderson, a psychology professor at

Amherst College, recently gave a talk, 'Positive Psychology: The Science of Happiness,' in which she described things that we think will make us happy but don't and things that really do. It turns out that a private plane would not make me happier. (I'm still not convinced.) It also turns out that people who have religious or spiritual beliefs are happier than those who don't, no matter what their beliefs."[33]

Despite these demonstrations of *faith*, *belief*, and *practice*, which are the foundation of all religions, past centuries have been rife with revolutions, uprisings, acts of genocide, and wars, which spread unhappiness through the Earth. Faith, belief, and practice helped to bring humanity out of the Middle Ages (Dark Ages) (AD 500–AD 1000), into an era of enlightenment.[34]

Why did human beings abandon such an impressive path and put its hope and trust in a materially driven life, punctuated by our postmodern age? We cannot change the past, but we can ask the present for forgiveness for past transgressions to bring about healing and happiness in the future.

Likewise, after six thousand years of recorded history, growth in the number of world religions, growth in the number of institutions of learning, and growth in human knowledge, we have exhibited a noticeable decline in "spiritual progress" as it lags behind "material progress."

Researchers have pointed us to the reasons for the decline in spirituality that began with the Enlightenment in the *premodern* world that extended to the *modern* world with the rise of the intellectual class and the increase in the influence of science and reasoning. The new era of assertiveness fostered the growth of the university network through the world and the scholarly narrative, which largely excludes God as Creator of the universe.

Religious (Spiritual) absolutes have mostly given way to Agnosticism, Neopaganism, Spiritism, Universalism, Humanism,

---

[33] Sally Quinn, January 24, 2014,
https://www.washingtonpost.com/national/religion/religion-is-a-sure-route-to-true-happiness/2014/01/23/f6522120-8452-11e3-bbe5-6a2a3141e3a9_story.html.

[34] http://www.britannica.com/event/Dark-Ages.

and Zoroastrianism, as well as the more familiar world religions, some of which date back to antiquity, and new religions that have come to the surface as alternatives to religious orthodoxy.

We have now arrived in the twenty-first century, somewhat confused and unhappy with the state of our *postmodern* world. We cannot go back to the *premodern* or *modern* world, but we can begin a new "search for spirituality," which is essentially a "search for happiness." Most will discover a more permanent state of "joy."

Why do we think that we no longer need God when we can make progress only through His gifts, His mercy, and His love? God alone enables our progress and our happiness. Can we make progress when we abandon belief in a Creator of the universe?

We can make progress when we relegate every conscious moment of our lives to the knowledge that happiness is our "spiritual" birthright. Human progress comes from obedience to the "Law of Love," which brings happiness; conversely, regression comes from the "Law of the Sword," which connotes any human action that brings unhappiness to any member of the human family.

Is it sufficient to display such qualities as *love*, *care*, and *compassion* to those who belong to our race, religion, culture, or social and economic class, and then provide a "moral alibi" for our behavior towards others?

There cannot be spirituality without prayer, prayer without hope, or hope without happiness. Our fervent prayer is what begins the transformation process in our lives when things go wrong. It is our faith that sustains us, but *faith*, *belief*, and *practice* must be congruent to be fruitful in our lives.

I experienced a diagnosis of a health challenge in the absence of any symptoms of the illness. As I contemplated surgery, I reached into the deep recesses of my mind as a reminder of my experience sitting and sharing with Aunt Ella-May (1915–1995) as she contemplated her mortality. She shared her *faith* and *hope* in the *present* and *afterlife* without any fears or regrets. Her contentment and happiness at her imminent transition were transcendental.

Aunt Ella-May was astutely aware that she was in the beginning phase of the third stage of her journey from *premortal* to *mortal* to *immortal*. This story is familiar to our respective families. Simultaneously, for many generations, members of our family have been practicing the following ten "Vertical Relationship" (VR), and ten "Horizontal Relationships" (HR), as an unscripted tradition, and we share those practices with you.

o   TEN VERTICAL RELATIONSHIP (VR) PRACTICES THAT STRENGHTEN OUR RELATIONSHIP WITH GOD:

1. *Obey* God's commandments *(Obedience)*.
2. *Read* inspirational books *(Meditation)*.
3. *Seek* spiritual guidance *(Worship)*.
4. *Forsake* revenge *(Forgiveness)*.
5. *Pray* daily *(Communion)*.
6. *Obey* human laws *(Civility)*.
7. *Seek* God's will *(Righteousness)*.
8. *Sanctify* our lives *(Consecration)*.
9. *Care* for God's creation *(Stewardship)*.
10. *Believe* in a higher moral authority *(Faith)*.

o   TEN HORIZONTAL RELATIONSHIP (HR) PRACTICES THAT STRENGHTEN OUR RELATIONSHIPS WITH OTHERS:

1. *Extend* unconditional love to others *(Caring)*.
2. *Apply* fairness and justice equitably *(Equity)*.
3. *Forgive* others unconditionally *(Forgiveness)*.
4. *Practice* nondiscrimination *(Humanity)*.
5. *Live* peacefully with all *(Humility)*.
6. *Sympathize* with others *(Empathy)*.
7. *Serve* others selflessly *(Servanthood)*.
8. *Commit* to one's relationships *(Loyalty)*.
9. *Consider* the poor and homeless *(Charity)*.
10. *Communicate* honestly with others *(Integrity)*.

These combined twenty "Vertical Relationship" (VR) and "Horizontal Relationship" (HR) practices constitute a blueprint for improving our relationship with God and neighbor, which are mutually inclusive as well. Despite the trials in our daily lives, these VR and HR practices will improve immensely one's state of contentment and will elevate one's "Happiness Index" (HI).

Daily practices of the above ten "Vertical Relationship" (VR) and "Horizontal Relationship" (HR) activities will improve immensely one's state of contentment and elevate his or her "Happiness Index" (HI) to a higher level. These combined twenty VR and HR practices are mutually inclusive, most beneficial as a concurrent practice.

Marjorie and I would not argue that these twenty VR and HR practices are simple to follow, but this blueprint, penned herein, brings hope in the postmodern era for happiness, anchored upon the foundation of the two great commandments that can inspire and inform tens of thousands of human laws (Matthew 22:37–40).

However, the higher relationship with God (VR) serves to establish the foundation for a right relationship with our neighbor (HR). These relationships inform the stability of the human family and transcend happiness as a world-changing imperative from "happiness" as a material imperative to "Optimum Happiness" (OH) underpinned by "joy," which is a "spiritual imperative," but for many, spirituality is a confusing human narrative.

On December 21, 2015, while sitting in the waiting room of a Goodyear Dealership in Milton, Ontario, Canada, I discovered an excerpt from Lisa Miller's work that resonated with our multigenerational experiences. It was a captivating introduction to her work. I share this excerpt with you. Her research may also inspire your interest in the seemingly mystical nature of spirituality.

Lisa Miller, Director of Clinical Psychology at Columbia University's Teachers College, in her new book *The Spiritual Child*, out later this spring: "She is convinced not only of spirituality's health benefits for people in general, but of its particular importance for young people during a stage of human development when we are most vulnerable to impulsive, risk or damaging behaviors. In fact, Miller declares, spirituality, if properly fostered in children's formative years, will pay off in spades in adolescence. An intensely felt, transcendental sense of a relationship with God, the universe, nature or whatever the individual identifies as his or her 'higher power.'"[35]

---

[35] *Maclean's Magazine*, April 6 & 13, 2015, Volume 128, Number 13 & 14, p. 45.

Our multigenerational families have been bastions of religious instruction handed down for generations. It has been the stabilizing force in the lives of generations of families. Our mother's family, recently referred to as the "Saunders Clan," dates back to the late 1800s.

We have also observed a kind of "spiritual osmosis" that played itself out among the youths in our family from the past to the present generation. Nonetheless, the postmodern age we live in has limitations on what each generation perceives vital to their growth and survival.

Our families have lived the experience for generations, and we have frequent conversations with youths in the family regarding the immeasurable benefits of spirituality and religion in our lives and the lives of our children, and the lessons that we teach them.

"Train up a child in the way he should go [teaching him to seek God's wisdom and will for his abilities and talents]. Even when he is old he will not depart from it."

— *Proverbs 22:6 (AMP)*

The most critical advantage is when the spiritual path imbues the mind during early childhood training and development. The training acts as a recall mechanism as the child becomes a youth, and the world presents a different set of values and choices from what the first society, the home, offered.

Unfortunately, parents of past generations used physical discipline to reinforce their training of children, but the physical punishment of children has given way to more informed ways of bringing up children. Regardless of the noble intentions of parents to maintain the religious traditions of yesteryear, it is a considerable challenge today, because families have lost an important *ally* in schools that once reinforced religious education.

This political and religious bifurcation is problematic for nations because governments and religious organizations take distinctly different paths as they attempt to achieve similar goals for the creation of orderly societies. The result is that co-operation between the two in achieving their mutual goals is complicated in theory and challenging to secular and religious harmony in practice, underpinned by "Separation of Church and State."

The greater loss is in the transcendent "joy" that can come only from "spiritual nurturing." It alone can sustain the soul when material happiness fails to satisfy the minds of children. A "joyless" life can lead to anxiety and depression in children, adolescents, and adults as well.

JOY VERSUS HAPPINESS

"The glory of science is that it is freeing the soul — breaking the mental manacles — getting the brain out of bondage — giving courage to thought — filling the world with mercy, justice, and joy."

— *Robert G. Ingersoll (1833–1899)*

"Joy" comprehends "happiness," but "happiness" may not comprehend "joy." "Joy" is a *spiritual* attribute, and happiness is a *material* attribute. Material things satisfy the outer self, but the inner self can be satisfied only when it experiences "joy."

For many, "joy" is a familiar term, but it is not attributable to happiness because happiness for many is a material compulsion. Material possessions cannot explain the "joy" that radiates within. "Joy" is that indescribable feeling that has no material desire associated with it.

Moreover, "joy" is the "sentinel" that guards the soul when "Happiness" takes flight temporarily. Practice the spiritual attributes of loving, caring, giving, and sharing daily, and an overwhelming "joy" will spring up in your life. "Joy" surpasses happiness because it is within us as opposed to outside of us.

Happiness has a natural connection to that which is external, hence the tendency to give or receive something tangible to enter a temporary state of happiness. "Joy" helps us to overcome daily challenges, although we may become temporarily unhappy with a particular situation. However, it could be surmised that an appropriate mixture of happiness and "joy" is experienced in the material realm when receiving a gift or celebrating a significant event such as marriage.

Chronic illness can be a predicate of chronic unhappiness and resentment of life. Today, statements such as "death with dignity," "assisted suicide," and "right to die" are commonplace in the movement to legalize euthanasia, with equally opposing views generally based on religious principles.

Devout religious individuals understand the nature of "joy" that comes from exercising their *faith*, *belief*, and *practice*, even when faced with challenges in daily life. They know the difference in circumstances that transcends happiness and "joy." People can be unhappy with a situation but still maintain their "joy," which comes from knowing that God is in control despite the challenging circumstances. The Epistle of James informs of the benefits of "joy."

> "The word 'joy' comes from the Greek root word *chara* and means 'to be exceedingly glad.' James 1:2–4 (NIV) says, 'Consider it pure joy, my brothers and sisters, whenever you face trials of many kinds, because you know that the testing of your faith produces perseverance. Let perseverance finish its work so that you may be mature and complete, not lacking anything."
>
> "I have been told that happiness is external and based on situations, events, people, places, things, and thoughts. Therefore, happiness is the result of outside situations, people, or events that align with your expectations. Joy is internal and comes when you make peace with who you are, where you are, and why you are" (Psychology Today, https://www.psychologytoday.com/blog/pathological-relationships/201212/joy-vs-ha).[36]

Grandmothers sang an old song: *"I've got that joy, joy, joy, joy! Down in my heart..."*[37] Grandma's singing radiated throughout traditional households; she was trying to tell us that she derived "joy" from her spiritual heart connection. More importantly, no one could take "joy" away from her because it was down in her heart to stay. The outward evidence was a spirit imbued with kindness,

---

[36] http://catalystway.com/blog/2016/02/11/are-you-happy-and-full-of-joy/
[37] George Willis Cooke (1848–1923), born in Comstock, Michigan, USA.

generosity, gentleness, peacefulness, and happiness. We agree that "joy" is a spiritual attribute because of its persuasive power, but "joy" needs nurturing to remain uppermost in our mind. We share these twenty practices to cultivate "joy" in our lives to maintain a spiritual presence.

o   TWENTY PRACTICES TO CULTIVATE JOY IN OUR LIVES TO MAINTAIN A SPIRITUAL PRESENCE:

1. *Believe* in a higher purpose of existence.
2. *Visit* and entertain family and friends.
3. *Visit* residents in a nursing home.
4. *Work* from home (if it is feasible).
5. *Live* within your financial means.
6. *Be thankful* for everything.
7. *Read* inspirational books.
8. *Take* spontaneous vacations.
9. *Cultivate* a vegetable garden.
10. *Admire* the growth of plants.
11. *Listen* to inspirational music.
12. *Support* family and friends.
13. *Maintain* a positive attitude.
14. *Avoid* conflicts in your life.
15. *Hang* portraits together.
16. *Write* poetry together.
17. *Wear* relaxing clothes.
18. *Cook* meals together.
19. *Visit* the ocean.
20. *Daydream.*

These twenty activities are practical. When you practice them daily, they help to maintain a *spiritual* and *physical* connection with the universe and elevate mindfulness. They parallel the "joy" that we experienced as children, filled with the simpler things in life, despite the busyness of the postmodern family.

Have you ever considered where happiness goes when we fail to make the final draft pick on the football team, when a spouse files for a divorce, or when a company decides to downsize your position? When happiness takes flight because of a change in circumstances, "joy" remains the guardian of the soul and continues to shine the light on a path to happiness. It is on the platform of "joy" that happiness rests.

Happiness is elevated when we communicate with each other. For "better or for worse," our lives have become an extension of the world of "Artificial Intelligence" (AI). The relationships that we have formed with technology seem to distract us from our greater goal to establish and maintain our primary relationships with other human beings.

Observably, much of the conflict and the unhappiness that we experience in daily life may be due in part to the diminishing of communications between humans and the exponential rise of communications between people and machines.

Imagine the reduction in conflict, the avoidance of conflict, and the billions of dollars in savings that the world could benefit from if people merely communicated with each other in a more *effective*, *consistent*, and *wholesome* way. Imagine if we only recognized that lack of communication between parents and children on the one hand and between world leaders on the other hand encapsulates the greatest body of conflict in the world.

CONFLICT AVOIDANCE AND HAPPINESS

"There is neither happiness nor misery in the world; there is only the comparison of one state with another, nothing more. He who has felt the deepest grief is best able to experience supreme happiness."

— *Alexandre Dumas (1802-1870)*

We begin with "Conflict Avoidance and Happiness" because it is a higher imperative of human happiness's existence than "Conflict Management and Happiness." Conflict management is essential, but it is management after the fact. "Conflict Avoidance" is a more potent strategy than "Conflict Management," deserving of more *emphasis, research,* and *study.*

Conflict and happiness may appear as contradictory assertions. On the one hand, conflict connotes disagreement between and among people. It implies, rather falsely, that the opposing sides will struggle perpetually. On the contrary, happiness suggests a nonconflict situation, harmony, and good feelings among people and happy outcomes.

Despite childhood nurturing, conflict may appear as an unavoidable part of human life. It begins in infancy, and it maintains a trajectory throughout the teenage years to adulthood. It is the cause of unhappiness among individuals and nations. This brief discourse is an abbreviated commentary on why conflict persists, despite the nurturing of children and young adults.

Our goal is to try to understand the fundamental causes of conflict and principal ways to avoid conflict. Notwithstanding, the lessons that we learn as children to aid us to control conflict between siblings, to the lessons we learn as teenagers to manage teenage rivalry, to the challenges adults encounter in relationships, it seems as though we are always in a state of conflict at some level.

It is incumbent upon society to examine the influence of early childhood and teenage lessons on the insufficiency in preparedness for the adult world of conflict that seems unmanageable. It seems as if something monumental has gone wrong in human relationships that leads has led to conflict and unhappiness. The evidence is in conflict among religions, races, colors, cultures, and political competitors. Further proof is the increase in divorce rates, family fragmentation, the rivalry between street gangs, and conflict between nations.

This discourse proposes that conflict may begin with opposing views and disagreements, but it can end in disagreement and unhappiness for all those who are involved in the conflict. Likewise, it can end happily with all stakeholders in agreement with the outcomes.

Regardless of the issues at stake, conflict resolution begins with our attitude, but first, let us examine the broader perspectives of conflict. How does conflict arise between individuals and nations? Marjorie and I have discovered from *intellectual* and *empirical* observation that wherever there are differences, there is a potential for conflict.

The differences are either *intrinsic*, such as in our race or color, or *extrinsic*, such as in our religion, culture, social, economic, and our political "worldview." Among other political and economic factors, these differences have, for centuries, caused war, genocide, human suffering, and unhappiness in the world. They also demonstrate the challenge to the human family to tolerate differences without some form of *legal* or *moral* constraint.

We refer to this phenomenon as a "Conflict of Differences." These differences pose a particular problem for individuals and nations in our twenty-first century as people of different races, religions, colors, and cultures travel across continents. Likewise, mass immigration and refugee movements across continents have also landed human beings in the "global village" relatively unprepared to live as a "family."

Our preoccupation with physical differences and material well-being seem to define and characterize human existence more so than our common heritage and a mutual pursuit of life, hope, purpose, liberty, fairness, justice, and happiness.

Studies in sociology, psychology, and psychiatry and other studies in human behavior, whether *religious*, *scientific*, or *observational*, teach that the human species is a paradox. Humans are the only living species gifted with free will and the capacity to change our environment to suit our purpose, yet we often fail to mitigate or manage situations that we can predict with stealth accuracy.

The ability to manage conflicts comes from "Human Intelligence" (HQ), which is a gift from God to all human beings. We are free to use this ability for constructive or destructive purposes. We can negatively influence our destiny to promote *conflict* and unhappiness, or positively to foster *concord* and happiness, but is there a "frame of reference;" a source upon which to ensure that the future will not merely be a repeat of the past?

"Spiritual Intelligence" (SQ) enables us to comprehend things that the natural mind cannot understand because only the spiritual mind can discern those things that are spiritual. "This is what we speak, not in words taught us by human wisdom but in words taught by the Spirit, explaining spiritual realities with Spirit-taught words (1 Corinthians 2:13, NIV).

Fortunately, for the human family, we have always had access to SQ to enable us to tap into a higher source of intelligence to guide humankind along a path of fulfillment—the *past, present,* and *future.* Cindy Wigglesworth says:

"We build the multiple intelligences we need: cognitive or mental intelligence (IQ) and the related technical skills of our craft; emotional intelligence (EQ), or good interpersonal skills; physical intelligence (PQ), or good body management; and SQ. "Spiritual Intelligence" (SQ) is an essential component of both personal and professional development. With "Human Intelligence" (HQ) we access the voice of our noblest self—our higher self—and let it drive our lives."[38]

HQ is limited to material knowledge; hence, we have a great capacity to create "Artificial Intelligence" (AI) in machines. The overwhelming growth in AI has benefitted humankind and at the same time increased our capacity for conflict with disastrous results.

The evidence is the genius of the human mind with our vast storehouse of human knowledge over the centuries that produced "Weapons of Mass Destruction" (WMD).

Some political leaders and military strategists might proffer that the presence of WMD on the Earth engenders hope to humankind to forestall global conflict, but the opposite is true. The mere presence of WMD on the Earth is the greatest threat to human survival, thus requiring the highest need for "Conflict Avoidance" in the history of humanity. Fear of each other brings humankind closer to the brink of catastrophe with the horrors of ever-greater wars than those experienced in *World War I (1914–1918)*, *World War II (1939–1945)*, and the *Vietnam War (1954–1975)*, for example.

Human beings have not been effective at managing conflict, before or "after the fact." The results have often been catastrophic; hence, our primary focus is on "Conflict Avoidance" as a proactive strategy. The cost of "Conflict Avoidance" is marginal in comparison to the cost of "Conflict Management," which is unplanned and deficit-driven expenditures. The ten behaviors cited here, are the primary "cause" of conflict among people and nations,' cause much of the unhappiness in the world.

---

[38] Cindy Wigglesworth, Author of *SQ21*, Leadership Coach and Corporate Consultant, *Spiritual Intelligence: Living as Your Higher Self*.

o   TEN BEHAVIORS THAT ARE THE CAUSE OF CONFLICT
    AND UNHAPPINESS IN THE WORLD:

1. *Lack* of spirituality
2. *Lack* of empathy
3. *Desire* for revenge
4. *Violation* of contracts
5. *Aggressive* behavior
6. *Infidelity* in marriage
7. *Unfairness* and injustice
8. *Violation* of sovereignty
9. *Disobedience* to authority
10. *Disloyalty* in relationships

These ten behaviors delineated above can be prevalent in some marriages and families, and even within races, cultures, corporations, institutions, and nations. They cause conflict. In contrast, the ten behaviors (practices) below can "uproot" the cause of conflict and unhappiness in the world.

o   TEN BEHAVIORS THAT CAN UPROOT THE CAUSE OF
    CONFLICT AND UNHAPPINESS IN THE WORLD:

1. A *"Spiritually Driven"* life
2. *Empathy* for others
3. *Forfeit* vengeance
4. *Contract* compliance
5. *Peace* loving behavior
6. *Fidelity* in marriage
7. *Fairness* and justice
8. *Respect* for sovereignty
9. *Obedience* to authority
10. *Loyalty* in relationships

Regardless of the conflict among friends, family members, business associates, or nations, regardless of differences in opinion, attitude or worldview, and although it may require discipline and a consistent awareness of these ten behaviors, they are the most potent to avoid conflict in our daily lives.

The conflicts encountered in daily living originate from within the human heart. These problems manifest in outward actions such as genocide; war; racial, cultural, and religious intolerance; and, in general, acts of inhumanity to each other, though they are mere symptoms of "unhappiness" with the human condition.

Nevertheless, the human condition is not permanent but yielding because the "indomitable" spirit within people always leads to a higher purpose and our higher selves, despite challenges of each era, *premodern, modern,* and *postmodern.*

Conflict can arise in marriage, among family members, between cultures, and between business corporations and nations. Conflicts have different approaches to solutions, from village elders engaged in local conflict among village dwellers, to lawyers involved in the management of conflict between corporations, to the International Court of Justice (ICJ)'s involvement in a territorial dispute.

CONFLICT MANAGEMENT AND HAPPINESS

"Repay no one evil for evil, but give thought to do what is honorable in the sight of all."

— *Romans 12:18 (ESV)*

How do we manage conflict that causes unhappiness at different stages of life? The lessons that we learn, are they cumulative? As children and youths, our parents taught us to *love, care,* and *share.* For many of us, these lessons were an integral part of our upbringing and, in particular, our religious education.

When we enter the world as young children, and as we advance from elementary and secondary school to college or university, the language and learning become more sophisticated. We learn such words as *responsibility, accountability, discipline, fairness, justice, honesty,* and *empathy.* We never stop learning.

As we move along the "trajectory of life," we enter the corporate world, start a business, or manage a corporation. We are aware that nations create significant global organizations and institutions with considerable effort and expense to further educate, mitigate, and eradicate the human condition that causes conflict, suffering, unhappiness, and premature death in the world.

The evidence is not only in the genocide, wars, slavery, colonization, and apartheid of past decades, but also in the continuation of some of these atrocities into the twenty-first century in various parts of the world.

Despite the human "trajectory of learning" and acquiring knowledge from childhood to adulthood, observe the lasting effects of destructive activities throughout the ages and into the twenty-first century. Where did all the learning go?

The great benefits that twenty-first-century society brings, such as a happy outdoor lifestyle underpinned by global travel, are under a great threat. Is conflict innate? Is it a consequence of our competitive, scientific, and technological postmodern society?

Conflict and the rising threat to peace, safety, and security are the greatest preoccupation of individuals and nations in the crucible of the twenty-first century. Conflict has gone global in ways that no one would have imagined in an era of "sophisticated learning."

How does humanity shield itself against global conflict and unhappiness? Humanity has searched for answers for six thousand years of recorded human history. Political leaders, social scientists, religious leaders, philosophers, academics, counselors, and global human rights organizations have been unable to stem the tide of conflict in the world.

A universality of hope must spring from the spirit within us in an unquenchable desire to lift individuals and nations to the same level of hope we hold for ourselves. It is only in this context that hope can have meaning, and we can bring hope through the "diminishing of conflict" that affects the greater human family.

Conflict is a "double-edged sword." On the one hand, it can be good when it surfaces the inner higher qualities in us as we search for solutions as a mutual benefit that leads to peace, harmony, and happiness, often referred to as a "win-win" proposition where both parties benefit from the outcome.

On the other hand, conflict can take us to an impasse where the end result can be "disagreement," or "agreement to disagree," often leading to further conflict. When we enter the "arena of conflict," it should always be with minds preempted and imbued with universal love, peace, fairness, and justice as first imperatives.

These peaceful attributes reside in our deeper spiritual nature. They transcend all natural impulses to win and to seek revenge or retribution. "Spiritual Intelligence" (SQ) surpasses all other noble attempts to find an amicable resolution to the conflict.

Many unsolvable problems faced by individuals and nations have roots in the past. They have roots in our history of aggression (neighbor against neighbor) because of race; color; culture; nationality; religion; political ideology; the breaking of vows, pledges, contracts, bonds, and agreements; and the violations of sovereignty.

We are aware that the history of human conflict is a chronicle of the world's growing deficit financing of trillions of dollars extrapolated over the past century in the "pursuit of peace" as nations reap the harvest of war *unhappily.*

These actions threaten to unravel the religious, social, and economic fabric of nations. Furthermore, they threaten the existence and survival of humanity. They frustrate individuals, nations, and the international community and result in enormous financial burdens on the world economy. In monetary terms, "happiness" is a *surplus* in the economy, and "unhappiness" is a *deficit.*

Many families are preoccupied with the academic achievement of their children as the first imperative of their survival and their material survival, but a material-based education tends to shift the attention away from spiritual attributes and directs human activities in an imbalanced way toward competition, even unfair competition.

Competition is also a "double-edged sword." On the one hand, it is the engine to foster the growth of the economy, but on the other hand, it can foster unfairness and results in disparity and conflict. To manage conflict effectively means to mobilize the highest investments in human resources. These investments are primarily in the change of perspective, attitudes, and behaviors.

Our great efforts over the centuries have not sufficiently produced gross measurable statistical progress regarding a quantifiable reduction of national and international conflicts, genocide, hopelessness, poverty, hunger, depression, and human suffering. Our twenty-first century has not ushered in international peace and harmony, nor has it achieved universal social and economic equity goals engendered by nations.

Global meetings and conferences by the G8 and G20 countries seem to result in new mandates, but they tend to move deadlines for finding solutions to human problems into the future.

These problems grow more complex with each passing decade, such as trade wars, territorial wars, international terrorism, cyber wars, and wars for scarce resources. Listed below are fifteen general strategies to help avoid, mitigate, and manage conflict.

o FIFTEEN GENERAL STRATEGIES TO HELP AVOID, MITIGATE, AND MANAGE CONFLICT:

1. *Call* upon a higher "Spiritual" power for guidance.
2. *Begin* with a positive resolution to the conflict in mind.
3. *Know* that you will learn a valuable lesson from the conflict.
4. *Mutually* agree on the essential elements of the conflict.
5. *Consult* with proven expertise to present your position.
6. *Approach* the situation with a sociable predisposition.
7. *Maintain* a positive conflict management mindset.
8. *Produce* empirical data to validate your position.
9. *Maintain* a positive conflict avoidance mindset.
10. *Know* that conflict can have positive outcomes.
11. *Avoid* making unsubstantiated assumptions.
12. *Dismiss* any concept of winners and losers.
13. *Negotiate* with fairness and transparency.
14. *Strive* for calmness, openness, and objectivity.
15. *Strive* for a mutually agreeable conflict resolution.

The above fifteen general strategies have the potency to resolve any conflict when the parties in the conflict are predisposed to an amicable resolution. They are not essential elements of the conflict, but they help to create a "potent" environment upon which to predicate a solution.

Additionally, we provide the following seven steps (Reference: Table 1) to augment the fifteen general strategies above that will help to *avoid*, *mitigate*, and *manage conflict*. The high value of the Seven Steps Process to Manage Conflict (SSPMC) is when *all* involved in the conflict resolution are familiar with each step at a detailed level.

Each step may require extensive research and documentation to resolve a major conflict, or in minor circumstances, the individuals involved in the conflict can talk through each step to effect a resolution. The associated Generic Process Flowchart 1 (overleaf) is also an aid to following the process methodology.

SEVEN STEPS PROCESS TO MANAGE CONFLICT (SSPMC)

SEVEN STEPS:	SEVEN HIGH-LEVEL DEFINITIONS:
1. Document	Document the conflict.
2. Establish	Establish the solution criteria.
3. Assess	Assess the solution criteria against risks.
4. Decide	Decide on action the plan.
5. Develop	Develop and execute the plan.
6. Evaluate	Evaluate the plan and make adjustments.
7. Measure	Measure the resolution.

Table 1.

The high value of the Seven Steps Process to Manage Conflict (SSPMC) is when the decision to manage a conflict comes from an inner personal desire for resolution and is not necessarily influenced by others. Some conflict management objectives may require a commitment to caring for people other than oneself, such as in managing "irreconcilable differences" in marriage or caring for the elderly. Likewise, the conflict may be internalized and thus require a personal conviction, such as one who decides to embark on a "spiritual" journey.

From a general perspective of the Generic Process Flowchart 1, it provides a basis upon which to focus on strategic elements of the seven "Self-Improvement" (SI) steps (Reference: Table 1). Observe the feedback loops in the Generic Process Flowchart 1. The outcome-based approach provides the "Aspirant" with an opportunity to revisit and repeat specific steps to obtain the desired outcome before proceeding with the succeeding step.

GENERIC PROCESS FLOWCHART 1.
SEVEN STEPS PROCESS TO MANAGE CONFLICT (SSPMC)

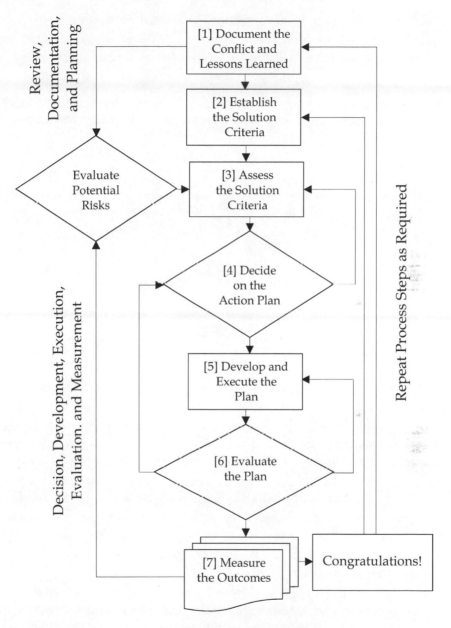

Generic Process Flowchart 1.

REPOSITIONING YOUR LIFE
— SEVEN STEPS TO A NEW YOU

"You can search throughout the entire universe for someone who is more deserving of your love and affection than you are yourself, and that person is not to be found anywhere. You, yourself, as much as anybody in the entire universe, deserve your love and affection."

— *Siddhartha Gautama Buddha (circa 563 BCE–483 BCE)*

Our search for happiness may demand that we reposition our lives and rethink our "worldview." This repositioning of our lives will help to foster better relations with others as we learn new things about others and ourselves. The following discourse comprises the thoughts of Kathy Gottberg (Kathy@smartliving365.com):

"A big part of living SMART 365 is recognizing and discovering new and beneficial ways to create a life of wellbeing and happiness. Like so many other things in life, the journey is not a destination—rather it is an ongoing process of growth, experience and expression.

"In some ways, it is similar to something that occurs in the commercial real estate field in the U.S. What? That's right, no matter how wonderful a property (or a life) has been in the past, there comes a time when it is necessary to 'reposition' it in order to experience its highest and best use. Although human lives are far more complex, we can learn a few things about change, creativity and feasibility by taking a deeper look at the art of repositioning....What is repositioning? In the commercial field, repositioning a property means to take that property and redirect it or turn it around in a significant way to maximize its potential. In the same way, repositioning a life is taking a closer look to discover exactly what is happening, evaluating that pattern, and then making necessary changes and choices that move it in a more positive and beneficial way.

"For example, a simple repositioning of a commercial property is analyzing whether it is being used effectively. A large office building in Hawaii showed on careful examination that both the rents were extremely low and the management was ineffective. Both of these could be improved upon rather easily and increase both the value and the benefit of the building.

"In exactly the same way, small changes in a person have the potential to dramatically increase the happiness and benefits of that person's life. Relatively small alterations like making a decision to eat in a more healthy way, to smile more often or to exercise daily, all can turn a person's life around in a positive way.

"A more dramatic example of property repositioning would be to completely change the use and appearance of the property. Taking an old dilapidated motel and turning it into a retreat-center or eldercare facility illustrates such a difference. A dramatic change when repositioning a life was when Thom and I decided to move from Colorado back to California.

"We clearly knew that we both preferred to live in a warm climate close to the beach and the mountains. Even though we uprooted ourselves from the security of what was familiar (jobs, income, friends, etc.), we knew we would be happier and more content in California over the long run.

"So how does one go about repositioning your life? Again, the commercial property comparison is helpful. When a commercial property broker meets with an owner, there is a list of important considerations to consider. A few of those that apply equally to repositioning a life are:

"Step 1:

"Uncovering Objectives. A good place to start is determining if a change is necessary in the first place and if there is enough motivation to do what it takes. Has your existing life gotten dull and repetitive? Is the stress of debt making you crazy? Are your relationships destructive? By facing the truth about where you are, where you want to be and if you will do what it takes is the first step to repositioning your life.

"Step 2:

"SWOT (strengths, weaknesses, opportunities and threats). Before making any big change these are important aspects to consider. While the word "threat" may seem strange, I think it addresses the fears we harbor (whether real or imagined). Identifying these positions can help us be honest about what regularly works for us and what works against us — and then act accordingly.

"Step 3:

"Highest and best use. I believe everyone needs purpose and meaning in one's life. This question asks you if you know what that is, and more importantly, whether you are living it. It also questions the depth of our lives in ways that can be life transforming.

"Step 4:

"Feasibility. How feasible is your desire to reposition your life in the way that you want? If you decide you want to be a professional ballerina after retirement that might not be humanly possible. If instead, you want to be a part of the ballet in a meaningful way — there are dozens of ways to go about that at any age. Honesty is critical when discussing feasibility.

"Step 5:

"Resources. In order to undertake any journey we need assets at hand. The more resources, friends, support, discipline, education, etc. that can gather-together, identify and create, the better. The bigger the change, the more necessary it is to have a large supply of things to help us on the path.

"Step 6:

"Action Plan. Any hope to reposition either a building or a life requires a general plan. While the plan does not have to be a complete blueprint, there needs to be enough details so we at least stay headed in the direction that we say we want to achieve.

"Step 7:

"Flexibility and Trust. Ultimately, no matter how carefully thought out any repositioning is, there are always surprises. A detailed plan does not mean that it will never alter, only that we are moving in one particular direction. In addition, flexibility opens us up to possibilities that we might not have even known about when we first started the journey (change). By staying open and trusting the process we may discover that the best opportunity remained hidden until we took that first step.

"Up until now, you may never have thought that the commercial real estate industry had anything to do with your life. The truth is, the world around us offers dozens of signs showing us the way to proceed. Much of that path is paying attention, staying conscious, having the desire, and refusing to settle for anything less. Unfortunately, far too many people seem to be content to be merely alive, rather than experience and celebrate *living*. There is a big difference—and SMART Living 365 is a resource to help make that happen."[39]

Kathy's SMART Living 365 resource on "Repositioning Your Life—Seven Steps to a New You" has inspired Marjorie and me, and we hope that you have been inspired as well because we have followed these and similar steps that have led us along "fruitful" paths of happiness. We hope that your "tree of life" also bears "abundant fruit."

---

[39] http://smartliving365.com/repositioning-your-life-seven-steps-to-a-new-you/. With kind permission of Kathy Gottberg, Kathy@smartliving365.com.

CHAPTER
5

THE "HAPPINESS INDEX" (HI) PROCESS
METHODOLOGY (HIPM)

"In questions of science, the authority of a thousand is not
worth the humble reasoning of a single individual."

— *Galileo Galilei (1564–1642)*

Design and development of the "Happiness Index" Planning
Process Methodology (HIPPM) began in the year 2000 with an
assertion that there is a rising tide of unhappiness in the world. The
postmodern world seems to be spiraling into a "crisis of
unhappiness" in various parts of the world. Marjorie and I have
observed this scene play out on the world stage throughout our
adult lives with worrisome thoughts of the future happiness of the
world.

Symptoms of this unhappiness are in the breakdown of marriage, personal and corporate failure, national and international litigation, exponential growth in the production of Weapons of Mass Destruction (WMD), growth in the Prison Industrial Complex (PIC), and growth in the Military Industrial Complex (MIC) of nations. In parallel with the growth of these institutions, is the phenomenal increase in world refugees fleeing the ravages of war, and persecution (http://www.unhcr.org/558193896.html).

World governments and world peace organizations struggle to find solutions as their emissaries circle the Earth on global peace missions that are generally "unfruitful." Our inquiry, penned herein, is a testimony to our hope for a higher understanding of the "power of happiness" to transform the world.

Great material wealth has failed to satisfy an inner emptiness, an inner struggle, and an inner hunger for a life of peaceful coexistence among people and nations. We make this conjecture not as a cliché, but with the profound belief that regardless of the calamity that confronts humankind, it all begins in the cradle and the breakdown of the first society — the family.

Trends in the breakdown of marriage, fatherless homes, intervention by social workers and the justice system in the affairs of the family, the rise of a new class of homeless individuals, youths escaping from domestic violence, abuse, loneliness, impoverishment, and elusive happiness support our assertion.

We embarked on the "Discovering Your Optimum 'Happiness Index' (OHI) Project" inspired by our empathy for millions around the world for whom these challenges are a part of daily life. Our journey was life-transforming, played out in real life not as academic research or clinical study, but on the world stage.

The "Happiness Index" Planning Process Methodology (HIPPM) endeavors to provide an approach for people to understand better the integration of the preceding narrative in Chapters 1–4. Your HI will help to confirm and validate our assertion that the world could be a better place when people are happier, not merely as a personal pursuit or "lifestyle happy" but as a desire to imbue happiness in others as well.

Marjorie and I decided on a HIPPM that focuses on "Ten Key Happiness Indicators" (TKHI) (Reference: Table 3), underpinned by achievements, attributes, and customs, unlike a pure lifestyle focus.

Our approach is common to our *conscious* and *subconscious* attitude and behavior bolstered by our nurturing, as opposed to inadvertent and spontaneous lifestyle habits. For many individuals, lifestyle is synonymous with success and happiness, but this misappropriation of *lifestyle* and *happiness* can be counterproductive to the real goals of happiness when the quality of lifestyle diminishes.

Lifestyle tends to be transient as opposed to the deeper influence and meaning of how achievements, attributes, and customs shape our "worldview" and our behavior. Furthermore, the response to our "Happiness Index" (HI) model is introspective.

In the preceding discourse (Reference: Chapters 1–4), we briefly examined the "search for happiness" and the human condition that makes us *happy* or *unhappy*. Often, we have allowed ourselves to become victims of our circumstances, for instance, the country of our birth, our religion, our race, our culture, our education, our childhood experiences, our material status, and our internal prejudices.

We recognize and acknowledge many schools of *thought*, *study*, and *research* methods that scientists use to determine the Gross National Happiness (GNH) of nations. The answers that they derive provide statistical evidence to support their inquiries at a national level. Our methodology focuses on the happiness of the individual, which aggregates to GNH.

For over a decade (2000–2015), Marjorie and I have observed empirically and have talked and dialogued with people, and informally interviewed, and surveyed them to garner a firsthand understanding of people's perspectives on *happiness* and *unhappiness*, more importantly how they celebrate these two diametrically opposed human conditions.

The conversation is not just with those whom we have encountered and with whom we have shared thoughts and exchanged ideas regarding the "quest for happiness," but each of us shares in a conversation of mindfulness of how our "spiritual" and "natural" nature enables human beings to cope in the postmodern era. We also endeavored to ascertain by self-directed methods how one could determine his or her "Happiness Index" (HI).

Our determination gave birth to the "HAPPINESS INDEX" PLANNING PROCESS METHODOLOGY (HIPPM) that underpins our proposition for a happier world. Our desire was to bring "new" but simple tools to the happiness industry and engage in the global conversation.

THE "HAPPINESS INDEX" PLANNING PROCESS
METHODOLOGY (HIPPM) KEYS

The key to understanding the "Happiness Index" Planning Process Methodology (HIPPM) is to comprehend the crucial foundation of the "Ten Key Happiness Indicators" (TKHI). These indicators (Categories 1–10) are as follows: (1) Career $^{(C100)}$, (2) Character $^{(C100)}$, (3) Education $^{(E100)}$, (4) Forgiveness $^{(F100)}$, (5) Health $^{(H100)}$, (6) Humility $^{(H100)}$, (7) Personality $^{(P100)}$, (8) Religion $^{(R100)}$, (9) Self-esteem $^{(S100)}$, and (10) Socialization $^{(S100)}$ (Reference: Table 3).

The TKHI provide the basis from which we created the matrix of ten diverse questions for each Questionnaire Category (QC) 1–10, correlated to the Questionnaire Template (QT) 1–10. They relate to both a Western "worldview" (a function of our Western heritage social, religious, and cultural orientation) and way of thinking. Notwithstanding, our methodology has universal application.

We have provided a brief definition of the TKHI under the heading STEP 2 (Reference: Table 2). As a composite, the Questionnaire Categories (QC) 1–10 relate to the way we understand life, our faith, our belief, and our practice. Whether we are aware that we hold a particular "worldview" or not, our behavior projects our "worldview," which places us in harmony or conflict with others. The questionnaire will surface the "worldview" of each "Aspirant," which is personal.

Each question embodies a *past*, *present*, and *future* outlook of the panorama of our lives. Arguably, when the "Aspirant" completes the process by answering (completely) the matrix of questions, it will probably be the *first* inventory of its kind that he or she will have explored. The HIPPM is a tool to enable you to navigate easily and respond to the myriad of questions in a "self-directed" way, and for you to answer each question without any external influence. This approach will yield the best results from the questionnaire.

The "Happiness Index" (HI) is analogous to a Body Mass Index (BMI) calculator. The BMI reference number may be an "Optimum" number for a particular weight and height, but the number is unique to the individual.[40]

---

[40] http://www.smartbmicalculator.com/.

Our "Happiness Index" Planning Process Methodology (HIPPM) is nonscientific, but it can complement research in behavioral science disciplines such as sociology or psychology. Our research led us to conclude that our "Happiness Index" (HI) has applications in science when modeled across large groups or populations for variance and standard deviation. Our hope is to seek to broaden the discourse through collaboration with a scientific organization in the future.

Our HIPPM does not attempt to *compare to* or *compete with* other tools that have a focus on lifestyles or other national perspectives on happiness. Our HIPPM is unique, compelling, and useful as a tool, indicative of spiritual, social, moral, intellectual, and physical health, happiness, and well-being. It takes the "Aspirant" on a journey of seven steps to discover his or her HI (Reference: Table 5). It also provides a simplified step-by-step breakdown of the method (Reference: Table 2). We have also included a compendium of tables, templates, flowcharts, and note pages that comprise the HIPPM.

Throughout the process, you can capture your thoughts on the note pages to expand on the precepts, useful for the next stage of Self-Improvement Planning (SIP), defined later in this chapter. Our desire is that these seven steps will inform your understanding of the HIPPM and inspire you to strive to achieve and sustain "Optimum Happiness" (OH) as a norm.

Similar to the first attempt at any new endeavor, the HI methodology may pose an initial challenge, but it will provoke your curiosity. Additionally, our desire is that you will realize the intrinsic benefits of the HIPPM, not only as a tool to inspire Self-Improvement (SI) but to help those with whom we interact daily. The innovative and compelling nature of the HI method will move you to share it with others.

Table 2 (Overleaf) depicts the Seven Steps "Happiness Index" Planning Process Methodology (SSHIPPM) to complete the HIPPM. Each step begins with a summary of the outcomes of the composite of each step's activity. We recommend that you complete all seven steps (STEP 1–7). More importantly, we recommend that you follow each step action (activity), which will become intuitive after the first attempt at completing the guide. The guide will inspire you to call to mind other questions that you may consider as salient to your happiness and OH.

SEVEN STEPS "HAPPINESS INDEX" PLANNING PROCESS METHODOLOGY (SSHIPPM)

o   STEP ONE _SUMMARY READ _A Self-Directed Guide to Your "Happiness Index" (HI) (Reference: Chapters 1–4)
o   STEP TWO _SUMMARY COMPLETE _The Ten Questionnaire Template (QT) 1–10 for each Questionnaire Category (QC) 1–10 (Reference: Table 3)
o   STEP THREE _SUMMARY POPULATE _The Summary Questionnaire Template (SQT) 11 (Reference: Table 4) with the Subtotal Scores (Y + N = T) from each Questionnaire Template (QT) 1–10
o   STEP FOUR _SUMMARY TRANSFER _The Total Score (Column "T") from the Summary Questionnaire Template (SQT) 11 (Reference: Table 4) to the "Happiness Index" Measurement Template (HIMT) 12 (Reference: Table 5) in the relevant score range
o   STEP FIVE _SUMMARY DEVELOP _A Self-Improvement Plan using Self-Improvement Planning Template (SIPT) 1–10 (Reference: Table 6)
o   STEP SIX _SUMMARY EXECUTE _The Self-Improvement Planning Process Methodology (SIPPM) (Reference: Table 7) (Generic Process Flowchart 2)
o   STEP SEVEN _SUMMARY CONCLUSION _You have successfully completed the "Happiness Index" Planning Process Methodology (HIPPM).

Table 2.

STEP ONE

SUMMARY

o   STEP ONE _SUMMARY

READ THE SELF-DIRECTED GUIDE TO YOUR "HAPPINESS INDEX" (HI) (REFERENCE: CHAPTERS 1–4).

STEP TWO

SUMMARY

o   STEP TWO _SUMMARY

COMPLETE THE QUESTIONNAIRE TEMPLATES (QT) 1–10
FOR EACH QUESTIONNAIRE CATEGORY (QC) 1–10
(REFERENCE: TABLE 3).

o   ACTIVITY 1:
READ _The Definition of Matrix of Questionnaire Template (QT)
versus Questionnaire Category (QC) versus Achievement, Attribute,
and Custom.

o   ACTIVITY 2:
READ _The Definition of Achievement, Attribute, and Custom.

o   ACTIVITY 3–3I:
READ _The Definition of Questionnaire Template (QT) 1–10 for each
Questionnaire Category (QC) 1–10
(QT 1 _Career — QT 10 _Socialization).

o   ACTIVITY 4:
READ _The Definition of Questionnaire Template
Scoring Methodology (QTSM) for each Category QT 1–10.

o   ACTIVITY 5–5I:
COMPLETE _The Questionnaire Template (QT) 1–10 for each
Questionnaire Category (QC) 1–10
(QT 1 _Career — QT 10 _Socialization).

STEP 2: ACTIVITY _1
DEFINITION OF THE MATRIX OF QUESTIONNAIRE TEMPLATE
(QT) VERSUS QUESTIONNAIRE CATEGORY (QC) VERSUS
ACHIEVEMENT, ATTRIBUTE, AND CUSTOM
(REFERENCE: TABLE 3)

Table 3. The matrix of Questionnaire Template (QT) versus Questionnaire Category (QC) versus Achievement, Attribute, and Custom provides the foundational basis of the "Happiness Index" Process Methodology (HIPPM).

We have observed the phenomenon of life and the profound influence that the ten Questionnaire Categories (QC) depicted in Table 3 (Overleaf) have in everyday life situations. Questionnaire Templates (QT) 1–10 represent each category.

The exponent (^{100}) indicates the maximum score of 100 points that an "Aspirant" can achieve for answering each of the ten questions depicted in each (QT). Each category can be a positive influence and engender happiness, or a negative influence and cause unhappiness. Therefore, each category can act as a counterbalance to the other.

For example, one can have an excellent education (a graduate degree) and a lucrative career and symbols of success and happiness, but be unhappy because of a lack of good health or the "spirit" of forgiveness.

The "Ten Key Happiness Indicators" (TKHI), underpinned by the three entities Achievement, Attribute, and Custom, characterize our daily existence. Together with QC, QT, and the compendium of questions, they comprise the "intelligence matrix" that undergirds the HIPPM.

Scientific researchers have deployed other methods to measure the happiness index of nations, but we have chosen to explore in our model the "Happiness Index" (HI) at a level that speaks to our interactions with fellow beings, punctuated by our behavior.

The model does not recognize any "weighted differences" in the categories to attribute levels of criticality of one category over another. The primary goal of the HI is to inspire the "Aspirant" to strive for parallel growth in all Questionnaire Categories (QC) 1–10 for a balanced "Happiness Index" (HI). The ultimate goal is "Optimum Happiness" (OH), which is most likely feasible for most "Aspirants."

MATRIX OF QUESTIONNAIRE TEMPLATE (QT) VERSUS
QUESTIONNAIRE CATEGORY (QC) VERSUS ACHIEVEMENTS,
ATTRIBUTES, AND CUSTOMS

TEN KEY HAPPINESS INDICATORS (TKHI)

QUESTIONNAIRE TEMPLATE (QT) VERSUS QUESTIONNAIRE CATEGORY (QT)		ACHIEVEMENTS, ATTRIBUTES, AND CUSTOMS
TEMPLATE	CATEGORY (Alphabetically)	
QT1.	Career (C^{100})	Achievement
QT2.	Character (C^{100})	Attribute
QT3.	Education (E^{100})	Achievement
QT4.	Forgiveness (F^{100})	Attribute
QT5.	Health (H^{100})	Achievement
QT6.	Humility (H^{100})	Attribute
QT7.	Personality (P^{100})	Attribute
QT8.	Religion (R^{100})	Custom
QT9.	Self-esteem (S^{100})	Achievement
QT10.	Socialization (S^{100})	Custom

Table 3.

STEP 2: ACTIVITY _2.
DEFINITION OF ACHIEVEMENT, ATTRIBUTE, AND CUSTOM
(REFERENCE: TABLE 3)

ACHIEVEMENT: We define ACHIEVEMENT as a demonstration of the capacity for "intelligent pursuits" such as education, employment, and career. Achievement allows us to actualize ourselves, to grow, and to help others to grow as well. Achievement demonstrates the human capacity to set goals and to overcome challenges and obstacles. High achievers contribute to the growth of civilization through creativity and innovation. Katharine Hansen in *What Good Is a College Education Anyway?* (2001) asks the question, "Is there anyone who wouldn't like to live a longer, healthier [happier] life?" Achievements are what give our life purpose and motivate us to be creative and innovative as we better our lives and the lives of others.

ATTRIBUTE: We define ATTRIBUTES as the qualities and characteristics that a person displays in his or her relationship with others. Attributes can be positive, such as honesty, humility, tolerance, patience, truthfulness, and thoughtfulness; or negative, such as dishonesty, arrogance, intolerance, impatience, untruthfulness, and thoughtlessness. It is critical for leaders to possess a balance of attributes in the "natural" realm, such as foresight, judgment, integrity, empathy, intelligence, and competence; likewise in the "spiritual" realm, such as love, peace, caring, sharing, compassion, longsuffering (patience), forgiveness, and mercy.

CUSTOM: We define CUSTOMS as behaviors practiced by groups of people who differentiate themselves from others by religious beliefs, social attitudes, or culinary practices. Often, some reject the customs of others as unacceptable to their culture. Cultures clash when they cannot reconcile their differences in *faith, belief, practice,* and values. Intrinsic and extrinsic perspectives also underpin customs such as race and color (intrinsic), and faith, belief, and practice (extrinsic). The above brief definitions of *achievement, attribute,* and *custom* also emphasize the philosophical platform that undergirds the "Happiness Index" Planning Process Methodology (HIPPM).

STEP 2: ACTIVITY _3–3I
DEFINITION OF QUESTIONNAIRE TEMPLATE (QT) 1–10
TEN KEY HAPPINESS INDICATORS (TKHI)
• QT 1 _CATEGORY: CAREER

We define CAREER as the path that one takes in life fostered by various levels of education, training, volunteerism, and personal activities. Education is the foundation upon which one seeks to build a long-term career, hopefully with the desired compensation in money and benefits.

A career can be a rewarding experience, underpinned by a "Wholesome Education." It can also be less than a rewarding experience regarding both compensation and lack of personal growth. Likewise, a person may feel as if he or she is not making a worthwhile contribution to the growth of a corporation, the nation, or the world.

Careers can transcend a sense of personal well-being when one experiences a feeling of worth and fairness in a context of employment equity. For a career to be fulfilling, the employee must practice diligent service to inspire a wholesome relationship with his or her employer. The employer must make available to the employee equitable opportunities for career advancement.

Good character helps to build great relations and great careers. One can experience rich rewards from his or her career when employers recognize *loyalty, deportment*, and *performance* as major factors to achieve corporate productivity and success.

When a "Wholesome Education" underpins careers, employers and employees are enlightened (spiritually, morally, socially, intellectually, and physically). They are empowered to create ethical ways to grow and manage successful corporations and shield the corporation from the uncertainties of economic downturns.

Enlightenment enables employer and employee to envision ethical ways to create wealth for the company and build happy relations between them; likewise to create mechanisms to shield the principals against the accumulation of superfluous wealth for a few that threatens the economic survivability and happiness of many. A meaningful and stable career is the foundation for stable and prosperous families, corporations, and nations. A rewarding career helps individuals to maintain a happy state of mind.

STEP 2: ACTIVITY _3A
DEFINITION OF QUESTIONNAIRE TEMPLATE (QT) 1–10
KEY HAPPINESS INDICATOR (KHI)
• QT 2 _CATEGORY: CHARACTER

We define CHARACTER as our mannerisms, our behavior, our attitude, our trustworthiness, our integrity, our loyalty, our caring, and our benevolence. Character determines how we respond to unfavorable situations in our relationships with others. Good character brings happiness; similarly, bad character brings unhappiness. It is one of the primary determinants of happiness or unhappiness because, above all other human attributes, *bad* character puts us in the judgment seat of our peers, our friends, and our family members.

Our character is the highest human trait that influences principles and behaviors that direct every aspect of our lives. Character traits can be positive, such as caring, respectfulness, discipline, compassion, and thoughtfulness; likewise, character traits can be negative, such as uncaringness, disrespectfulness, thoughtlessness, neglectfulness, resentfulness, and unfriendliness.

A person of *good* character is one who takes responsibility for his or her behavior even when the consequences are unfavorable. A person with questionable character weighs the consequences before he or she decides to accept or deny responsibility for his or her behavior. Our failures, our successes, our happiness, and our unhappiness undergird our character traits.

Children must be witnesses to acts that demonstrate honesty, compassion, forgiveness, patience, moral strength, and character in every facet of the daily lives of their parents. These examples are what help to set the foundation to build their character. Character ought to be the "first fruits" of education as the most powerful tool to build a strong "character fortress" for children's futures.

As an essential component, education ought to help build character. Character education ought to be an unbroken cord, beginning in kindergarten and extending all the way through high school, postgraduate school, graduate school, politics, business, and industry. A *good* character is the greatest enabler in every facet of life.

STEP 2: ACTIVITY _3B
DEFINITION OF QUESTIONNAIRE TEMPLATE (QT) 1–10
KEY HAPPINESS INDICATOR (KHI)
• QT 3 _CATEGORY: EDUCATION

We define EDUCATION as a human construct. Education is responsible for the phenomenal growth of human knowledge. Education is analogous to the horizon that appears to drift further away as we move toward it.

Education is not a finite concept that ends at high school, college, or university graduation. Without education, our spiritual, moral, social, intellectual, and physical growth would be limited, as would be our material well-being. Education must have the inherent capacity to mitigate lifestyle challenges such as obesity, smoking, drug abuse, child and elder abuse, and driving while impaired.

Education must help to correct cultural and social ills such as racial and religious intolerance, and social injustice. It must contribute to alleviating the conditions that inspire violence, genocide, war, breaking contracts, and violating territories.

Education must help to reduce the fear that overwhelms individuals and nations, and it must relieve anxiety for the future. It must heal the economic wounds of a nation through education and employment inequity programs.

Education must help mitigate the primary causes of divorce and its consequential impact on the lives of children. It must liberate the individual and the nation. However, only a "Wholesome Education" can achieve these objectives.

A "Wholesome Education" is an approach to education that focuses on the following five essential types of foundations of a student's development: Spiritual (religious), moral, social, intellectual, and physical. The potency of education rests on these foundations. They must have measurable outcomes, similar to Academic Information Literacy (AIL) and numeracy measures.

A "Wholesome Education" underlies the solutions to *all* of the daily problems faced by individuals, nations, and international communities. A "Wholesome Education" can lead to success, a successful career, a happy family, a successful life, a strong health environment, and a happy nation.

STEP 2: ACTIVITY _3C
DEFINITION OF QUESTIONNAIRE TEMPLATE (QT) 1–10
KEY HAPPINESS INDICATOR (KHI)
• QT 4 _CATEGORY: FORGIVENESS

We define FORGIVENESS as the act of asking for and extending forgiveness between the offender and the offended person. When the offender asks for forgiveness, he or she must make a solemn promise or resolve not to repeat the offense. Furthermore, he or she must make restitution for the wrong, in some way reverse the harmful effects of the wrong, and, where possible, bring healing and happiness.

Forgiveness is not merely a natural act; it is a "Spiritual" command according to Christian doctrine and other world religions. Forgiveness recognizes the human family as one indivisible whole with a common need for universal love, "joy," peace, patience (longsuffering), compassion, gentleness, kindness, forgiveness, and happiness (Mark 11:25, ESV).

Whether an action is *intentional* or *unintentional*, forgiveness is an essential healing virtue. The offender must ask for forgiveness. Likewise, the offended person must extend forgiveness, not merely from the *head* but also the *heart,* and without any reservation. Otherwise, real restitution, healing, and happiness become nonexistent, and forgiveness becomes a mere mechanical exercise. Forgiveness heals both the offender and the offended. Anger, hate, the need for revenge, and unhappiness among individuals and nations may inspire a lack of forgiveness.

Many individuals and nations have risen beyond personal and national pride and asked for forgiveness for transgressions against other people and nations. Conversely, some individuals and nations cannot bring themselves to ask for forgiveness for fear that it is an admission of culpability. Forgiveness and mercy portray great character and strength, and they open doors of "reciprocal returns."

A more critical but unrealized benefit of forgiveness is the positive influence that forgiveness has on the health of those who choose to make forgiveness a way of life. Forgiveness in action can often stave off the conflict that may follow a destructive path that leads to unmanaged conflict and unhappiness.

STEP 2: ACTIVITY _3D
DEFINITION OF QUESTIONNAIRE TEMPLATE (QT) 1–10
KEY HAPPINESS INDICATOR (KHI)
• QT 5 _CATEGORY: HEALTH

We define HEALTH as a general good feeling of our spiritual, mental, and physical well-being. Although we might feel well, our health entails more than the absence of the conditions that cause diseases. We have general control of our health, nutrition, nurturing, knowledge of health matters, personal behavior, and environment in which we live, but health maintenance is paramount.

Maintenance of health requires *nutrition* and *nurturing*. Nutrition is the appropriate quantity and quality of foods and fuel (air, water, exercise, and sunlight) that are necessary to sustain our physical bodies. Notwithstanding the absence of disease, a sudden illness can impair one's health and thrust one's family members into a state of spiritual, emotional, physical, and financial unhappiness.

Nurturing is the spiritual and mental stimulation that helps to maintain our spiritual and mental balance, which enables us physically. Physical health complements spiritual and mental health through daily physical exercise and nutritious foods. A healthy you is a happy person with spiritual, mental, and physical balance; likewise, an unhealthy you can cause spiritual, mental, and physical imbalance and make you unhappy.

Paradoxically, the concerns in past decades were for the spiritual and medical health of children and adults, but a "new" invasion in the form of mental health appears on the horizon as the next major human health dilemma. Unfortunately, our busy lifestyles seem to diminish interpersonal communications and thus enable some mental conditions that may go undetected until some individuals (mostly young males) act out in violence, which causes great unhappiness for families, the larger community, the criminal justice system, and the nation.

Immediate family members and the wider community need to become more aware of poor mental health as a significant threat to individual and national happiness. Furthermore, families must do all that they can to ensure that our relationships with others help rather than hinder our *spiritual*, *mental*, and *physical* health and well-being.

STEP 2: ACTIVITY _3E
DEFINITION OF QUESTIONNAIRE TEMPLATE (QT) 1–10
KEY HAPPINESS INDICATOR (KHI)
• QT 6 _CATEGORY: HUMILITY

We define HUMILITY as one of the most beneficial human attributes. The antonym of *humility* is *pride* or *arrogance*. The humble person renders service to others, subordinating self-will to the respect of others. Humility characterizes strength rather than weakness.

Humility is the most significant aspect of the original and only right relationship between human beings. Humility does not demand that we humiliate ourselves or eliminate character or personal integrity, but rather that we give preference and honor to others.

Humility and its twin human attribute servanthood are the great cornerstones of leadership. Humility ought to be our capable guide and our example to the world and others who seek to understand what motivates us rather than question our *faith, belief,* and *practice*. Lack of humility can cause conflicts while humility demonstrates strength of character and enhances relationships. Humility empowers the humble person, imbues happiness, and helps to increase one's "Happiness Index" (HI).

Despite the significant advances we have made in science, medicine, and exploration, human pride remains a barrier to humility and servanthood in leadership, which are two of the great cornerstones of enlightened leadership.

These higher spiritual and mental attributes incorporate love, kindness, sharing, caring, compassion, and meekness, and they appeal to higher moral imperatives. Pride, on the other end of the leadership spectrum, is one of the most destructive human attributes, with no redeeming virtues.

Pride bolsters all of the ideological wars that history has recorded. Personal pride may influence (negative or positive) relationships within the family. National pride can have a great benefit to nations on the one hand, and on the other hand be a national tragedy for individuals and nations in the absence of *humility* and *servanthood* as salient leadership virtues, witnessed by the downfall of many ancient civilizations.

STEP 2: ACTIVITY _3F
DEFINITION OF QUESTIONNAIRE TEMPLATE (QT) 1–10
KEY HAPPINESS INDICATOR (KHI)
• QT 7 _CATEGORY: PERSONALITY

We define PERSONALITY as a great asset or liability as it resonates positively or negatively on a first encounter. A friendly personality is noticeable, appealing, and welcoming.

An attractive personality is apt to create an environment of friendliness and to imbue happiness in others. Conversely, an unfriendly personality is likely to establish a climate of unfriendliness and to inculcate unhappiness in others.

> Oldham and Morris (1995): "Your personality style is your organizing principle. It propels you on your life path. It represents the orderly arrangement of all your attributes, thoughts, feelings, attitudes, behaviors, and coping mechanisms. It is the distinctive pattern of your psychological functioning—the way you think, feel and behave—that makes you definitely you."[41]

Interestingly, as we grow, our personality can change from friendly to unfriendly or vice versa, depending on our experiences. Change in personality can be a potent indicator of mental health problems or other circumstances that cause unhappiness in one's life. Families and friends can play a vital role in observing and helping others by seeking mental healthcare for the individual and extending care and concern for visible changes in their behavior.

Everyone can improve on his or her personality, but it is our family and "circle of friends" who point out the need to us. The layperson may conclude that antisocial behavior is merely arrogant behavior, but social scientists may diagnose individuals who are incapable of maintaining stable relationships with others as a personality disorder. To heal our nature is to cure the world of perpetual unhappiness.

---

[41] Copyright © 1995 by John M. Oldham, M, D., and Lois B. Morris. All rights reserved.

STEP 2: ACTIVITY _3G
DEFINITION OF QUESTIONNAIRE TEMPLATE (QT) 1–10
KEY HAPPINESS INDICATOR (KHI)
• QT 8 _CATEGORY: RELIGION

We define RELIGION (Spirituality) as the *purest* and *noblest* of belief systems and customs, but false religion has contributed to some of the greatest atrocities throughout the ancient world and up to the present age.

Religion should elevate humanity to great heights of hope for the world unified among races, cultures, colors, and creeds. Pure religion, founded in spirituality, is distinct from religion that is self-serving or commercialized, that is complicit with egregious acts against humanity, or that does not act in the best interests of humankind. The latter sort of religion can only bring about mistrust, disbelief in religion, and unhappiness.

Spirituality enables human beings to rise to the highest state of humanity and to reach the deepest depths to lift up humanity, demonstrated by a remarkable display of the love for humankind, in particular those whom we deem undeserving of love.

Spirituality is the highest human attribute that can help to overcome fear, anger, apprehension, violence, revenge, and other social ills, and to bring sustained happiness, which is "joy." "Joy" is the singular spiritual attribute that can help us to reach our "*Optimum*" state of happiness.

Religion brings about happiness when its adherents demonstrate "Spiritual" virtues by exercising the kind of love for fellow beings encouraged and taught by religions. Imagine if *all* faiths modeled the life-transforming attributes that highlight right action, such as love, "joy," peace, patience, kindness, goodness, faithfulness, gentleness, and self-control. Happiness would blossom largely throughout the world.

We need to reexamine the high potential for pure religion (spirituality) to heal the incalculable wounds that have resulted from wars among nations over the past centuries up to the present, some in the name of religion. These acts are contrary to the preservation of the human family because religion ought to reign supreme in our lives as a common denominator for human survival.

STEP 2: ACTIVITY _3H
DEFINITION OF QUESTIONNAIRE TEMPLATE (QT) 1–10
KEY HAPPINESS INDICATOR (KHI)
• QT 9 _CATEGORY: SELF-ESTEEM

We define SELF-ESTEEM as a trait that begins within the family. Children are born into homes with happy and loving parents regardless of those parents' circumstances or the environment of birth. None of us can choose the family that we are born into, and the environment in which we grow can have a positive or negative impact on our overall development regarding *self-image, self-worth,* and *self-esteem.*

When we were children, we never envisaged that the nineteenth, twentieth, and twenty–first centuries would offer opportunities to remodel our bodies and reshape our images physically. The images that many seek to attain often appear to dictate the way they feel about themselves.

An inordinate number of audio, visual, and personal images influence the way children and adults view themselves physically. Images considered ideal compel them to compare and evaluate themselves against others regarding color, looks, height, hair, weight, size, clothes, and even education and intelligence.

The material demands and social pressures of our postmodern era often shake the confidence and self-esteem in some children and adults, and cause unhappiness. The transition from youth to adulthood seems to occur at a pace that is incompatible with their development and their understanding of real-world issues such as dating, intimate relationships, and money management.

From the poor, dispossessed, and disenfranchised to the wealthiest of individuals, even brief periods of low self-esteem can cause individuals to lose self-control and to adopt self-destructive behaviors.

It will take nothing less than a national and international state of emergency to rebuild some of the important "self-esteem happiness infrastructures" for the benefit of future generations. Positive self-esteem leads to successful living. It can enable us to cope with and manage the many challenges in our lives, such as personal health, marriage, work–life balance, career, and family.

STEP 2: ACTIVITY _3I
DEFINITION OF QUESTIONNAIRE TEMPLATE (QT) 1–10
KEY HAPPINESS INDICATOR (KHI)
• QT 10_CATEGORY: SOCIALIZATION

We define SOCIALIZATION as the social fabric that reinforces human relationships. When something goes wrong within our society, we look to our governments for answers because governments have the responsibility and the macro-administrative mechanisms to address problems of society. However, we ought to look at our families, our religious institutions, our corporations, and our schools for solutions as well.

What is the impetus behind human behavior, good or bad? The family is the tree from which all members of society have sprung. The judge, the lawyer, the police officer, the delinquent, and the offender all are the products of families.

The scientist, the engineer, the doctor, the nurse, the principal, the teacher, and the student all have their roots in the family. The murderer and the victim also have roots in the family foundation. The family, then, becomes the first place to look when something goes wrong in society. The family is the "first society" for social development. It is the primary gateway to all other institutions and institutions of learning.

Where, when, and how do human beings develop patterns of unsocial behavior? The socialization process begins with our childhood nurturing and development.

From the moment a child is born, he or she begins to experience the effects of his or her first social environment—the home. The traditional and cardinal rules for raising children are good manners, personal discipline, responsibility, and respect for others who are directly or indirectly responsible for their care.

Family love for and attention to each other are the hallmarks of household relations, particularly in caring for infants and elder family members. Respect for elder members of society and persons in uniform were the pillars of society. In other words, social behavior was, and is today, paramount to the stability of the family and nations, and integral to the social contract that humans share with each other.

STEP 2: ACTIVITY _4
QUESTIONNAIRE TEMPLATE (QT) 1–10 SCORING
METHODOLOGY (QTSM)
(REFERENCE: QT 1_CATEGORY: CAREER, p. 174)

PREAMBLE: The Questionnaire Template (QT) is the tool that is central to the "Happiness Index" Planning Process Methodology (HIPPM) and is simple to comprehend. The Questionnaire Template Scoring Methodology (QTSM) is a comparison between the "Personal Answer Score" (Y + N = T) versus the "Reference Optimum Answer Score" (Y + N = T).

Designating the "Reference Optimum Answer Score" is an important aspect of the methodology. The "Optimum Answer Score" is not a character judgment but a benchmark to which we ascribe, based on the nobles of the Western "worldview," despite the liberal postmodern age in which we live. They are the predicate of universal practices; generally accepted religious, social, and cultural norms; and civil society.

The "Reference Optimum Answer Score" is also synonymous with a Body Mass Index (BMI) calculator, which is not a personal judgment as well, but a reference measurement to inspire contemplation and action in the future for personal betterment.

Many individuals will agree that there is an "Optimum Answer Score" to each question. Likewise, a relative level of *happiness* or *unhappiness* correlates to each question. Some of the "Aspirant's" responses will evidently be at variance with the "Reference Optimum Answers Score," reflected in the Questionnaire Template (QT) 1–10.

Some questions may not be relevant to a particular "Aspirant." For this reason, each range in the "Happiness Index" Measurement Template (HIMT) 12 (Reference: Table 5) is within a typical range of approximately (200 points); for instance, Very Unhappy (0–200), Unhappy (201-400), Happy (401–600), Very Happy (601–800), and "Optimum Happiness" (OH) (801–1,000) points.

There are ten Questionnaire Templates (QT) 1–10, representing the ten Questionnaire Categories (QC) 1–10. The goal is to present a broad range of questions that "Aspirants" can easily understand and recognize as common to daily activities and decision-making. It is critical to answering all ten questions in all ten categories to attain the highest integrity of outcomes of the methodology.

The "Happiness Index" Planning Process Methodology (HIPPM) is an approach from five perspectives, defined as follows:

SCORING APPROACH 1.

Questionnaire Template (QT) 10 Questions X 10 points per question = 100 points. This is the maximum number of points (score) that "Aspirants" can achieve for answering each QT 1-10. (Reference: QT 1 — CATEGORY: CAREER, p. 174).

SCORING APPROACH 2.

The maximum of 100 points per template X 10 Templates = 1,000 points (score). This is the maximum number of points (score) that an "Aspirant" can achieve for answering the questions in all 10 Questionnaire Templates QT 1-10 relative to the designer's Optimum Answer Score (Reference: QT 1 — CATEGORY: CAREER, p. 174).

SCORING APPROACH 3.

The Questionnaire Template (QT) 1-10 requires answers (either "0" or "10") in columns "Y" and "N." The "0" and "10" answer range is critical to avoid ambiguity in the answers, which represent your personal response (score) to each Questionnaire Category (QC). Typically, the profile of each answer is as follows: $(Y + N = T)$ $(10 + 0 = 10)$, $(0 + 10 = 10)$, or $(0 + 0 = 0)$. (Reference: QT 1 — CATEGORY: CAREER, p. 174).

SCORING APPROACH 4.

If your response to a question in the "PERSONAL ANSWER SCORE" is different from the "OPTIMUM ANSWER SCORE" (Column Y or N), where the answer is "10," then place "0" in the corresponding column. We predicate the answers on absolutes to eliminate any ambiguity in response and to advance the cause for Self-Improvement by removing a variable response, which benefits the "Aspirant" if his or her quest is to achieve "Optimum Happiness" (OH) (Reference: QT 1 — CATEGORY: CAREER, p. 174).

SCORING APPROACH 5.

The scores (points) for each Questionnaire Template QT 1–10 are then summed "horizontally" in columns (Y + N = T), and then summed vertically for the subtotal of each column (Y + N = T). (Reference: QT 1 — CATEGORY: CAREER, p. 174).

The following pages list the ten Questionnaire Templates QT 1–10, also referred to as the Ten Key Happiness Indicators (TKHI) Templates.

o   TEN KEY HAPPINESS INDICATORS (TKHI) TEMPLATES:

    1. Career $^{(C100)}$ (Achievement)
    2. Character $^{(C100)}$ (Attribute)
    3. Education $^{(E100)}$ (Achievement)
    4. Forgiveness $^{(F100)}$ (Attribute)
    5. Health $^{(H100)}$ (Achievement)
    6. Humility $^{(H100)}$ (Attitude)
    7. Personality $^{(P100)}$ (Attribute)
    8. Religion $^{(R100)}$ (Custom)
    9. Self-esteem $^{(S100)}$ (Achievement)
  10. Socialization $^{(S100)}$ (Custom)

The accompanying notes pages associated with each Questionnaire Template (QT) are useful to record the "Aspirant's" thoughts, concerns, and personal observations for future reference. The notes also provide a personal chronicle that the "Aspirant" can use to direct his or her Self-Improvement Planning (SIP) strategy using Self-Improvement Planning Template (SIPT) 1–10 to develop plans for his or her Self-Improvement (SI) (Reference: Table 6).

STEP 2: ACTIVITY_5–5I
QUESTIONNAIRE TEMPLATE (QT) 1–10
- QT 1_CATEGORY: CAREER

<table>
<tr><td colspan="8">HI Questionnaire Template (QT) 1 _Category: CAREER
A Self-Directed Guide to Your "Happiness Index" (HI)</td></tr>
<tr><td colspan="2" rowspan="2">Legend: Y (Yes) + N (No) = T
(Total)</td><td colspan="3">Personal Answer Scores</td><td colspan="3">Reference Optimum Answer Scores</td></tr>
<tr><td>Y</td><td>N</td><td>T</td><td>Y</td><td>N</td><td>T</td></tr>
<tr><td>Q</td><td>QUESTIONS:</td><td>Y</td><td>N</td><td>T</td><td>Y</td><td>N</td><td>T</td></tr>
<tr><td>Q1.</td><td>Are you completely satisfied with your current career level at this stage of your life?</td><td></td><td></td><td></td><td>10</td><td>0</td><td>10</td></tr>
<tr><td>Q2.</td><td>Do you believe that you have reached a career ceiling?</td><td></td><td></td><td></td><td>0</td><td>10</td><td>10</td></tr>
<tr><td>Q3.</td><td>Does your career provide you with job satisfaction?</td><td></td><td></td><td></td><td>10</td><td>0</td><td>10</td></tr>
<tr><td>Q4.</td><td>Do you worry about your capacity for higher education?</td><td></td><td></td><td></td><td>0</td><td>10</td><td>10</td></tr>
<tr><td>Q5.</td><td>Has promotion been denied because you do not have a degree?</td><td></td><td></td><td></td><td>0</td><td>10</td><td>10</td></tr>
<tr><td>Q6.</td><td>Do you have well-defined career plans for your future?</td><td></td><td></td><td></td><td>10</td><td>0</td><td>10</td></tr>
<tr><td>Q7.</td><td>Have you ever contemplated changing careers due to lack of job satisfaction?</td><td></td><td></td><td></td><td>0</td><td>10</td><td>10</td></tr>
<tr><td>Q8.</td><td>Do you have the appropriate level of education for your current career?</td><td></td><td></td><td></td><td>10</td><td>0</td><td>10</td></tr>
<tr><td>Q9.</td><td>Does your career path lead to a higher-paid position?</td><td></td><td></td><td></td><td>10</td><td>0</td><td>10</td></tr>
<tr><td>Q10.</td><td>Do you believe lifelong learning is truly the key to career advancement?</td><td></td><td></td><td></td><td>10</td><td>0</td><td>10</td></tr>
<tr><td colspan="2">SUBTOTAL =</td><td></td><td></td><td></td><td>60</td><td>40</td><td>100</td></tr>
</table>

NOTES

STEP 2: ACTIVITY_5A
- ## QT 2_CATEGORY: CHARACTER

HI Questionnaire Template (QT) 2 _Category: CHARACTER A Self-Directed Guide to Your "Happiness Index" (HI)							
Legend: Y (Yes) + N (No) = T (Total)		Personal Answer Scores			Reference Optimum Answer Scores		
Q	QUESTIONS:	Y	N	T	Y	N	T
Q1.	Would you say that you are a person of good character?				10	0	10
Q2.	If you found a large sum of money, would you disclose it?				10	0	10
Q3.	Would you create a deception to protect yourself from a wrong you had committed?				0	10	10
Q4.	Would you blame someone for an act he/she did not commit?				0	10	10
Q5.	Would you accept credit for work done by someone else?				0	10	10
Q6.	Would you cheat on an exam if you were confident that it would be unknown?				0	10	10
Q7.	Would you call in sick from work even if you were not sick?				0	10	10
Q8.	If you received more money than was due, would you return the excess amount?				10	0	10
Q9.	Would you speak to a friend or family member who makes racist slurs?				10	0	10
Q10.	Do you make promises that you know you will not fulfill?				0	10	10
	SUBTOTAL =				40	60	100

NOTES

STEP 2: ACTIVITY_5B
- ## QT 3_CATEGORY: EDUCATION

HI Questionnaire Template (QT) 3 _Category: EDUCATION A Self-Directed Guide to Your "Happiness Index" (HI)						
Legend: Y (Yes) + N (No) = T (Total)		Personal Answer Scores			Reference Optimum Answer Scores		
Q	QUESTIONS:	Y	N	T	Y	N	T
Q1.	Are you completely satisfied with your current level of education?				10	0	10
Q2.	Will you achieve the educational goals you have planned?				10	0	10
Q3.	Do you have the financial capacity to attend college or university?				10	0	10
Q4.	Were you ever denied a position because you lacked the relevant qualifications?				0	10	10
Q5.	Does your present educational level cause stress?				0	10	10
Q6.	Do you have clear educational plans for your future?				10	0	10
Q7.	Do you struggle to learn new concepts?				0	10	10
Q8.	Do you believe that higher education is a privilege?				0	10	10
Q9.	Do you have a strong aptitude and love for learning?				10	0	10
Q10.	Do you believe lifelong learning is truly the goal of education?				10	0	10
SUBTOTAL =					60	40	100

NOTES

_____

_____

_____

_____

_____

_____

_____

_____

_____

_____

_____

_____

_____

_____

_____

_____

_____

_____

STEP 2: ACTIVITY_5C
- QT 4_CATEGORY: FORGIVENESS

HI Questionnaire Template (QT) 4 _Category: FORGIVENESS A Self-Directed Guide to Your "Happiness Index" (HI)							
Legend: Y (Yes) + N (No) = T (Total)		Personal Answer Scores			Reference Optimum Answer Scores		
Q	QUESTIONS:	Y	N	T	Y	N	T
Q1.	Do you exercise forgiveness regardless of the wrong?				10	0	10
Q2.	Would you forgive anyone regardless of his or her race, color, culture, or religion?				10	0	10
Q3.	Would you ask for forgiveness if you hurt someone?				10	0	10
Q4.	Do you consider forgiveness an excuse for the person's actions?				0	10	10
Q5.	Have you ever refused to forgive someone for his or her wrongs?				0	10	10
Q6.	Do you believe that one must deserve forgiveness to receive it?				0	10	10
Q7.	Do you resurface issues after you have forgiven someone?				0	10	10
Q8.	Do you believe that unforgiveness can be harmful?				10	0	10
Q9.	Do you believe that some people do not deserve forgiveness?				0	10	10
Q10.	Do you believe that forgiveness is a "spiritual" attribute?				10	0	10
SUBTOTAL =					50	50	100

NOTES

STEP 2: ACTIVITY_5D
- QT 5_CATEGORY: HEALTH

| HI Questionnaire Template (QT) 5 _Category: HEALTH
A Self-Directed Guide to Your "Happiness Index" (HI) | | | | | | | |
| Legend: Y (Yes) + N (No) = T (Total) | | Personal Answer Scores | | | Reference Optimum Answer Scores | | |
Q	QUESTIONS:	Y	N	T	Y	N	T
Q1.	Are you in good general mental and physical health?				10	0	10
Q2.	Do you ever experience feelings of loneliness and depression?				0	10	10
Q3.	Would you say that your life is in a well-balanced state?				10	0	10
Q4.	Are you easily frustrated with and intolerant of others?				0	10	10
Q5.	Do you get depressed feelings over lack of money?				0	10	10
Q6.	Do you have any illnesses that incapacitate you in any way?				0	10	10
Q7.	Would a catastrophic illness cause you to become depressed?				0	10	10
Q8.	Do you have a strong family social network in your life?				10	0	10
Q9.	Are your relationships with others generally wholesome?				10	0	10
Q10.	Do you have any challenges in forgiving others?				0	10	10
SUBTOTAL =					40	60	100

NOTES

_____

_____

_____

_____

_____

_____

_____

_____

_____

_____

_____

_____

_____

_____

_____

_____

_____

_____

STEP 2: ACTIVITY_5E
- QT 6_CATEGORY: HUMILITY

HI Questionnaire Template (QT) 6 _Category: HUMILITY A Self-Directed Guide to Your "Happiness Index" (HI)							
Legend: Y (Yes) + N (No) = T (Total)		Personal Answer Scores			Reference Optimum Answer Scores		
Q	QUESTIONS:	Y	N	T	Y	N	T
Q1.	Are you a humble person in your dealings with people in general?				10	0	10
Q2.	Do your peers refer to you as a humble person?				10	0	10
Q3.	Do you consider people who are humble as weak?				0	10	10
Q4.	Has anyone ever referred to you as one who is full of false pride?				0	10	10
Q5.	Do you wait for someone whom you have harmed to ask for forgiveness?				0	10	10
Q6.	Do you believe that leaders should exercise humility in leadership?				10	0	10
Q7.	Do you consider a humble person as an inept person?				0	10	10
Q8.	Do you believe that humility builds character?				10	0	10
Q9.	Do you let personal pride affect your humility?				0	10	10
Q10.	Do you consider humility and servanthood as salient attributes of leadership?				10	0	10
SUBTOTAL =					50	50	100

NOTES

STEP 2: ACTIVITY_5F
- QT 7_CATEGORY: PERSONALITY

HI Questionnaire Template (QT) 7 _Category: PERSONALITY A Self-Directed Guide to Your "Happiness Index" (HI)						
Legend: Y (Yes) + N (No) = T (Total)		Personal Answer Scores			Reference Optimum Answer Scores		
Q	QUESTIONS:	Y	N	T	Y	N	T
Q1.	Do you have a well-balanced and likeable personality?				10	0	10
Q2.	Do you constantly compare yourself with others?				0	10	10
Q3.	Do you constantly voice frustration with friends, neighbors, and associates?				0	10	10
Q4.	Do you have strong family ties with parents and siblings?				10	0	10
Q5.	Do you get along well with your peers and others?				10	0	10
Q6.	Were your teenage years "wholesome" and happy years?				10	0	10
Q7.	Did you grow up in a family with strong religious beliefs?				10	0	10
Q8.	Does your family have strong and positive family values?				10	0	10
Q9.	In general, are you happy with your family relationships?				10	0	10
Q10.	Do people with unlikeable personalities frustrate you?				0	10	10
	SUBTOTAL =				70	30	100

NOTES

STEP 2: ACTIVITY _5G
- ## QT 8_CATEGORY: RELIGION

HI Questionnaire Template (QT) 8 _Category: RELIGION A Self-Directed Guide to Your "Happiness Index" (HI)							
Legend: Y (Yes) + N (No) = T (Total)		Personal Answer Scores			Reference Optimum Answer Scores		
Q	QUESTIONS:	Y	N	T	Y	N	T
Q1.	Do you subscribe to any form of religious belief?				10	0	10
Q2.	Do you believe that you are your brother's keeper?				10	0	10
Q3.	Do you believe that human beings originated from a common species?				10	0	10
Q4.	Do you believe that life would be better if we discarded every concept of God?				0	10	10
Q5.	Do you believe that religion is the primary cause of world problems?				0	10	10
Q6.	Do you believe that human authority is supreme?				0	10	10
Q7.	Do you believe that life is a series of random events?				0	10	10
Q8.	Would you pray for a relative or friend who became seriously ill?				10	0	10
Q9.	If you became seriously ill, would you let someone pray for you?				10	0	10
Q10.	Are you a loving, caring, and compassionate person?				10	0	10
	SUBTOTAL =				60	40	100

NOTES

_____

_____

_____

_____

_____

_____

_____

_____

_____

_____

_____

_____

_____

_____

_____

_____

_____

_____

_____

STEP 2: ACTIVITY _5H
- QT 9_CATEGORY: SELF-ESTEEM

HI Questionnaire Template (QT) 9 _Category: SELF-ESTEEM A Self-Directed Guide to Your "Happiness Index" (HI)							
Legend: Y (Yes) + N (No) = T (Total)		Personal Answer Scores			Reference Optimum Answer Scores		
Q	Questions:	Y	N	T	Y	N	T
Q1.	Are you a person with high self-esteem?				10	0	10
Q2.	Do your peers highly regard your position on issues?				10	0	10
Q3.	Do you ever entertain feelings that people do not like you?				0	10	10
Q4.	Do you wish that you could change your physical features?				0	10	10
Q5.	Are you comfortable in a roundtable discussion?				10	0	10
Q6.	Would you feel at ease speaking in front of an audience?				10	0	10
Q7.	Are you self-conscious regarding your physical appearance?				0	10	10
Q8.	Do you look toward TV personalities as your role models?				0	10	10
Q9.	Have you discovered your purpose in life?				10	0	10
Q10.	Do you feel secure and confident in your life?				10	0	10
SUBTOTAL =					60	40	100

NOTES

_____

_____

_____

_____

_____

_____

_____

_____

_____

_____

_____

_____

_____

_____

_____

_____

_____

_____

_____

_____

_____

STEP 2: ACTIVITY _5I
- ## QT 10_CATEGORY: SOCIALIZATION

HI Questionnaire Template (QT) 10 _Category: SOCIALIZATION A Self-Directed Guide to Your "Happiness Index" (HI)						
Legend: Y (Yes) + N (No) = T (Total)		Personal Answer Scores			Reference *Optimum* Answer Scores		
Q	QUESTIONS:	Y	N	T	Y	N	T
Q1.	Do your peers acknowledge you as a sociable person?				10	0	10
Q2.	Do you have close personal friendships with people of another race, color, culture, or religion?				10	0	10
Q3.	Do you have a strong relationship with any member(s) of your family?				10	0	10
Q4.	Do you feel comfortable attending big family functions?				10	0	10
Q5.	Do you know by name at least two families in your neighborhood?				10	0	10
Q6.	Do you seek opportunities to get to know your neighbors?				10	0	10
Q7.	Do you seek opportunities to get to know your associates at work?				10	0	10
Q8.	Do you have any discomfort attending social functions?				0	10	10
Q9.	Would your name be at the top of anyone's social event listing?				10	0	10
Q10.	Do you care what people think about your social attitude?				10	0	10
SUBTOTAL =					90	10	100

NOTES

STEP THREE

SUMMARY:

o STEP THREE _SUMMARY

POPULATE THE "HAPPINESS INDEX" (HI) SUMMARY
QUESTIONNAIRE TEMPLATE (SQT) 11 (REFERENCE: TABLE 4)
WITH THE SUBTOTAL SCORES (Y + N = T) FROM EACH
QUESTIONNAIRE TEMPLATE QT 1–10.

- ACTIVITY 1

READ _The Definition of "Happiness Index" (HI) Summary
Questionnaire Template SQT 11. (Reference: Table 4).

- ACTIVITY 2

POPULATE _The "Happiness Index" (HI) Summary Questionnaire
Template (SQT) 11 (Reference: Table 4) with the Subtotal Scores
(Y +N = T) from each Questionnaire Template (QT) 1–10.

STEP 3_ACTIVITY _1.
DEFINITION OF THE "HAPPINESS INDEX" (HI) SUMMARY
QUESTIONNAIRE TEMPLATE (SQT) 11.
(REFERENCE: TABLE 4)

We define the "HAPPINESS INDEX" (HI) SUMMARY
QUESTIONNAIRE TEMPLATE (SQT) 11 (Reference: Table 4) as the
tool used to summarize the subtotal scores for each of the 10
Questionnaire Templates (QT) 1–10. The sum is the Total Points
(Score) attained by the "Aspirant" on completion of all 10
Questionnaire Templates for all 10 Questionnaire Categories
(Reference: Table 4).

The SQT 11 (Reference: Table 4) is a summary comparison of the
"Personal Answer Scores" versus the "Reference *Optimum* Answer
Scores." The SQT 11 provides an immediate overview of the
variance between the two scores and a quick reference point for
contemplating Self-Improvement Planning (SIP).

    SUMMARY APPROACH 1.

Using the Subtotal scores (points) (Y + N = T) from each individual
Questionnaire Template (QT) 1–10, POPULATE the corresponding
columns and cells (Y + N = T) in the "Happiness Index" (HI)
Summary Questionnaire Template (SQT) 11.

    SUMMARY APPROACH 2.

Sum the "Personal Answer Scores" (Subtotal) vertically down each
column (Y + N = T) for the "Total Score" of all of the Questionnaire
Template (QT) 1–10.

    SUMMARY APPROACH 3.

Sum the scores horizontally across the bottom column (Y + N = T)
of the "Personal Answer Scores" to derive "Total Score" in the
column "T." The "Total Score" in column "T" is the score that the
"Aspirant" transfers to the "Happiness Index" Measurement
Template (HIMT) (Reference: Table 5) as the "Aspirant's"
"Happiness Index" (HI) score.

"Real happiness is not of temporary enjoyment, but is so interwoven with the future that it blesses forever."

—James Lendall Basford (1845–1915)
Sparks from the Philosopher's Stone, 1882

STEP 3: ACTIVITY _2.
"HAPPINESS INDEX" (HI)_SUMMARY QUESTIONNAIRE
TEMPLATE (SQT) 11.

"Happiness Index" (HI) Summary Questionnaire Template (SQT) 11 (A composite of all ten Questionnaire Templates (SQT) 1–10 A Self-Directed Guide to Your "Happiness Index" (HI)							
Legend: Y = Yes, N = No, T = Total		Personal Answer Scores			Reference Optimum Answer Scores		
SQT Template	QC Category	Y	N	T	Y	N	T
SQT1.	Career (C100) (Attribute)				60	40	100
SQT2.	Character (C100) (Achievement)				40	60	100
SQT3.	Education (E100) (Achievement)				60	40	100
SQT4.	Forgiveness (F100) (Attribute)				50	50	100
SQT5.	Health (H100) (Achievement)				40	60	100
SQT6.	Humility (H100) (Attribute)				50	50	100
SQT7.	Personality (P100) (Attribute)				70	30	100
SQT8.	Religion (R100) (Custom)				60	40	100
SQT9.	Self-Esteem (S100) (Achievement)				60	40	100
SQT10.	Socialization (S100) (Custom)				90	10	100
TOTAL SCORE =					580	420	1,000

Table 4.

NOTES

STEP FOUR

SUMMARY:

o   STEP FOUR _SUMMARY

TRANSFER THE TOTAL SCORE FROM THE "HAPPINESS INDEX" (HI) SUMMARY QUESTIONNAIRE TEMPLATE (SQT) 11 (Reference: Table 4) TO THE "HAPPINESS INDEX" MEASUREMENT TEMPLATE (HIMT) 12 (REFERENCE: TABLE 5).

- ACTIVITY 1.

READ _The Definition of "Happiness Index" Measurement Template (HIMT) 12. (Reference: Table 5).

- ACTIVITY 2.

TRANSFER _The total score (Column "T") from the "Happiness Index" (HI) Summary Questionnaire Template (SQT) 11 (Reference: Table 4) to the "Happiness Index" Measurement Template (HIMT) 12 (Reference: Table 5) in the relevant Level, Range, Score.

STEP 4: ACTIVITY _1.
DEFINITION OF THE "HAPPINESS INDEX" MEASUREMENT
TEMPLATE (HIMT) 12. (REFERENCE: TABLE 5)

Table 5. The "Happiness Index" Measurement Template (HIMT) 12 is the measurement tool that compares the "Aspirant's" "Happiness Index" (HI) Score[2] versus Range versus Score[1]. The HIMT acts as a barometer that measures atmospheric pressure, a thermometer that measures temperature in degrees Centigrade or Fahrenheit, or a glucometer that measures the amount of glucose (mmol/l) in a patient's blood. Though nonscientific, our HIMT measures the "Aspirant's" HI in a self-directed way.

STEP 4: ACTIVITY _2.
TRANSFER THE SCORE COLUMN"T" FROM QT 11. TO
THE "HAPPINESS INDEX" MEASUREMENT
TEMPLATE (HIMT) 12. (REFERENCE: TABLE 5).

"HAPPINESS INDEX" (HI) SCORE VERSUS RANGE VERSUS LEVEL					
LEVEL	Level 1.	Level 2.	Level 3.	Level 4.	Level 5.
RANGE	Very Unhappy	Unhappy	Happy	Very Happy	Optimum Happiness (OH)
SCORE[1]	0–200 Points	201-400 Points	401-600 Points	601-800 Points	801-1,000 Points
SCORE[2]			√		

Table 5.

The "Happiness Index" Measurement Template (HIMT) 12 (Table 5) depicts your "Happiness Index" (HI) (Level, Range, and Score). Your HI is an association between the *quantitative* and *qualitative* measures of happiness that is the outcome of the self-directed exercise. Score[1] is the reference score, and Score[2] is the score you achieved. The results are private and confidential unless you choose to share them with others for a group discussion. The HIMT measurement approach is as follows:

o   HIMT MEASUREMENT APPROACH 1.

The "Aspirant" places a "tick" mark in the appropriate column or the actual score that is within the range shown in the "Happiness Index" Measurement Template (HIMT) 12 (Reference: Table 5).

o   HIMT MEASUREMENT APPROACH 2.

The HIMT 12 displays the correlation among the three measurement criteria (Level, Range, and Score). The mean index Level 3 (401–600) points) depicts "Happy," and Level 5 (801–1,000) depicts the "Optimum Happiness" (OH).

The HIMT 12 (Reference: Table 5) provides the basis to determine if the "Happiness Index" (HI) level merits consideration for Self-Improvement (SI). The decision is entirely in the jurisdiction of the "Aspirant." He or she alone decides if he or she can benefit from Self-Improvement Planning (SIP) using the Self-Improving Planning Template (SIPT) 1–10 (MATRIX OF SELF-IMPROVEMENT PLANNING TEMPLATES (Reference: Table 6).

Marjorie and I recognize that each "Aspirant" will make his or her assessment of the validity and usefulness of the Seven Steps "Happiness Index" Planning Process Methodology (SSHIPPM) (Reference: Table 2), and, moreover, if the model has practical value to his or her life, or whether the discourse in Chapters 1–4 has any influence on his or her "worldview" or happiness.

The intelligent observer would call into question an urgent need for a new *epoch* in happiness to help transform the postmodern world to a state of *hope, happiness*, and "*joy.*" This "new" state is essential to counteract prevailing world conditions such as apathy for leadership, global economic challenges, 'global warming' the rise in the mass movement of refugees, escalating wars, and international terrorism.

This forward-looking postmodern age is possible. The world does not need huge expenditures to institute "new" educational and scientific systems of learning or "new" scientific intervention to make us happy. The transformation begins with a deeper understanding of "happiness," elevated to *OH*, which is a "higher value" proposition for human survival as a viable species.

All that is required is "new" thinking and a "new" desire to rise to a "higher depth" to cultivate a happier world with a focus on the future of the next generations. It requires us to rise beyond clichés that have led us to believe that we could make ourselves happy to the exclusion of others. It obliges us to come to a "new" understanding that our interdependence must be foremost in our "quest for happiness." The foregoing narrative in Chapters 1–4 (pp. 1-147), presents a "blueprint" of our transformation from "Happiness" to "Optimum Happiness" (OH).

THE ULTIMATE GOAL

The ultimate goal is to initiate a Global "Happiness Index" (HI) Movement (GHIM), even if it may be a *silent* or *salient* movement. Moreover, Marjorie and I encourage you to revisit your response to each of questions tabled in the Questionnaire Template (QT) 1–10 to determine if Self-Improvement (SI) is a necessary next step in your "happiness journey."

> "When it is obvious that the goals cannot be reached, don't adjust the goals, adjust the action steps."
>
> — *Confucius (551 BCE–479 BCE)*

STEP
FIVE

SUMMARY:

o STEP FIVE _SUMMARY

DEVELOP A SELF-IMPROVEMENT PLAN USING
SELF-IMPROVEMENT PLANNING TEMPLATE (SIPT) 1–10
REFERENCE: MATRIX OF SELF-IMPROVEMENT PLANNING
TEMPLATES (SIPT) 1–10 (REFERENCE: TABLE 6).

• ACTIVITY 1.
READ _The Definition of Self-Improvement Planning (SIP).

• ACTIVITY 2.
REVIEW _The Matrix of Self-Improvement Planning Templates
(SIPT) 1–10) (Reference: Table 6).

• ACTIVITY 3.
DEVELOP _A Self-Improvement Plan using Self-Improvement
Planning Template (SIPT) 1–10.

STEP 5: ACTIVITY _1.
SELF-IMPROVEMENT PLANNING (SIP)

"Let us strive to improve ourselves, for we cannot remain stationary; one either progresses or retrogrades."

— *Madame Marie du Deffand (1697–1780)*

DEFINITION OF SELF-IMPROVEMENT PLANNING (SIP)

Self-Improvement Planning (SIP) defines the process to create strategic plans for improving one's "Happiness Index" (HI). It is useful to individuals who perceive a need to "Optimize" their HI. The Seven Steps "Happiness Index" Planning Process Methodology (SSHIPPM) (Reference: Table 7) is our proposal for SIP.

Similar to any improvement initiative, the intrinsic value of the SSHIPPM lies in its ability to guide the "Aspirant" through a systematic process methodology. It begins with recognizing the need and ending with measuring the process outcomes that ought to be positive.

All people experience some challenges in daily life. Hence, all can benefit from some level of SI. What is important is how one copes with circumstances and situations when the outcomes are not favorable. A higher "Happiness Index" (HI) ought to have a positive influence on those within our immediate "Circle of Influence" and extend outwards.

No one can deny that some degree of Self-Improvement (SI) will help all individuals to deal with daily challenges, but you alone decide if there are valid reasons to consider if your beliefs, perceptions, behaviors, achievements, attitudes, and customs foster the happy life you deserve.

Any one of these attributes can be the trigger for your transformation from "Very Unhappy" to "Optimum Happiness" (OH), which is feasible. Immediately, what comes to mind are the challenges in marriage, family, raising children, developing a career, or managing during bad economic times; then there are personal challenges with one's character, integrity, personality, or self-esteem. Having delineated measures help to maintain objectives, such as:

o   1. SELF-IMPROVEMENT (SI) PLANNING OBJECTIVES

The objectives of a Self-Improvement (SI) Plan should be *personal*, *realistic*, *clear*, and well considered. They should describe the goals and targets within a realistic timeframe (short, medium, or long-term). Furthermore, you should make a commitment to follow through on all commitments, to be prepared to repeat the process if necessary, and to read the guide to re-establish the context of your SI objectives.

> "A strong man cannot help a weaker unless the weaker is willing to be helped, and even then the weak man must become strong of himself; he must, by his own efforts, develop the strength which he admires in another. None but himself can alter his condition."
>
> — *James Allen (1864–1912)*

o   2. SELF-IMPROVEMENT (SI) MEASURES

One principal area of SI that most individuals contemplate is his or her career. One's career helps to establish one of the foundation pillars for a better life through stable employment and financial stability and mobility. SI has a threefold perspective associated with empirical measures; for instance:

o   2.1. UNIVERSAL MEASURES

Self-Improvement (SI) can have universal norms, behaviors, and adequate measures that groups display while working within an organization, a steering committee, or a "think tank."

o   2.2. INDIVIDUAL MEASURES

Self-Improvement (SI) can have self-inspired measures after completing the "Happiness Index" Planning Process Methodology (HIPPM) that the individual strives to achieve as improvement in his or her character, career, or personality.

o   2.3. RECOMMENDED MEASURES

Professionals in the field of Self-Improvement (SI) may make a formal recommendation to a client for Self-Improvement in such areas as career development, behavior modification, physical fitness, or diet or nutrition to improve one's health.

For instance, there is a demonstrated justification for higher education to boost one's career. Statisticians tell us that the lifetime income of families headed by individuals with a bachelor's degree will be more than $1.0 million more than the incomes of families headed by those with a high-school diploma; likewise, quality of work and job satisfaction are greater. Research indicates that the average income for a male aged twenty-five or over who holds a bachelor's degree is more than double that of a male with a high-school diploma. In fact, the more educated the general population, the more vibrant the economy and the better the health and happiness of nations.

The headline reads "Self-improvement: [Six] 6 things you can do to enhance yourself and career." Posted by Chad O'Connor, September 20, 2012, 11:00 a.m., by Ellen Keiley, who states, "Regardless of your career level, there is always room for improvement. Often the focus tends to be on obstacles rather than strategies. There are numerous things you can do to improve yourself starting with setting goals and developing a plan of action that includes professional development, physical fitness, and even getting a little creative."

Ellen Keiley suggests the following [six activities] are some possibilities to try:

1. Take a Communication Skills Class
2. Read Motivational Books
3. Tap Into Your Inner Creativity
4. Take Up Pilates, Yoga, and Other Exercise
5. Find a Mentor
6. Get Involved with a Non-profit Organization or join a Committee[42]

STEP 5: ACTIVITY _2.
REVIEW THE MATRIX OF SELF-IMPROVEMENT
PLANNING TEMPLATES (SIPT) 1–10
(REFERENCE: TABLE 6).

Overleaf is a Matrix of Self-Improvement Planning Template (SIPT) 1–10 (Reference: Table 6), which shows a correlation between the Template Number versus Self-Improvement (SI) Category versus Achievement, Attitude, and Custom.

STEP 5: ACTIVITY _3.
CREATE A SELF-IMPROVEMENT PLAN USING SELF-
IMPROVEMENT PLANNING TEMPLATE (SIPT) 1–10.

DEVELOP a high-level Self-Improvement Plan (SIP) objective using the Self-Improvement Planning Templates (SIPT) 1–10. You could also use other types of instruments and seek other professional services for their expert guidance. The "Aspirant" can divide each high-level plan statement into as many detail statements as are necessary to examine all of the circumstances of the Self-Improvement objectives.

---

[42] Ellen Keiley, CPC, is President of the MBA Women International Boston Chapter Board of Directors, a member of the City Year and United Way Boston Women's™ Leadership Initiatives, and a Boston World Partnerships Connector. Used with permission. Contact: atellenmkeiley@gmail.com, http://www.boston.com/business/blogs/global-business-hub/2012/09/self_improvemen.html.

STEP 5: ACTIVITY _2.
MATRIX OF SELF-IMPROVEMENT PLANNING TEMPLATES
(SIPT) 1–10. (TEMPLATES VERSUS CATEGORY, VERSUS
ACHIEVEMENTS, ATTRIBUTES, AND CUSTOMS)

PLANNING TEMPLATE VERSUS CATEGORY		ACHIEVEMENTS, ATTRIBUTES, AND
TEMPLATE (Numerically)	CATEGORY (Alphabetically)	CUSTOMS (Alphabetically)
SIPT1. Template	Career$^{(C100)}$	Achievement
SIPT2. Template	Character$^{(C100)}$	Attribute
SIPT3. Template	Education$^{(E100)}$	Achievement
SIPT4. Template	Forgiveness$^{(F100)}$	Attribute
SIPT5. Template	Health$^{(H100)}$	Achievement
SIPT6. Template	Humility$^{(H100)}$	Attribute
SIPT7. Template	Personality$^{(P100)}$	Attribute
SIPT8. Template	Religion$^{(R100)}$	Custom
SIPT9. Template	Self-Esteem$^{(S100)}$	Achievement
SIPT10. Template	Socialization$^{(S100)}$	Custom

Table 6.

NOTES

STEP 5: ACTIVITY _3.
CREATE A SELF-IMPROVEMENT PLAN
USING SELF-IMPROVEMENT PLANINING TEMPLATE
(SIPT) 1–10.
SIPT 1_CATEGORY: CAREER

A Self-Directed Guide to Your "Happiness Index" (HI) Self-Improvement Planning Template SIPT 1 _CATEGORY: CAREER	
QUESTION:	SELF-IMPROVEMENT PLANNING (SIP):
Q1.	High-level Self-Improvement Plan Objectives
Q2.	High-level Self-Improvement Plan Objectives
Q3.	High-level Self-Improvement Plan Objectives
Q4.	High-level Self-Improvement Plan Objectives
Q5.	High-level Self-Improvement Plan Objectives
Q6.	High-level Self-Improvement Plan Objectives
Q7.	High-level Self-Improvement Plan Objectives
Q8.	High-level Self-Improvement Plan Objectives
Q9.	High-level Self-Improvement Plan Objectives
Q10.	High-level Self-Improvement Plan Objectives

NOTES

_____

_____

_____

_____

_____

_____

_____

_____

_____

_____

_____

_____

_____

_____

_____

_____

_____

_____

_____

_____

STEP 5: ACTIVITY _3A.
CREATE A SELF-IMPROVEMENT PLAN.
SIPT 2_CATEGORY: CHARACTER

A Self-Directed Guide to Your "Happiness Index" (HI) Self-Improvement Planning Template SIPT 2 _CATEGORY: CHARACTER	
QUESTION:	SELF-IMPROVEMENT PLANNING (SIP):
Q1.	High-level Self-Improvement Plan Objectives
Q2.	High-level Self-Improvement Plan Objectives
Q3.	High-level Self-Improvement Plan Objectives
Q4.	High-level Self-Improvement Plan Objectives
Q5.	High-level Self-Improvement Plan Objectives
Q6.	High-level Self-Improvement Plan Objectives
Q7.	High-level Self-Improvement Plan Objectives
Q8.	High-level Self-Improvement Plan Objectives
Q9.	High-level Self-Improvement Plan Objectives
Q10.	High-level Self-Improvement Plan Objectives

NOTES

_____

_____

_____

_____

_____

_____

_____

_____

_____

_____

_____

_____

_____

_____

_____

_____

_____

_____

_____

STEP 5: ACTIVITY _3B.
CREATE A SELF-IMPROVEMENT PLAN.
SIPT 3_CATEGORY: EDUCATION

A Self-Directed Guide to Your "Happiness Index" (HI) Self-Improvement Planning Template SIPT 3 _CATEGORY: EDUCATION	
QUESTION:	SELF-IMPROVEMENT PLANNING (SIP):
Q1.	High-level Self-Improvement Plan Objectives
Q2.	High-level Self-Improvement Plan Objectives
Q3.	High-level Self-Improvement Plan Objectives
Q4.	High-level Self-Improvement Plan Objectives
Q5.	High-level Self-Improvement Plan Objectives
Q6.	High-level Self-Improvement Plan Objectives
Q7.	High-level Self-Improvement Plan Objectives
Q8.	High-level Self-Improvement Plan Objectives
Q9.	High-level Self-Improvement Plan Objectives
Q10.	High-level Self-Improvement Plan Objectives

NOTES

STEP 5: ACTIVITY _3C.
CREATE A SELF-IMPROVEMENT PLAN.
SIPT 4_CATEGORY: FORGIVENESS

A Self-Directed Guide to Your "Happiness Index" (HI) Self-Improvement Planning Template SIPT 4 _CATEGORY: FORGIVENESS	
QUESTION:	SELF-IMPROVEMENT PLANNING (SIP):
Q1.	High-level Self-Improvement Plan Objectives
Q2.	High-level Self-Improvement Plan Objectives
Q3.	High-level Self-Improvement Plan Objectives
Q4.	High-level Self-Improvement Plan Objectives
Q5.	High-level Self-Improvement Plan Objectives
Q6.	High-level Self-Improvement Plan Objectives
Q7.	High-level Self-Improvement Plan Objectives
Q8.	High-level Self-Improvement Plan Objectives
Q9.	High-level Self-Improvement Plan Objectives
Q10.	High-level Self-Improvement Plan Objectives

NOTES

STEP 5: ACTIVITY _3D.
CREATE A SELF-IMPROVEMENT PLAN.
SIPT 5_CATEGORY: HEALTH

A Self-Directed Guide to Your "Happiness Index" (HI) Self-Improvement Planning Template SIPT 5 _CATEGORY: HEALTH	
QUESTION:	SELF-IMPROVEMENT PLANNING (SIP):
Q1.	High-level Self-Improvement Plan Objectives
Q2.	High-level Self-Improvement Plan Objectives
Q3.	High-level Self-Improvement Plan Objectives
Q4.	High-level Self-Improvement Plan Objectives
Q5.	High-level Self-Improvement Plan Objectives
Q6.	High-level Self-Improvement Plan Objectives
Q7.	High-level Self-Improvement Plan Objectives
Q8.	High-level Self-Improvement Plan Objectives
Q9.	High-level Self-Improvement Plan Objectives
Q10.	High-level Self-Improvement Plan Objectives

NOTES

STEP 5: ACTIVITY _3E.
CREATE A SELF-IMPROVEMENT PLAN.
SIPT 6_CATEGORY: HUMILITY

A Self-Directed Guide to Your "Happiness Index" (HI) Self-Improvement Planning Template SIPT 6 _CATEGORY _HUMILITY	
QUESTION:	SELF-IMPROVEMENT PLANNING (SIP):
Q1.	High-level Self-Improvement Plan Objectives
Q2.	High-level Self-Improvement Plan Objectives
Q3.	High-level Self-Improvement Plan Objectives
Q4.	High-level Self-Improvement Plan Objectives
Q5.	High-level Self-Improvement Plan Objectives
Q6.	High-level Self-Improvement Plan Objectives
Q7.	High-level Self-Improvement Plan Objectives
Q8.	High-level Self-Improvement Plan Objectives
Q9.	High-level Self-Improvement Plan Objectives
Q10.	High-level Self-Improvement Plan Objectives

NOTES

_____

_____

_____

_____

_____

_____

_____

_____

_____

_____

_____

_____

_____

_____

_____

_____

_____

_____

STEP 5: ACTIVITY _3F.
CREATE A SELF-IMPROVEMENT PLAN.
SIPT 7. CATEGORY_PERSONALITY

A Self-Directed Guide to Your "Happiness Index" (HI) Self-Improvement Planning Template SIPT 7 _CATEGORY _PERSONALITY	
QUESTION:	SELF-IMPROVEMENT PLANNING (SIP):
Q1.	High-level Self-Improvement Plan Objectives
Q2.	High-level Self-Improvement Plan Objectives
Q3.	High-level Self-Improvement Plan Objectives
Q4.	High-level Self-Improvement Plan Objectives
Q5.	High-level Self-Improvement Plan Objectives
Q6.	High-level Self-Improvement Plan Objectives
Q7.	High-level Self-Improvement Plan Objectives
Q8.	High-level Self-Improvement Plan Objectives
Q9.	High-level Self-Improvement Plan Objectives
Q10.	High-level Self-Improvement Plan Objectives

NOTES

STEP 5: ACTIVITY _3G.
CREATE A SELF-IMPROVEMENT PLAN.
SIPT 8_CATEGORY: RELIGION

A Self-Directed Guide to Your "Happiness Index" (HI) Self-Improvement Planning Template (SIPT) 8 SIPT 8 _CATEGORY: RELIGION	
QUESTION:	SELF-IMPROVEMENT PLANNING (SIP):
Q1.	High-level Self-Improvement Plan Objectives
Q2.	High-level Self-Improvement Plan Objectives
Q3.	High-level Self-Improvement Plan Objectives
Q4.	High-level Self-Improvement Plan Objectives
Q5.	High-level Self-Improvement Plan Objectives
Q6.	High-level Self-Improvement Plan Objectives
Q7.	High-level Self-Improvement Plan Objectives
Q8.	High-level Self-Improvement Plan Objectives
Q9.	High-level Self-Improvement Plan Objectives
Q10.	High-level Self-Improvement Plan Objectives

NOTES

STEP 5: ACTIVITY _3H.
CREATE A SELF-IMPROVEMENT PLAN.
SIPT 9_CATEGORY: SELF-ESTEEM

A Self-Directed Guide to Your "Happiness Index" (HI) Self-Improvement Planning Template SIPT 9 _CATEGORY: SELF-ESTEEM	
QUESTION:	SELF-IMPROVEMENT PLANNING (SIP):
Q1.	High-level Self-Improvement Plan Objectives
Q2.	High-level Self-Improvement Plan Objectives
Q3.	High-level Self-Improvement Plan Objectives
Q4.	High-level Self-Improvement Plan Objectives
Q5.	High-level Self-Improvement Plan Objectives
Q6.	High-level Self-Improvement Plan Objectives
Q7.	High-level Self-Improvement Plan Objectives
Q8.	High-level Self-Improvement Plan Objectives
Q9.	High-level Self-Improvement Plan Objectives
Q10.	High-level Self-Improvement Plan Objectives

NOTES

STEP 5: ACTIVITY _3I.
CREATE SELF-IMPROVEMENT PLAN.
SIPT 10_CATEGORY: SOCIALIZATION

A Self-Directed Guide to Your "Happiness Index" (HI) Self-Improvement Planning Template (SIPT) 10 SIPT 10_CATEGORY: SOCIALIZATION	
QUESTION:	SELF-IMPROVEMENT PLANNING (SIP):
Q1.	High-level Self-Improvement Plan Objectives
Q2.	High-level Self-Improvement Plan Objectives
Q3.	High-level Self-Improvement Plan Objectives
Q4.	High-level Self-Improvement Plan Objectives
Q5.	High-level Self-Improvement Plan Objectives
Q6.	High-level Self-Improvement Plan Objectives
Q7.	High-level Self-Improvement Plan Objectives
Q8.	High-level Self-Improvement Plan Objectives
Q9.	High-level Self-Improvement Plan Objectives
Q10.	High-level Self-Improvement Plan Objectives

NOTES

_____

_____

_____

_____

_____

_____

_____

_____

_____

_____

_____

_____

_____

_____

_____

_____

_____

_____

_____

STEP
SIX

SUMMARY:

o   STEP SIX _SUMMARY

EXECUTE THE SELF-IMPROVEMENT PLANNING PROCESS
METHODOLOGY (SIPPM) (REFERENCE: TABLE 7)
(REFERENCE: GENERIC PROCESS FLOWCHART 2).

• ACTIVITY 1

READ _The Definition of the Self-Improvement Planning Process
Methodology (SIPPM).

• ACTIVITY 2

EXECUTE _The Seven Steps Self-Improvement Planning Process
Methodology (SSSIPPM) using the Generic Process Flowchart as a
Guide (Reference: Table 7) (Reference: Generic Process Flowchart 2).

STEP 6: ACTIVITY _1.
THE SELF-IMPROVEMENT
PLANNING PROCESS METHODOLOGY (SIPPM)

"One ought, every day at least, to hear a little song, read a good poem, see a fine picture, and, if it were possible, to speak a few reasonable words."

— *Johann Wolfgang von Goethe (1749–1832)*

DEFINITION OF SELF-IMPROVEMENT PLANNING
PROCESS METHODOLOGY (SIPPM)

The Self-Improvement Planning Process Methodology (SIPPM) is a process designed to *evaluate*, *assess*, and *develop* strategies to improve in areas that will enhance one's "Happiness Index" (HI). It is similar to a critical Continual Improvement Process (abbreviated as CIP or CI in corporations), defined as an ongoing effort to improve products, services, or processes.

The goal of the SIPPM is to guide you through some basic process steps to maintain and optimize your desired "Happiness Index" (HI) level, but we begin by revisiting our trajectory of happiness.

There are numerous self-help gurus and professional services available to assist in your Self-Improvement (SI) journey. You can conduct research from reputable Internet websites of accredited universities, university hospitals, and other global organizations.

We did not follow any complicated formula even though much of life in our postmodern world is complex. Complexity is a good teacher for simplicity to become simple. We strive to live a spiritual, philosophical, and humanitarian life, and to look for the good in every human action and not the evil in human reaction. We provide the following twenty activities for Self-Improvement (SI) to help to achieve your Optimum "Happiness Index" (OHI) goals.

o   TWENTY ACTIVITES FOR SELF-IMPROVEMENT (SI) TO HELP ACHIEVE YOUR "OPTIMUM HAPPINESS" (OH) GOALS:

1. *Strive* to maintain loyalty to family, friends, and associates.
2. *Read* books that *engage, enlighten,* and *empower* the mind.
3. *Maintain* close relations with family and friends.
4. *Pen* realistic goals, and strive to achieve them.
5. *Maintain* an active and objective mind.
6. *Write* letters and poetry in handwriting.
7. *Strive* to learn something new each week.
8. *Take* regular walks with a friend in a greenbelt.
9. *Share* life experiences with others.
10. *Maintain* a proper diet and exercise regime.
11. *Share* your dreams and thoughts with others.
12. *Forgive* others, and avoid feelings of revenge.
13. *Listen* attentively to conversation.
14. *Learn* about other people and cultures.
15. *Take* a course in a different language.
16. *Give* generously to the less fortunate.
17. *Strive* to maintain a positive outlook.
18. *Set* high educational goals.
19. *Listen* to relaxing music.
20. *Avoid* conflict situations.

Practice the following twenty SI activities with a presence of mind, hope, peace, and happiness. It will begin a process of transformation, not just of ourselves but also of the environment around us, which is the primary objective of this Self-Directed Guide to Your "Happiness Index" (HI).

Furthermore, the twenty activities listed also constitute a basis upon which to establish your high-level Self-Improvement Planning (SIP) objectives. Other researchers have different "schools of thought" regarding the "search for happiness."

You have read the account of our journey, and we are confident that the questions you have answered in the ten questionnaire worksheet categories were personal and revealing in ways that you might never have contemplated.

Your "Happiness Index" (HI) score is personal and confidential, but "Optimum Happiness" (OH) is celebratory. Our desire is that you have found the path to OH between the covers of this pioneering work that will transform your life to a higher state of happiness (which is "joy") than you may be experiencing. All that it requires is for you to believe in yourself and the inner goodness of fellow human beings, always expecting the best of others and giving your best to others as you shine the light along a path to happiness so that others can follow.

Our "Happiness Index" Planning Process Methodology (HIPPM) presents "Aspirants" with the opportunity to achieve the goals of OH. The significance of the methodology is the increased likelihood of achieving your Self-Improvement (SI) objectives when you follow a method.

The method we present constitutes seven simple steps. These seven steps provide the basis upon which to execute your Self-Improvement (SI) Plan. Each step can be broken down into additional substeps and multiple action plans depending on the complexity of the challenge.

In this discourse, SI means to "uplift" every aspect of our being, such as spiritual, moral, social, intellectual, and physical aspects. These five attributes will enable human beings to build a better human civilization with peace and security, and happiness for individuals, families, nations, and the international community.

For SI to be "wholesome," it must begin with self, but there must also be a wilful understanding of the aggregate benefits that are inherent when it becomes a totally conscious state within the individual, family, and nation. Overleaf, Seven Steps Self-Improvement Planning Process Methodology (SSSIPPM) (Reference: Table 7), should facilitate any SI initiative, whether it is to improve character or self-esteem.

STEP 6: ACTIVITY _2.
SEVEN STEPS SELF-IMPROVEMENT
PLANNING PROCESS METHODOLOGY (SSSIPPM)

SEVEN STEPS:	SEVEN HIGH-LEVEL DEFINITIONS:
1. Recognize	Recognize the need for Self-Improvement (SI).
2. Document	Document the SI need.
3. Assess	Assess the SI criteria.
4. Decide	Decide on the SI action plan.
5. Develop	Develop and execute the SI plan.
6. Evaluate	Evaluate the SI plan and make adjustments.
7. Measure	Measure SI outcomes and repeat as required.

Table 7.

The high value of the Seven Steps Self-Improvement Planning Process Methodology (SSSIPPM) occurs when the decision for Self-Improvement comes from a personal desire for it and is not necessarily influenced by others. Some SI objectives may require a commitment to *study*, *research*, and *training*, such as in career improvement, while others may need a personal conviction, such as with one who decides to embark on a spiritual journey.

From a general perspective, the Generic Process Flowchart provides a basis upon which to focus on strategic elements of the seven Self-Improvement (SI) steps. The outcome-based approach provides the "Aspirant" with an opportunity to revisit and repeat specific steps to obtain the desired outcome before moving on to the succeeding step.

STEP 6: ACTIVITY _2.
GENERIC PROCESS FLOWCHART 2.
SEVEN STEPS SELF-IMPROVEMENT PLANNING PROCESS
(SSSIPP)

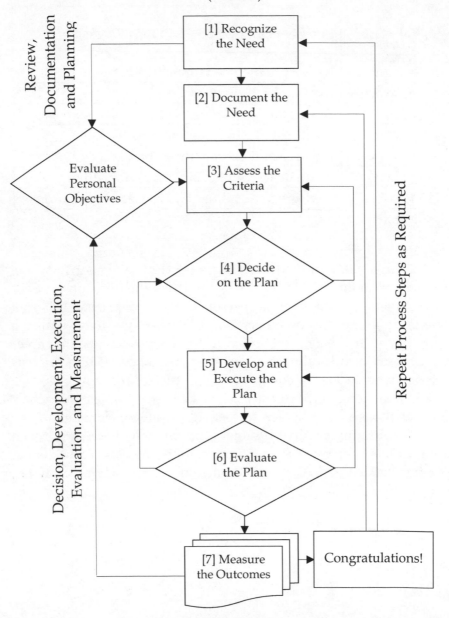

Generic Process Flowchart 2.

STEP SEVEN

CONCLUSION!

You have successfully completed the "Happiness Index" Planning Process Methodology (HIPPM).

CONGRATULATIONS!

It gratifies Marjorie and me that you have taken this remarkable journey with us in your "search of happiness." We also hope that you have discovered the "awe-inspiring" purpose of your existence and the great privilege that we have to share the resources of the Earth, freely given by our Creator for our well-being and happiness. We wrote this book out of a sincere desire for anyone who lives outside of the boundaries of the poignant words of Thomas Jefferson (1743–1826), third President of the United States.

> "We hold these truths to be self-evident: that all men are created equal; that they are endowed by their Creator with certain unalienable rights; that among these are life, liberty, and the pursuit of happiness."(United States Declaration of Independence in Congress, July 4, 1776)

In this chronicle, we have achieved our objective to embark on a comprehensive journey into some of the complex dimensions of happiness that we have discovered. It is a testament to the account of our experiences as we set our goals on "Optimum Happiness" (OH) not merely for ourselves but for our readers. We trust that you have accomplished your goals as well. We invite you to visit our comprehensive website: *www.ffhdwritersinc.com*.

"Twenty years from now you will be more disappointed by the things you didn't do than by the ones you did do. So throw off the bowlines, sail away from the safe harbor. Catch the trade winds in your sails. Explore. Dream. Discover."

— Mark Twain (1835–1910)

APPENDICES

ACRONYMS

AD	Anno Domini
AIL	Academic Information Literacy
BAA	Business Accounting Assistant
BBA	Bachelor of Business Administration
BC	Before Christ
BCE	Before the Christian Era
BMI	Body Mass Index
BOE	Board of Education
CET	Certified Engineering Technologist
CEV	Contemporary English Version
CHI	Corporate Happiness Index
CI	Continuous Improvement
CIP	Continuous Improvement Process
CSI	Continuous Self-Improvement
EQ	Emotional Intelligence
ESV	English Standard Version
GDP	Gross Domestic Product
GHIM	Global Happiness Index Movement
GNP	Gross National Product
GSP	Gross Social Progress
HA	Happiness Audit
HCSB	Holman Christian Standard Bible
HG	Happiness Gap
HI	Happiness Index
HIMT	Happiness Index Measurement Template
HIPM	Happiness Index (HI) Process Methodology
HIPPM	Happiness Index Planning Process Methodology
HQ	Human Intelligence
HR	Horizontal Relationship
IIQM	Incarceration Index Questionnaire Model
IHI	International Happiness Index
ICJ	International Court of Justice
IQ	Intelligent Quotient
ISBN	International Standard Book Number
MBA	Master of Business Administration
NAFTA	North American Free Trade Agreement
NHAP	National Happiness Awareness Program
NHI	National Happiness Index

NIV	New International Version
NKJV	New King James Version
OECD	Organisation for Economic Co-operation and Development
OH	Optimum Happiness
OHI	Optimum Happiness Index
ONC	Ordinary National Certificate
PHI	Personal Happiness Index
PI	Poverty Index
PMP	Project Management Professional
PQ	Physical Intelligence
QC	Questionnaire Category
QT	Questionnaire Template
QTSM	Questionnaire Template Scoring Methodology
SI	Self-Improvement
SIP	Self-Improvement Planning
SIPPM	Self-Improvement Planning Process Methodology
SIPT	Self-Improvement Planning Template
SQ	Spiritual Intelligence
SQT	Summary Questionnaire Template
SSHIPPM	Seven Steps Happiness Index Planning Process Methodology
SSPMC	Seven Steps Process to Manage Conflict
SSSIPPM	Seven Steps Self-Improvement Planning Process Methodology
SWOT	Strengths, Weaknesses, Opportunities, and Threats
TKHI	Ten Key Happiness Indicators
TOC	Table of Civilization
UK	United Kingdom
UN	United Nation
UNCED	United Nations Conference on Environment and Development
UNESCO	United Nations Education, Scientific and Cultural Organization
UNHCR	United Nations High Commissioner for Refugees
VR	Vertical Relationship
WMD	Weapons of Mass Destruction

TABULAR LISTINGS

CHAPTERS 1–5

246

SELECT BIBLIOGRAPHY

Our bibliography sets out a sample of books read or researched as stimulants to thought over several decades. The nature of this discourse obliges us to recognize some writers with similar interests in making the world a better place where human beings can live and strive for *peace, harmony,* and *happiness.*

The list includes many diverse works in the fields of religion, leadership, philosophy, psychology, psychiatry, sociology, and other academic areas. We hope that these reference books will add to the rich repository of human knowledge that is available to humankind for the creation of a better and happier world envisioned by Thomas Jefferson (1743–1826) and other higher thinkers of our *premodern, modern,* and *postmodern* age.

Adler, Mortimer J. *Six Great Ideas.* New York, New York: A Touchstone Book Published by Simon & Schuster, 1981.

Allison, J., & Gediman, D. (Eds.). *This I Believe – The Personal Philosophies of Remarkable Men and Women* (1st ed.). New York, New York: Holt Paperbacks, 2007.

Anderson, Greg. *The 22 {Non–Negotiable} Laws of Wellness (Feel, Think, and Live Better Than You Ever Thought Possible).* New York, New York: HarperCollins Publishers, 1995.

Anderson, Ken. *Bible–Based Prayer Power (Using Relevant Scriptures to Pray with Confidence for All Your Needs).* Nashville, Tennessee: Thomas Nelson Publishers, 2000.

Angelou, Maya. *Even the Stars Look Lonesome.* New York, New York: Random House, 1997.

Ankerberg, John, & Weldon, John. *The Facts on World Religions.* Eugene, Oregon: Harvest House Publishers, 2004.

Aultman, Donald S. (Editor), Contributors: Conn, Paul, Fisher, Robert W., Goff, Doyle, & Hammond, Jerome. *Understanding Yourself and Others.* Cleveland, Tennessee: Pathway Press, 2001.

Barna, George. *A Fish Out of Water (9 Strategies to Maximize your God–Given Leadership Potential).* Brentwood, Tennessee: Integrity Publishers, A Division of Integrity Media, Inc., 2002.

Barna, George. *Leaders on Leadership (Wisdom, Advice and Encouragement on the Art of Leading God's People).* Ventura, California: Regal Books – A Division of Gospel Light, 1997.

248

Böckle, Franz. *Moral Theology – War Poverty Freedom (The Christian Response)*. New York, New York/Glen Rock, NJ: Paulist Press, 1966.

Collins, Gary R., PhD. *Christian Counseling (A Comprehensive Guide)*. Waco, Texas: Word Books Publisher, 1980.

Colson, Charles. *Who Speaks for God? (Confronting the World with Real Christianity)*. Westchester, Illinois: Crossway Books, a division of Good News Publishers, 1985.

Covey, Stephen R. *The Seven Habits of Highly Effective People (Powerful Lessons in Personal Change)*. New York, New York: Simon & Schuster, 2013.

Datta, Dhirendra Mohan. *The Philosophy of Mahatma Gandhi*. Madison, Wisconsin: The University of Wisconsin Press, 1953.

Dawood, N. J. *The Koran*. Middlesex, England: Penguin Books, 1956.

Desai, Mahadev. *M. K. Gandhi: An Autobiography or The Story of My Experiments with Truth*. New York, New York: Penguin Books, 1927.

Dillenberger, John (Editor). *Martin Luther: Selections from His Writings*. New York, New York: Doubleday, 1961.

Dobson, James, Dr., and Bauer, Garry L. *Children at Risk (The Battle for the Heart and Minds of Our Kids)*. Dallas, London, Vancouver, Melbourne: Word Publishing, 1990.

Ellis, Desmond, & Anderson, Dawn. *Conflict Resolution (An Introductory Text)*. Toronto, Canada: Edmond Montgomery Publications Limited, 2005.

Ford, Leighton. *Transforming Leadership (Jesus' Way of Creating Vision, Shaping Values & Empowering Change)*. Downers Grove, Illinois: InterVarsity Press, 1991.

Fox, Emmet. *Find and Use Your Inner Power*. New York, New York: HarperSanFrancisco, 1937.

Fox, Emmet. *The Sermon on the Mount*. New York, New York: HarperSanFrancisco, 1934.

Freud, Sigmund. *Civilization and Its Discontents*. New York, New York: W. W. Norton & Company, Inc., 1961.

Friedman, George. *The Next 1000 Years*. A Forecast for the 21st Century. Melbourne, Victoria 3000, Australia: Black Inc., 2009.

Gibbs, Errol, & Grey, Philip. *Five Foundations of Human Development (FFHD)*. Bloomington, Indiana: AuthorHouse, 2011.

Gilbert, Elizabeth. *Eat, Pray, Love – A Woman's Search for Everything*. New York, New York: Penguin Books, 2008.

Haywood, Dale M., Nash, Timothy G., & Amin, R. John. *When We Are Free* (Third Edition). Midland, Michigan: Northwood Institute Press, 1981.

Helms, Ludger. *Poor Leadership and Bad Governance: Reassessing President and Prime Ministers in North America, Europe and Japan.* Northampton, Massachusetts: Edward Elgar Publishing Limited, 2012.

Hendricks, Howard G. *Teaching to Change Lives.* Portland, Oregon: Multnomah Press, 1987.

Hüng, Hans. *Does God Exist? (An Answer for Today).* Garden City, New York: Doubleday & Company, 1980.

Johnstone, Patrick. *Operation World (The Day-to-Day Guide to Praying for the World).* Cleveland, Tennessee: Zondervan Publishing House, 1983.

King, Martin Luther, Jr. *Why We Can't Wait.* New York, New York: Signet, Signet Classics, Signette, Mentor and Plume Books, 1963, 1964.

Krishnamurti, R. J. *Talks and Dialogues (The Intelligence That Transcends Thought).* New York, New York: Avon Books, 1968.

LaHaye, Tim. *The Battle for the Public Schools (Humanism's Threat to Our Children).* Old Tappan, New Jersey: Fleming H. Revell Company, 1983.

Lewis, C. S. *Mere Christianity.* New York, New York: Macmillan Publishing Company, 1943.

Marturano, Antonio. *Leadership and the Humanities* (2014, Volume 2, Number 1). Abingdon, Oxfordshire, UK, 2014.

Maxwell, John C. *Developing the Leader Within You.* Nashville, Tennessee: Thomas Nelson, Inc., 1993.

Maxwell, John C., & Dornan, Jim. *Becoming a Person of Influence (How to Positively Impact the Lives of Others).* Nashville, Tennessee: Thomas Nelson, Inc., 1997.

McDowell, Josh, & Hostetler, Bob. *Right from Wrong (What you need to know to help youths make right choices).* USA: WordPublishing, 1994.

Melina, Ruskai L., Burgress, Gloria J., & Falkman, Lena Lid. *The Embodiment of Leadership.* San Francisco, California: Jossey–Bass, 2013.

Moore, Thomas. *Care of the Soul (A Guide for Cultivating Depth and Sacredness in Everyday Life).* New York, New York: HarperPerennial –A division of HarperCollins Publishers, 1992.

Murray, Andrew. *Humility.* New Kensington, PA: Whitaker House, 1982.

Nehil, Thomas E. *A Cultural Guide to the Global Village.* Midland, Michigan: Simon & Schuster Custom Publishing, 1997.

Paul, John, II. *Crossing the Threshold of Hope.* Toronto, Ontario, Canada: Alfred A. Knopf Canada, 1994.

Peale, Norman Vincent. *The Power of Positive Thinking*. New York, New York: Ballantine Books, 1952.

Peale, Stafford Ruth. *A Lifetime of Positive Thinking*. Pawling, New York: Guideposts, 2001.

Peter, Laurence J., Dr. *The Peter Plan (How to get things straight: An optimistic proposal for survival)*. New York, New York: Bantam Books, 1977.

Peters, Tom, & Austin, Nancy. *A Passion for Excellence (The Leadership Difference)*. New York, New York: Warner Books, 1985.

Pritchett, Price. *During Unrelenting High-Pressure Change (Business as Unusual)*. Dallas, Texas: Pritchett, 2009.

Pritchett, Price. *New World Habits for a Radically Changing World (13 Ground Rules for Job Success in the Information Age)*. Dallas, Texas: Pritchett, 2008.

Rourke, John T. *Taking Sides (Clashing Views on Controversial Issues in World Politics* (Eighth Edition). Guilford, Connecticut: Duskin/McGraw-Hill, A division of McGraw-Hill Companies, Inc., 1998.

Schuyler, Goldman Kathy. *Leading with Spirit, Presence & Authenticity*. San Francisco, CA: Jossey-Bass 2014.

Schuyler, Goldman Kathy, Baugher, Eric John, & Jironet, Karin. *Creative Social Change (Leadership for a Healthy World)*. Wagon Lane, Bingley, UK: Emerald Group Publishing Limited, 2016.

Sheenan, James. *The Law of Second Chances*. New York, New York: St Martin's Press, 2008.

Smalley, Gary. *Hidden Keys of a Loving Lasting Marriage*. Grand Rapids, Michigan: Zondervan Publishing House, 1984, 1988.

Sowcik, Matthew. *LEADERSHIP 2050 (Critical Challenges, Key Contexts, and Emerging Trends)*. Wagon Lane, Bingley, UK: Emerald Group Publishing Limited, 2015.

Taylor, Susan L. *Lessons in Living*. New York, New York: An Anchor Book – Published by Doubleday, 1995.

Vanzant, Iyanla. *One Day My Soul Just Opened Up (40 Days and 40 Nights toward Spiritual Strength and Personal Growth)*. New York, New York: Simon & Schuster Inc., 1998.

Vanzant, Iyanla. *Until Today (Daily Devotions for Spiritual Growth and Peace of Mind)*. New York, New York: Simon & Schuster, 2000.

Warren, Rick. *The Purpose Driven Life (What on Earth Am I Here For?)*. Grand Rapids, Michigan: Zondervan, 2002.

Weaver, Grady Henry. *The Mainspring of Human Progress*. Irvington-on–Hudson, New York: The Foundation of Economic Education, Inc. 1997.

Weeks, Dudley. *Conflict Resolution (Preserving Relationships at Work, at Home, and in the Community)*. New York, New York: G. P. Putnam's Sons, 1992.

Williams, Eric. *Capitalism and Slavery*. (Introduction by D. W. Brogan) London, England: Andre Deutsch Limited, 1944.

Williams, Eric. *From Columbus to Castro (The History of the Caribbean)*. New York, New York: Vintage Books, a Division of Random House, 1984. Originally published by Andre Deutsch Limited, London, England, in 1970.

Wright, Judith, & Wright, Bob. *TRANSFORMED: The Science of Spectacular Living*. Nashville, Tennessee: Turner, 2013.

Yancey, Philip. *Disappointment with God (Three questions no one asks aloud)*. Grand Rapids, Michigan: Zondervan Publishing House, 1988.

Yogananda, Paramahansa. *Where There Is Light*. Los Angeles, California: Self Realization Fellowship, 1988.

Zacharias, Ravi. *Can Man Live Without God* (Foreword by Charles Colson). Dallas, London, Vancouver, Melbourne: Word Publishing, 1994.

Ziglar, Zig. *Confessions of a Happy Christian*. Gretna, Louisiana: Pelican Publishing Company, 1978.

AUTHORS' BIOGRAPHY

Errol and Marjorie Gibbs are humanitarians. They are avid readers, self-inspired researchers, and writers. They are Canadian citizens who reside in Milton, Ontario. Religious, scientific, educational, philosophical, and humanitarian pursuits highlight their work. Multigenerational family life, nurturing children, community, business, and corporate experience bolster their seminal work, *"Discovering Your Optimum 'Happiness Index' (OHI)."*

Research, study, and religious and philosophical perspectives underlie their life's purpose. They embrace every opportunity to create literature and the human condition that inspire happiness for themselves and others. Errol and Marjorie have dedicated their lives to promoting the good in humanity by their work and relationships with people they encounter on their "journey of happiness," which began in earnest in the year 2000.

Marjorie and Errol have combined experiential knowledge, intellectual and empirical observation, and global travel on four continents—Africa, Europe, North America, and Oceania—in approximately twelve countries, twenty-four states, and about one hundred cities, towns, and villages over several decades. They have benefitted from a "panoramic view" of the human landscape as they have observed how people in several parts of the world experience happiness and unhappiness coexisting in a cultural mix of wealth (plenty) and poverty (scarcity), and more importantly, how peoples' "worldview" influences their relationships, their happiness, and their futures.

Marjorie and Errol live "Optimum Happy" lives. "Optimum Happiness" (OH) does not mean to have great wealth, to live in a mansion, to drive exotic automobiles, or to socialize with prominent figures in society. Their perspective on happiness is to reverence a higher moral authority, love for humanity, integrity in business, and care for family, friends, community, and nation. They contend that these fundamental imperatives of happiness underpin a successful life, not merely as "lifestyle happiness" but as perpetual "joy."

Marjorie brings to OHI the great instincts of the "heart" that she inherited from her mother. She inherited the "head" leadership from her father, who was an "old school" farmer and businessperson, and through her education and corporate experience. She holds a Bachelor of Business Administration (BBA) degree (summa cum laude), a

Business Accounting and Assistant Diploma (BAA), and certificates in Conflict Management and Environment Technology. Marjorie practices in the field of Accounting Management, where she meets and interacts with people from all "walks of life." These meetings help to enrich her "happiness journey" even when she is not reading or traveling.

Errol has a polytechnic engineering background, primarily in the energy industry. Errol has practiced for twenty-five years in both thermal and nuclear power generation. He is a certified Project Management Professional (PMP) and a Certified Engineering Technologist (CET), and he holds a Full Technological Certificate (Instrumentation Maintenance Technology) (energy sector). He also holds the equivalent of the Ordinary National Certificate (ONC) in Mechanical Engineering and Applied Physics from City and Guilds of London Institute in London, England.

During his career, Errol has held positions such as Senior Engineering Technician, Scientific Technologist, Planning and Scheduling Engineer/Officer, Project Management Analyst, Senior Process Designer, and Project Management and Business Consultant. In 2002, Errol relinquished his technical career to pursue a higher understanding of human development from religious, humanitarian, and philosophical perspectives; likewise to write and speak on issues that impede human growth and peaceful coexistence.

Among a host of technical and nontechnical presentations over the years (2000–2015), in July 2015, Errol presented at a conference ("Visions of a Future World") hosted by the Women's Federation for World Peace (WFWP), Toronto, Ontario. In October 2014, Errol presented at the International Leadership Association (ILA) 16th Annual Leadership Conference in San Diego, California, USA. In October 2013, Errol spoke at a conference ("Should Canada See Itself as a Welcoming Family?") hosted by the Women's Federation for World Peace (WFWP) in Ottawa, Ontario, Canada.

In 2008 and 2010 respectively, Errol presented at the 17th and 19th Annual Science Symposium, sponsored by Visions of Science Network for Learning (VOSNL) in Toronto, Ontario, Canada. Errol had the privilege to speak on the same circuit as distinguished former NASA astronaut Captain Winston E. Scott (Captain, USN, RET) and Professor and Dr. Mercedes T. Richards (1955–2016), Department of Astronomy & Astrophysics, Pennsylvania State University, USA.

In September 2000, Errol wrote and copresented a "White Paper" entitled "Manufacturing Engineering Project Office (MEPO) — A Critical Link to Supplier Integration." He presented the paper at the

Project Management Institute's (PMI®) Global Symposium on Project Management in Houston, Texas, USA.

The solution perspectives that Errol and Marjorie bring to the challenges of the postmodern world begin with a "new" understanding of the human capacity to change the course of history. *"Discovering Your Optimum 'Happiness Index' (OHI)"* is their way to engage people, communities, and nations in a dialogue about the intrinsic benefits of happiness as a positive human emotion. Whether you live in the Orient or the Occident, whether you are rich or poor, an academic or a layperson, religious or irreligious, the writers invite you to join them in a Global "Happiness Index" (HI) Movement (GHIM) as a critical enabler in the pursuit of happier world.

Errol and Marjorie put forward that "Optimum Happiness" (OH) is a "higher value" proposition for human survival as a viable species than "Happiness." They proffer that OH is the road to travel as they seek to help inspire others in their search for lives filled with peace, hope, happiness, and optimism for the future. Some of the ideas in their book might be different from what you have learned about happiness and taken for granted regarding "happiness" as a lifestyle. Their hope is that you will consider their perspectives as "new" discoveries that can aid in your quest for OH, underpinned by "joy," a "spiritual" imperative that can sustain your OHI." Moreover, "joy" is the "sentinel" that guards the soul when "Happiness" takes flight — temporarily.

HAVE WE INSPIRED YOU?

Dear Aspirant,

We thank you for taking the journey with Marjorie and me. We trust that you have read *"Discovering Your Optimum 'Happiness Index' (OHI)"* in its entirety. We hope that you have also completed the matrix of questions that underpin the "Happiness Index" Planning Process Methodology (HIPPM). You have discovered your "Happiness Index" (HI) and are poised to achieve the next goal of Self-Improvement (SI) in areas that will elevate you from mere "Happiness" to *"Optimum Happiness"* (*OH*). This new journey will shed a bright light on your path in your quest to discover your OHI.

We also invite you to visit our website and share our work with others.
www.gibbshappinessindex.com

AVAILABLE AT:

www.authorHouse.com
www.amazon.com
www.barnesandnoble.com
www.chapters.indigo.ca
www.waterstones.com

Ask for these books—*"Discovering Your Optimum 'Happiness Index' (OHI)"* and *"Discovering Your Optimum 'Happiness Index' (OHI) Quotes Handbook"365Q* —at your local bookstore or locate them on the website of your preferred online book retailer.

SPEAKING ENGAGEMENTS

CONTACT

Errol A. Gibbs
Marjorie G. Gibbs
Email: info@gibbshappinessindex.com
Website: www.gibbshappinessindex.com

102 OPTIMUM "HAPPINESS INDEX" (OHI) QUOTES
— READERS' BONUS

ONE HUNDRED AND TWO OPTIMUM "HAPPINESS INDEX" (OHI) QUOTES TO ENGAGE, ENLIGHTEN, AND EMPOWER YOUR SEARCH FOR "OPTIMUM HAPPINESS" (OH)[43]

1. "Optimum Happiness" (OH) is a higher value proposition than *happiness*.
2. With the right tools, people can improve their "Happiness Index" (HI).
3. The "pursuit of pleasure" is not the same as the "pursuit of happiness."
4. Happy people are at peace and are less anxious than unhappy people.
5. Happy people have high expectations of themselves and others.
6. The labyrinth of the mind stores both *happy* and *unhappy* thoughts.
7. "Joy" and "Happiness" can help to mitigate violence in the world.
8. Happiness lives between the twin towers of *attitude* and *gratitude*.
9. The grand design of the universe will be incomplete without you.
10. Happy people are less destructive and easy to foster relations with.
11. Happy employees are more dependable and more productive.
12. Our "interdependent nature" nurtures the "roots of happiness."
13. You can achieve a higher state of "Optimum Happiness" (OH).
14. Happy thoughts create happy feelings, emotions, and actions.
15. Much of human behavior is counterproductive to happiness.
16. Children are the "Emperors" and "Empresses" of happiness.
17. A happy world hinges on our desire to make others happy.
18. Happy people are more generous than unhappy people.
19. Loyalty is the bedrock of *longevity* in all relationships.
20. Happy people are more calm, creative, and productive.
21. A happy world hinges on a happy marriage and family.
22. Forgive the past; enjoy the present; plan for the future.
23. Strive to do better, to achieve more, and to give more.
24. The soul "searches for joy" when happiness takes flight.
25. "Spirituality" and "Happiness" are mutually inclusive.
26. "Lifestyle" and "Happiness" are only distant cousins.
27. Guard against actions that impede your happiness.
28. Happiness is *personal* and *interpersonal*.
29. Happiness is also *transactional* and *transformational*.
30. Happy employees are more loyal and more creative.
31. Money can bring both *happiness* and *unhappiness*.
32. Happiness exists in the "spiritual" and the "physical."
33. Without happiness, unhappiness will reign supreme.
34. Believe that the ultimate state of happiness is "joy."
35. Happiness is not possessing but being and doing.
36. Neither rich nor poor are happier than the other.
37. Eat foods from the ground, the tree, and the sea.

---

[43] Some quotes were taken from this text, *"Discovering Your Optimum 'Happiness Index' (OHI),"* —A Self-Directed Guide to Your "Happiness Index" (HI) (Including Questionnaire and Self-Improvement [SI] Templates). © 2016 Errol A. and Marjorie G. Gibbs. All rights reserved.

ONE HUNDRED AND TWO OPTIMUM "HAPPINESS INDEX" (OHI) QUOTES TO ENGAGE, ENLIGHTEN, AND EMPOWER YOUR SEARCH FOR "OPTIMUM HAPPINESS" (OH)[44] (Continued)

38. "Spiritual Intelligence" (SQ) imbues happiness.
39. Material *success* is not the same as a *successful life*.
40. Happy leaders are better managers of people.
41. Do not worry if the "Joneses" get ahead of you.
42. Unhappiness does not have to be permanent.
43. Seek knowledge, wisdom, and understanding.
44. Happy people have a friendly predisposition.
45. Today can be a happier day than yesterday.
46. Happiness is *spiritual, emotional,* and *physical*.
47. You can make others happy and vice versa.
48. Happy people are healthier emotionally.
49. Strive for family loyalty as a primary goal.
50. Be positive, and avoid negative situations.
51. "Joy" is a higher imperative of happiness.
52. Happy people have a forgiving attitude.
53. Good character traits imbue happiness.
54. Money may not bring lasting happiness.
55. A good character underpins happiness.
56. There are specific keys to a happier life.
57. Live a high-integrity and worry-free life.
58. Strive to live peacefully with all people.
59. Forgive others, and ask for forgiveness.
60. Everyone has a "Happiness Index" (HI).
61. Happiness is a companion of the soul.
62. Your purpose is to live, love, and serve.
63. Happy people have a forgiving spirit.
64. Demand your birthright to be happy.
65. Happy thoughts lead to right actions.
66. "Joy" brings peace and happiness.
67. Counter criticisms with compliments.
68. Make your spouse your best friend.
69. Never strive to win in an argument.
70. Maintain openness and objectivity.
71. Travel widely and read extensively.
72. Get adequate rest and relaxation.
73. Your life is part of a grand design.
74. A happy mind is a creative mind.
75. Seek "Optimum Happiness" (OH).
76. Paint your home in mood colors.
77. Laugh out loud (LOL) regularly.
78. Be a prudent money manager.

---

[44] Some quotes were taken from this text, *"Discovering Your Optimum 'Happiness Index' (OHI),"* —A Self-Directed Guide to Your "Happiness Index" (HI) (Including Questionnaire and Self-Improvement [SI] Templates). © 2016 Errol A. and Marjorie G. Gibbs. All rights reserved.

ONE HUNDRED AND TWO OPTIMUM "HAPPINESS INDEX" (OHI) QUOTES TO *ENGAGE, ENLIGHTEN,* AND *EMPOWER* YOUR SEARCH FOR "OPTIMUM HAPPINESS" (OH)[45] (Continued)

79. Seek and discover your genius.
80. Happiness is music to the soul.
81. Personal integrity is happiness.
82. Go to sleep with mood music.
83. Live by faith and not by fear.
84. Volunteer in your community.
85. De-clutter your surroundings.
86. Seek the advice of the elders.
87. Carpe diem (Seize the day).
88. Count your blessings daily.
89. Doing your best is happiness.
90. All human beings are one.
91. Happiness is your birthright.
92. Fulfill your promises made.
93. Unhappiness brings war.
94. Prayer infuses happiness.
95. Happiness is contagious.
96. You can find happiness.
97. Care for elderly persons.
98. Happiness is a *surplus*.
99. Unhappiness is a *deficit*.
100. Happiness is contagious
101. Be happy, be healthy.
102. Love, listen, laugh.

FINALLY

"Have regular hours for work and play; make each day both useful and pleasant, and prove that you understand the worth of time by employing it well. Then youth will bring few regrets, and life will become a beautiful success."

— *Louisa May Alcott, Little Women (1832–1888)*

---

[45] Some quotes were taken from this text, *"Discovering Your Optimum 'Happiness Index' (OHI),"* —A Self-Directed Guide to Your "Happiness Index" (HI) (Including Questionnaire and Self-Improvement [SI] Templates). © 2016 Errol A. and Marjorie G. Gibbs. All rights reserved.

Printed in the United States
By Bookmasters